Hollywood romantic comedy

Manchester University Press

Hollywood romantic comedy

States of the union, 1934–65

KATHRINA GLITRE

Manchester University Press
Manchester and New York
distributed exclusively in the USA by Palgrave

Published by Manchester University Press
Oxford Road, Manchester M13 9NR, UK
and Room 400, 175 Fifth Avenue, New York, NY 10010, USA
www.manchesteruniversitypress.co.uk

Distributed exclusively in the USA by
Palgrave, 175 Fifth Avenue, New York,
NY 10010, USA

Distributed exclusively in Canada by
UBC Press, University of British Columbia, 2029 West Mall,
Vancouver, BC, Canada V6T 1Z2

British Library Cataloguing-in-Publication Data
A catalogue record for this book is available from the British Library

Library of Congress Cataloging-in-Publication Data applied for

ISBN 0 7190 7078 3 *hardback*
EAN 978 0 7190 7078 5

ISBN 0 7190 7079 1 *paperback*
EAN 978 0 7190 7079 2

First published 2006

15 14 13 12 11 10 09 08 07 06 10 9 8 7 6 5 4 3 2 1

Typeset in Minion
by Graphicraft Limited, Hong Kong
Printed in Great Britain
by CPI, Bath

Contents

Preface

This book has been a long time coming. I started writing about screwball comedy for my MA dissertation nearly ten years ago and the main body of this research comes from my doctoral thesis. As the years passed, I have been extremely fortunate to come into contact with a wide range of people – friends and colleagues – who have all impacted on the book in one way or another. Doug Pye supervised both the MA and PhD research with good humour and patience and I would like to thank him for his invaluable expertise and advice. Thanks also to Jane Arthurs, Caroline Bainbridge, Jonathan Bignell, Anita Biressi, Mark Bould, Andrew M. Butler, Josie Dolan, Suzy Gordon, Jim Hillier, Iris Luppa, Samantha Matthews, John Mercer, Steve Neale, Lib Taylor and Greg Tuck (who comes last only through the accidents of alphabet) for advice and encouragement at various crucial points in the development of this book. A special thanks to Iris and to Celestino Deleyto for helping me track down copies of hard to get films.

A shorter version of Chapter 2 was published in *CineAction*, no. 54, under the title 'The same, but different: The awful truth about marriage, remarriage and screwball comedy'. My thanks to Robin Wood for his kind words and advice. Thanks also to the wonderful staff at Manchester University Press.

Finally, this book would never have been started without the unfailing support and encouragement of Gillian Glitre; but it would never have been finished without Mark Bould. This book is for them.

Introduction

Everyone knows how Hollywood romantic comedies end: with a kiss. It is extremely rare for a romantic comedy to end without the union of a couple; it is equally rare for the union to involve people other than the two lead actors. In other words, we usually know how the plot will be resolved just by looking at the opening credits. The fact of this happy ending has conventionally been understood by critics to prove the conservative nature of the genre – a movement from stability through disruption to the reaffirmation of the status quo. The genre's dramatic antecedents reinforce this sense of tradition, as if the cultural meanings of love, romance and marriage have remained unchanged in all this time. Such generalised, common-sense knowledge invariably reduces historical and cultural variation to monolithic, normative assumptions.

This book aims to explore the *changing* representation of the couple in 'classical' Hollywood romantic comedy, between 1934 and 1965.[1] There are, of course, some things that do not change in this period. The couple is always white, heterosexual and (basically) monogamous. In focusing on representations of such a couple, I am not intending to reinforce the erasure of difference, but to acknowledge the ways in which dominant ideology is reproduced. My intention is to recognise the ruptures and contradictions in this ideology, precisely to challenge the assumption that these are 'norms'. Because the genre is centrally concerned with romantic love, this book focuses primarily on discourses around gender and sexuality, but issues around class and ethnicity will also be touched upon.

Closer inspection of the films certainly reveals a more varied and complex version of events, in which the fact of the union becomes less important than the state of that union. Compare the endings of two versions of the same plot: the 1936 screwball comedy, *My Man Godfrey*, and the glossy 1957 remake of the same title. In the original, the chaotic force of the screwball heroine defies convention and male prerogatives. Irene Bullock (Carole

Lombard) arrives uninvited at Godfrey Parke's (William Powell) apartment with enough supplies for a week, but without a minister or marriage licence ('It's funny, I never thought of that,' she says). Godfrey has little choice in the matter, but cohabitation is avoided by the appearance of Mayor Courtney (Reginald Mason), who agrees to marry them without a licence (bringing legality into question). As the bridal party take their places, the bride (dressed in a long, drab overcoat) proclaims, 'Stand still, Godfrey, it'll all be over in a minute.' Without a kiss, the film fades to 'The End'.

In the remake, the feisty heroine (June Allyson) does chase after her man Godfrey (David Niven), but there is a much stronger sense of his willingness (replying 'I do' to Irene's proposal of 'Godfrey, don't you want to marry me?') and of Irene's conventional feminine potential as supportive wife. Both Irene and Godfrey express their desire to get married. The ship's Captain (Fred Essler) is under the impression that Irene is pregnant, but he cannot marry them until they are out of American waters, which will take two hours. The film ends with Irene asking Godfrey, 'Can you wait that long?'. They exchange looks, presumably agreeing to marry and allowing him to take control of the situation. He embraces her and, as they kiss, the camera pans to the porthole, framing the Statue of Liberty. This final image adds a secondary level of institutional sanction and affirmation. The reason they are on a ship is because (in this version) Godfrey is an illegal immigrant – an Austrian aristocrat who jumped ship and fell in love with America, as well as Irene. He has turned himself in, hoping to return to America legally, at which point he would marry Irene; he explicitly rejects the possibility of marrying Irene in America now, because this would bring his motives for marriage into question. In this respect, leaving American waters before marrying authenticates the venerable status of their marriage.

In a general sense, both films end entirely as predicted: a white, heterosexual couple is united on the verge of marriage. However, in the particular context of each film, this union has very different connotations. The screwball ending emphasises the heroine's chaotic logic, which treats marriage as an afterthought, and this instability exposes the conventional function of the institution. The ending of the remake does something quite different: the function of marriage is explicitly linked to issues of legitimacy and, although premarital consummation is implied, the overall effect is far more conservative than the original ending.

Why does the remake change the details of the ending? This is a film that relies quite heavily on the original in most respects, repeating basic plot events and even some of the original dialogue, but clearly some elements of the original no longer seem relevant or appropriate (for example, the Depression era sub-plot about converting the city dump into a swanky nightclub). Such changes are influenced by (at least) three interrelated dynamic processes – genre, industry and culture – all of which will be considered in this book.

In effect, these changes are also about the processes of ideology and the ways in which discourses of love are reinvented and recuperated for each generation. I have identified three key aspects for exploration: marriage, equality and desire.[2] These are among the most common themes of romantic comedy, but (while closely interdependent) each one seems to dominate the genre in successive decades, suggesting shifting cultural priorities. It is for this reason that I have singled out three cycles of romantic comedy: screwball comedy in the thirties; the career woman comedy in the forties; and the sex comedy in the late fifties.[3] By analysing three separate cycles of romantic comedy, it is possible to give due attention to the contemporary cultural discourses surrounding marriage, equality and desire. In each case, these discourses are also embodied by an iconic star couple: Myrna Loy and William Powell; Katharine Hepburn and Spencer Tracy; and Doris Day and Rock Hudson.

All three couples correspond with what Andrew Britton describes as the 'democratic' type of Hollywood star team (1995: 178), as opposed to the more 'romantic' couplings of stars such as Fred Astaire and Ginger Rogers, or Greta Garbo and John Gilbert. The 'democratic' couple embodies the possibility of social, sexual and professional equality, but this possibility is predominantly articulated in terms of the heterosexual love relationship. The sense of the star couple's equality is partly illusory, relying on the individual case and resolving ideological contradictions by the union of opposites (see Chapter 5). However, the prevalence of such star couples is telling in itself, suggesting a cultural fascination with the possibility of sexual equality in America at this time.

A foundational assumption of this book, then, is that meaning is contextual. By placing the genre in context – critically, historically, culturally – it is possible to discern a much more complex variety of meaning. This contextual approach provides an anchoring framework for the book's primary methodology: close textual analysis. It is not my intention to create a canon of 'superior' texts, but to elucidate the conventions of a mass-produced, popular genre. Some critics mistrust close textual analysis for relying on subjective interpretations. If the analyst is claiming such interpretations as authoritative truth then this mistrust is well deserved; I make no such claims. On the contrary, I believe all knowledge is partial, both in the sense of 'not total or entire' and 'having a preference'. As Elizabeth Grosz argues, 'all readings are *interpretive* through and through [. . .]. Interpretations come from particular perspectives and represent particular values' (1990: 141). Bearing this in mind, I should acknowledge my own particular perspective. My understanding of Hollywood romantic comedy is unavoidably informed by my own social positioning as a Western European, white, middle-class, basically heterosexual, left-of-liberal, feminist academic. I am not claiming this book as an authoritative version of Hollywood romantic comedy, therefore, but as an additional perspective on a critically neglected genre. My arguments are offered in the spirit of critical debate, as a way of rethinking the genre.

Just as my method moves from context to text, the structural tendency of this book is to move from the general to the particular, not only from genre to cycle, but also from cycle to individual film and its star couple. Part I provides a more substantial introduction to some of the generic, critical and industrial issues around Hollywood romantic comedy, as well as describing some of the basic genre conventions. This includes further theorisation of the happy ending, reviewing conventional arguments about classical narrative and resolution. The choices open to the couple are certainly constrained by the dominant ideology of heterosexual monogamy, but constraint is not equivalent to affirmation, and Hollywood romantic comedy's ideological conflicts are rarely resolved convincingly. The industrial context of the Production Code Administration also plays a part in these ideological negotiations. Chapter 1 then narrows the field, outlining the cycles of screwball comedy, career woman comedy and the sex comedy, and their place in the development of Hollywood romantic comedy.

Part II interrogates the representation of marriage – and divorce – in screwball comedy, drawing on cultural discourses around companionate marriage, leisure and 'fun morality'. Screwball comedy is distinguished by its unconventional courtship patterns, often resulting in precariously unstable resolutions. Gender inversion, play and spontaneity are common tropes, as women learn to take control of their desires, and men learn they are not all-powerful. The state of the union is invariably fragile, often occurring at the very last minute and involving the couple's withdrawal from society. Films discussed in Chapter 2 include *It Happened One Night* (1934), *Theodora Goes Wild* (1936), *The Awful Truth* (1937), *Holiday* (1938), *Bringing Up Baby* (1938) and *The Lady Eve* (1941). Four of these films have also been discussed by Stanley Cavell as 'Hollywood comedies of remarriage' (1981). Cavell's work has influenced most subsequent critical writing on romantic comedy, necessitating some detailed consideration of his arguments here. Chapter 3 takes the exploration of screwball comedy a stage further, through detailed analysis of *Libeled Lady* (1936). The film's thematic interest in publicity and privacy proves especially illuminating, and leads on to consideration of the film's star couple, Myrna Loy and William Powell. Still best remembered as Nick and Nora Charles in *The Thin Man* film series, Powell and Loy embodied the 'perfect' on-screen marriage. The chapter investigates the exact nature of this perfection in relation to companionate marriage and equality.

Part III examines the theme of equality in relation to the career woman comedy, drawing on cultural discourses around gender roles, 'momism' and popular Freudianism. The cycle usually features a woman in a powerful public position who is represented as 'lacking' femininity, while the man occupies a subordinate position. Thus, gender inversion is again a common trope, but here such inversion is represented as 'unnatural' and the cause of conflict. Courtship involves the correction of this inversion, with the woman taking up a more conventionally female role as wife. Of the three cycles, the career woman comedy offers the most conservative resolution, but it often seems forced and unconvincing – exposing the cultural and ideological imperatives underpinning the union. Films discussed in Chapter 4 include *Ninotchka* (1939), *Design for Scandal* (1941), *Take a Letter, Darling* (1942), *They All Kissed the Bride* (1942), *Lady in the Dark* (1944) and *June Bride* (1948). Critical writing has tended to focus on the cycle's 'punishment' of the career woman, but it is important to recognise that – within the logic of forties' gender politics – the couple's union still represents a version of 'equality'. Gender is constructed as complementary, creating the different but 'equal' couple. Chapter 5 expands further on this idea of complementary equality, focusing on the partnership of Katharine Hepburn and Spencer Tracy, primarily in *Woman of the Year* (1942), but also discussing *Without Love* (1945), *Adam's Rib* (1949) and *Pat and Mike* (1952). The star persona of the Hepburn/Tracy couple is built upon the romantic notion that opposites attract, creating a complex binary hierarchy, articulated in terms of not only gender, but also class and ethnicity.[4]

Part IV explores the confusion of consumer and sexual desire in the sex comedy, specifically in relation to contemporary discourses around dating etiquette, lifestyles and advertising. The standard plot centres on the twin themes of virginity and seduction, and key tropes include masquerade and miscommunication. The union of the couple often foregrounds sexual reproduction, pre-empting marriage; the normative state of this union is sometimes compromised further by coda sequences emphasising possibilities beyond heterosexuality. Films discussed in Chapter 6 include *The Moon Is Blue* (1953), *The Tender Trap* (1955), *Ask Any Girl* (1959), *It Started with a Kiss* (1959) and *That Touch of Mink* (1962). Often dismissed as glossy, superficial and sexist, the sex comedy's gender (and sexual) politics are far more complex than they might first appear. The prevalence of the interior design, fashion and advertising industries signals that image has become all-important, and the characters' construction of identity is repeatedly acknowledged. Chapter 7 analyses *Pillow Talk* (1959) in which Doris Day and Rock Hudson epitomise the 'bedroom problems' encountered in the sex comedy: the hero's seduction techniques manoeuvre the virginal heroine into acting on her own desires, but simultaneously bring his own sexuality into question. *Lover Come Back* (1961) and *Send Me No Flowers* (1964) are also discussed.

As this brief summary indicates, the state of the union in all three cycles is relatively unstable, but in different ways and for different reasons. The instability of the happy ending points to the impossibility of the ideal couple's existence, at least within patriarchal society. In this respect, the state of their union is extra-ordinary: it is an ideal which can only exist elsewhere and off-screen. The book concludes by evaluating the ideological implications of this extraordinary status and the limitations of the ideal.

Notes

1 For reasons that will become apparent in Chapter 1, the neoformalist descriptor 'classical' is misleading in relation to Hollywood romantic comedy. From this point on, I will simply refer to Hollywood romantic comedy, but this should be taken to imply the classical studio era. The year 1934 is a turning point for Hollywood romantic comedy (see Chapter 1) and also marks the beginning of the screwball comedy cycle; 1965 is a more arbitrary cut-off point, marking the release of the sex comedy, *Sex and the Single Girl.*

2 Equality is considered here primarily in terms of gender, although many romantic comedies stress class and economic issues as well. Sexual and racial differences are very rarely explicit issues during this period, owing to the 1930 Production Code's prohibitions against 'sex perversion' and 'miscegenation' ('The Production Code' 1996: 140), but queer meanings may slip in at thc 'sophisticated' level of implication and innuendo (see Chapters 1 and 7).

3 Historical eras do not have clearly defined boundaries; by referring to the era (the thirties) rather than the decade (the 1930s), I am implying a sense of continuity between these developments. References to the '1930s' indicate the specific years between 1931 and 1940.

4 A note on usage: throughout this book I use the singular 'persona' to refer to the image of the star couple, as well as individual stars. The couple's persona will obviously be effected by the individual stars' personae, but it also involves a specific formulation that does not carry across to the stars' films with other partners.

Part I

Hollywood romantic comedy

Clark Gable and Claudette Colbert in *It Happened One Night* (1934).
Courtesy of Columbia Tristar.

1

Genre, cycles and critical traditions

How do we know a romantic comedy when we see one? According to Brian Henderson, 'definition, even delimitation, is difficult or impossible because all Hollywood films (except some war films) have romance and all have comedy' (2001: 312). While the pervasive presence of romance and comedy is undeniable, Henderson is conflating different levels of representational convention. All Hollywood genres implicitly belong to the broader traditions of American narrative film (Pye 1975: 31); romance and comedy are common narrative conventions, hence their ubiquity. Romance and comedy can also be understood as fictional modes – that is, as ways of treating the narrative or, more precisely, as particular ways of imagining the diegetic world. However, these various functions do not preclude the existence of a recognisable genre, 'romantic comedy'. The quickest indication is to consider the use of descriptive terms. *Star Wars* (1977) has both romance and comedy, but no one would call it a 'romantic comedy', while *When Harry Met Sally* (1989) is unlikely to be described as anything else. The reason is simple: in *Star Wars* romance and comedy are secondary concerns; in *When Harry Met Sally* they are integral and interdependent.

The Russian formalist concept of the 'dominant' is useful here. According to Roman Jakobson, the dominant is 'the focusing component of a work of art: it rules, determines, and transforms the remaining components. It is the dominant which guarantees the integrity of the structure' (1978: 81). As Steve Neale explains, 'on this basis, particular genres can be characterized not as the only genres in which given elements, devices, and features occur, but as the ones in which they are dominant, in which they play an overall organizing role' (1995: 179). Thus, the formation of a couple takes place in many fictional texts as a narrative convention, but it plays the dominant, organising role in two genres: romance and romantic comedy. While romance treats the affair seriously, romantic comedy is more light-hearted. The romance,

Love Story (1970), wishes to evoke tears; the romantic comedy, *Love Crazy* (1941), aims for laughter.

In other words, 'genres do not consist only of films: they consist also, and equally, of specific systems of expectation and hypothesis that spectators bring with them to the cinema and that interact with films themselves during the course of the viewing process' (Neale 1995: 160). Genre expectations are based on convention – our mutual understanding that certain things happen in certain ways in certain kinds of texts. Thus, one of our expectations when watching a romantic comedy is that the film will end with the union of a couple. This expectation may be frustrated, as in *Annie Hall* (1977), but this forms part of the film's conscious engagement with the genre. This frustration is very different, then, to a film such as *Titanic* (1997), in which we expect the couple to meet a tragic end. These genre expectations are partly about such elusive things as tone and mood. The world of Hollywood romantic comedy is brightly lit, and accompanied by upbeat music in major keys. We have the sense of a benevolent world, in which destiny (rather than fate) may play a magical part and coincidence has positive results (whereas in melodrama it is the harbinger of doom).

These moods have much to do with the Hollywood modes of romance and comedy, as outlined by Deborah Thomas. She compares the comedic and melodramatic modes, arguing, 'it is a central aspect of comedic films [. . .] that the social space within them is transformable into something better than the repressive, hierarchical world of melodramatic films, so that fantasies of transformation within this space replace fantasies of escape to a space elsewhere' (2000: 14). Thomas identifies the romantic mode as being structured around the fantasy of mutual erotic desire (2000: 22), but feels this mode is less autonomous than comedy and melodrama and is necessarily intertwined with one or the other. She also makes a distinction between 'comic' and 'comedic', using the former to refer to the 'intention to make us laugh' (2000: 17) and the latter to refer to the specific structure of fantasy found in the mode of comedy (a usage I will maintain). Thus, the comedic mode is not necessarily funny, and comic genres may be treated in a melodramatic mode. While most romantic comedies involve the comedic fantasy of transformation and the romantic fantasy of mutual desire, neither mode is essential to the genre, and individual films may also shift between different modes. However, irrespective of which modes operate across which films, romantic comedy is still a comic genre: it always aims to make us laugh.[1]

For the purposes of this book, then, I take the dominant, organising element of the romantic comedy genre to be the comic formation of a (heterosexual) couple[2]: dominant – but not definitive. The vast majority of romantic comedies fit this pattern, but there is always room for variation and hybridisation. Most importantly, to seek to define a genre mistakes the processes of genre development, which work through repetition and difference. Genres change over time.

Theories of genre

Genre theorists have become increasingly critical of transhistorical approaches to the subject. Such approaches have treated genres as stable and discrete. They focus on identifying and defining exclusive limits, and treat the development of genres as teleological, evolving from a ritual archetype towards a final point of decay or collapse. This is part of the source of Henderson's difficulty. Despite recognising that 'a workable subset "romantic comedy" might refer to those films in which romance and comedy are the primary components' (2001: 312), he feels unable to pin this down categorically enough to fix or define the genre. However, the problem is not (as he suggests) that romantic comedy is too pervasive to be a genre, but that any definition of a genre is inherently temporal and transitory.

Genre development is better understood as a dynamic process, rather than a linear evolution of a stable type. While genre recognition undoubtedly depends upon the repetition of easily comprehended conventions, mere repetition is pointless (negating the need for more than one text). Each new genre text will repeat some elements, but vary others; individual texts will even introduce new elements which will in turn become conventionalised. 'In this way the elements and conventions of a genre are always *in* play rather than being simply *re*played' (Neale 1995: 170). Thus, genre operates in (at least) two temporal dimensions: there must be a synchronic sense of continuity, produced by the repetition of conventions; but there must also be a diachronic sense of change, produced by history.

One way of visualising this model is to think of a genre as a family. Alistair Fowler draws on Wittgenstein's idea of 'family resemblances' to theorise genre: 'representatives of a genre may then be regarded as making up a family whose septs and individual members are related in various ways, without necessarily having any single feature shared in common by all' (1982: 41). Thus, while still sharing many commonalities, each individual member will also be unique; and while the possibilities of cross-breeding are abundant, each generation will still bear some connection to the last.

What is particularly useful about this analogy is the cultural existence of such resemblance: descendants may look like their ancestors, but they are unlikely to behave like them. Even when conventions do continue or reoccur across a period of time, this is no guarantee that their function and meaning remain unchanged. While genre variation may simply involve challenging the audience's expectations to offer new pleasures, it may also be a response to shifting cultural ideology. This is crucial to a genre such as romantic comedy, which foregrounds social and sexual mores. Even the dominant is not immune to this process. The 'union' used to mean marriage; it now implies monogamy, but this too may change (in fact, since the 1990s, the wedding has again become central to contemporary Hollywood romantic comedy). The heterosexuality of the couple used to be assured, but there are now numerous romantic comedies with gay and lesbian couples. There is even the possibility that the genre may move beyond the couple altogether. For these reasons, among others, I refer to generic tendencies throughout this book, not hard and fast rules.

Critical traditions I: dramatic ancestry

Transhistorical approaches privilege synchronic time, assuming a stable, unified tradition. In terms of romantic comedy, this tradition has been back-dated to the New Comedy plays of Menander, Plautus and Terence (fourth, third and second centuries BC, respectively).[3] It has become a critical commonplace to identify Hollywood romantic comedy with the structures of New Comedy (for example, see Horton 1991: 10–11, Karnick and Jenkins 1995: 73–5 and Rowe 1995: 108–9), but there are a number of problems with this formulation. Northrop Frye defines the plot structure of New Comedy as formulaic: 'what normally happens is that a young man wants a young woman, that his desire is resisted by some opposition, usually paternal, and that near the end of the play some twist in the plot enables the hero to have his will' (1990: 163). Or, as Gerald Mast summarises the structure, 'boy meets girl; boy loses girl; boy gets girl' (1979: 4). The patriarchal gender assumptions contained within the New Comedy structure are misleading in relation to studio-era Hollywood romantic comedy. The girl in New Comedy often plays such a minor role that she has little or no dialogue (in Menander's *Dyskolos* (*The Grouch*) she does not even warrant a name). In Hollywood romantic comedy, the girl's role is central: it is more commonly *she* who meets the boy and, whether she has immediate designs on him or not, she often initiates the narrative at the very least. It is also quite common for the hero and heroine to know each other already (most obviously in comedies of remarriage). Neither does the rest of the clichéd pattern fit most Hollywood romantic comedies: the 'boy' and 'girl' are adults, not adolescents, and they do not lose each other, but rather resist, frustrate, battle and ignore each other. Consequently, the opposition is rarely paternal; it comes from within the couple themselves.

In this respect, Hollywood romantic comedy is more intimately related to the battling sexes tradition of Shakespearean comedy (*The Taming of the Shrew*, *Much Ado about Nothing*, *A Midsummer Night's Dream*), but this is where a further problem arises: a number of critics conflate Shakespearean comedy with New Comedy.[4] Where New Comedy is formulaic, Shakespearean comedy moves towards a 'profounder pattern, the ritual of death and revival' (Frye 1984: 80) developed from the English folk tradition – a tradition which Frye calls 'the drama of the green world' (1984: 80). For Frye, the green world represents a structural principle of Shakespearean comedy, and involves a movement from the tyranny of the everyday social world, to a magical natural realm (usually a forest) in which festive play renews society. Kathleen Rowe is mistaken, therefore, to associate the green world with New Comedy (1995: 108); as Frye argues, the green world is precisely what distinguishes Shakespeare's *The Two Gentlemen of Verona* from the New Comedy tradition (1984: 80).

While this may seem like pedantic nit-picking, my point is that this confusion and conflation of terms not only misrepresents Hollywood romantic comedy, but also reinforces generalised assumptions of romantic comedy as an unchanging, transhistorical tradition. There is a critical tendency to rely on the perceived similarities between the dramatic tradition and the Hollywood genre, at the expense of recognising developments. The structures of comedy may have remained relatively consistent, but their functions and meanings have shifted with changing circumstances. The green world is a good example. Rather than addressing the specificities of this space, recent critics have tended to treat it as a broad convention, conflating the green world with the carnivalesque and liminality.[5] While these elements have things in common, the differences are lost in the mix. The importance of distinguishing between different kinds of spaces becomes clearer if we consider Celestino Deleyto's 1998 analysis of *Alice* (1991): 'in a film in which the characters never move out of Manhattan "physically", the "other" space of romantic comedy – the forest or foreign city of Shakespearean comedy in which inhibitions are lifted and a new identity is found – is represented, on the one hand, by Alice's interior space and, on the other, by Dr Yang's apartment in Chinatown' (1998: 135). Here the complexity and diversity of historically, geographically and culturally specific spaces are reduced to the neat and tidy binary logic of the 'other'. There are two things to clarify: how often does the green world (as opposed to *any* 'other' space) occur? and what is its function? In fact, a movement into a green world is found in only a few Hollywood romantic comedies, and these are almost all screwball comedies. For this reason, I will return to the function of the green world in Chapter 3, once a clearer understanding of screwball comedy has been reached.

I should clarify, I am not claiming Shakespearean comedy as the 'true' progenitor of Hollywood romantic comedy, but recognising multiple and diverse antecedents; the genre's development is not unilinear.[6] There is a need to distinguish the broad genre 'romantic comedy' from the historically specific forms of that genre produced by the studio system; there is also a need to distinguish Hollywood romantic comedy from the critical paradigms of classical Hollywood narrative.

Critical traditions II: 'classical' Hollywood narrative

Classical Hollywood narrative has been repeatedly characterised as linear, goal-oriented and dependent on psychologically motivated, causal action. The neoformalist model articulated by David Bordwell and his collaborators relies most heavily on the concept of a 'cause-and-effect' chain of events, leading to a logical and complete resolution. The spectator's part in this process is formulated in terms of posing hypotheses and receiving knowledge: 'each sequence, every line of dialogue, becomes a way of creating or developing or confirming a hypothesis; shot by shot, questions are posed and answered' (Bordwell, Staiger and Thompson 1988: 39). By the end of the film the range of hypotheses has narrowed to one likely outcome, which is invariably confirmed; the high degree of closure places the spectator in a reassuring position of omniscience. This is indeed a 'classical' model of narrative. According to Aristotle, plot action 'ought to be both unified and complete, and the component events ought to be so firmly compacted that if any one of them is shifted to another place, or removed, the whole is loosened up and dislocated' (1983: 32).

The discourses of unified action reduce narrative complexity to the constant linear structure of beginning–middle–end as representing stability–disruption–stability. Ideologically, this structure has been understood in terms of the conservative reaffirmation of order after a period of transgression and disorder. What is most striking about such discourses is the privileging of the teleological project. As Richard Neupert asserts, 'the ending is the final product of all the narrative's labors – the end is privileged both during and after the viewing as a source of validation of the reading process' (1995: 32). According to the neoformalist model, 'The End' is the meaning.

However, this model cannot account for a variety of elements typical of Hollywood film. As Dirk Eitzen argues, elements such as spectacle, emotional intensity and comedy have very little to do with answering hypothetical questions of causal motivation; on the contrary, they seem 'to be tied up with a more visceral, less cerebral sort of pleasure' (1999: 398). Hollywood cinema is above all a commercial entity: mass-produced texts intended for mass consumption. To maximise profits, its pleasures must be diverse, and the pleasurable meanings of stars, *mise-en-scène*, special effects and so on (hereon referred to as 'spectacle') all tend to function in excess of causal motivation. By containing meaning within 'The End', the neoformalist model not only privileges the traditional unity of high art, but also cognitive processes over emotional responses, and 'classical' narrative at the expense of mass entertainment.

Comedy provides a particularly clear example of the limitations of the classical model. Comic meaning is rarely stable or unified; it depends instead upon double meanings and mistaken identities. Moreover, the process of 'getting the joke' tends to involve looking backward to reassess what just happened, rather than projecting forward to hypothesise what will happen next. Thus, comic elements interrupt the linear movement of narrative. Far from a straightforward chain of causal events, the structure of narrative comedy tends to be associated with the convolutions of accident, coincidence, repetition, reversal and surprise. In other words, the comic effect is the unexpected outcome of an inconsequential cause; hypothetical logic has nothing to do with it.

For these reasons, I reject the description 'classical' to refer to Hollywood romantic comedy of the studio era. In contrast to the unified trajectory of cause-and-effect, ending in the victory (or death) of an individual, Hollywood romantic comedy (like the Hollywood musical) tends to involve a 'dual-focus' narrative (Altman 1987: 16–27). Such a narrative places equal emphasis on the hero and heroine, alternating between their points of view, leading to patterns of simultaneity, repetition, parallelism and comparison, rather than cause-and-effect progression. The dual focus usually works to articulate the conflict between male and female, but there is invariably a 'secondary but essential opposition alongside the primary sexual division: each sex is identified with a particular attitude, value, desire, location, age or other characteristic attribute' (Altman 1987: 24). This may begin to suggest a conventional binary structure, which would assume the woman represents the inferior, wrong position, to be corrected by the superior Mr Right. However, in practice, the dual-focus narrative usually involves a process of compromise, not conquest. Where classical narrative privileges the values of the hero by villainising his opposite in a good-versus-evil conflict, dual focus narrative lends positive weight to both sides of the argument, continually renegotiating the balance of power and creating a more egalitarian structure of desire. Indeed, this process may include the reversal of the couple's original positions, enabling a degree of mutual re-education to take place and suggesting the potential for change. (Such reversals involve more than temporary inversion, therefore, and should not automatically be assumed to end in the reassertion of the status quo.) As Altman argues, the union of the couple thereby resolves not only the sexual dichotomy, but also mediates between the terms of the secondary thematic opposition (1987: 50). He concludes, 'in most cases [. . .] we are not permitted to verify whether this apparent solution is actually a workable one: the couple is united, the film ends, and we must accept on faith the implied assertion that they lived happily ever after. By convention, *time stops* when the couple kisses, and *change is forevermore banished* from their life together' (1987: 51, my emphasis).

This is a fairly typical formulation of romantic union in Hollywood narrative: static, stable and eternal. However, as far as Hollywood romantic comedy is concerned, this formulation is largely mistaken. There are two related aspects to consider here: union as stability; and union as social integration. Both play an important part in critical assumptions about the conservative ideological function of romantic comedy.

Happily ever after

Bordwell's understanding of the happy ending involves three factors: the motivated achievement of the narrative goal; the convincing resolution of the ideological conflict which has previously prevented this achievement; and an epilogue that 'functions to represent the final stability achieved by the narrative: the characters' futures are settled' (1982: 4). The union of the heterosexual couple is often understood to underwrite this stability (reaffirming the patriarchal status quo). The only problem is that these factors are rarely true of Hollywood romantic comedy. The union of the couple is not a secondary consideration designed to reinforce the unity of the main plot action; it *is* the main plot action. Indeed, the formation of the couple is a foregone conclusion. The very predictability of the ending undermines the cause-and-effect teleology. If we already know what is going to happen, why bother hypothesising?

In romantic comedy, the happy ending is determined by generic convention, rather than narrative logic.[7] Indeed – far from a 'motivated' resolution to the conflict – Hollywood romantic comedy often draws attention to the gap between reality and fiction by embracing artifice. As Zvi Jagendorf contends, 'the preposterous end [of comedy . . .] is not necessarily a victory for pleasure over necessity. Rather it is the parading of a fiction at a point where that fiction is most fragile' (1984: 14). Although a motivated, stable happy ending is, of course, entirely possible, Hollywood romantic comedy tends to be 'fragile' in this way. This has important implications for the resolution of the ideological conflict, which may be far from convincing. Indeed, the final union can be treated in an off-hand or ironic manner – as unavoidable rather than inevitable. Even the supposedly ubiquitous romantic clinch is often absent (see Chapter 2). This paradox is deepened by the function of the epilogue. Far from reinforcing the return of the status quo, as Bordwell suggests, the Hollywood romantic comedy epilogue tends to destabilise the final union by the return of a source of conflict, as in the codas to *The Palm Beach Story* (1942) and *Pillow Talk*.

Nonetheless, no matter how unlikely or unconvincing or unstable the final union of the couple may seem, most critics still argue that Hollywood romantic comedy achieves the hegemonic aim: the union of the couple reaffirms the patriarchal status quo. Andrew Horton is typical: 'the characters, no matter how much they have turned the everyday world upside down during the narrative, must act like "adults" to the degree of committing themselves to each other and thus to life within society. They change; society remains the same. [. . .] in the end, order is restored, and the rules of society are maintained' (1991: 11; see also Leach 1977: 81, Schatz 1981: 171 and Neupert 1995: 181). The assumption of union as social integration is crucial to such arguments.

According to Frye, the theme of comedy is 'the integration of society, which usually takes the form of incorporating a central character into it' (1990: 43). The final integration tends to involve 'some kind of party or festive ritual, which either appears at the end of the play or is assumed to take place immediately afterward. Weddings are most common' (1990: 163). For example, *Much Ado About Nothing* ends with festive dancing prior to a double wedding; the obstacles to union have not only been overcome, but expelled from society, reinstating an idyllic status quo. However, this kind of return to order is not essential. A different kind of emphasis can suggest the society has moved forward to a new situation. Thus, in *As You Like It*, the unions of the couples represent the rejection of the old world and the formation of a new and typically utopian society. To quote Jagendorf, 'if one model implies the achievement of balance within accepted norms of behavior, the other entertains the possibility of change and of a reappraisal of norms of behavior exhibited in the play. Most comic endings move between these two possibilities, and often contain features of both' (1984: 18). In other words, union as social integration has both conservative and progressive potential. It is not enough to claim that The End is the meaning – that, simply by ending with the union of the heterosexual couple, romantic comedy is about the traditional institutions of patriarchal society and must be inherently conservative. The context of The End must be taken into account.

The issue of social integration is further complicated in Hollywood romantic comedy by the rarity with which the films actually end with a social occasion, even when a wedding is involved. It is more common for the couple to withdraw from society, and some even reject it altogether (see Chapter 2). *Some Like It Hot* (1959) is a useful example: although the film ends with Joe/Josephine/Junior (Tony Curtis) revealing his true identity and forming a heterosexual couple with Sugar Kane/Kowalczyk (Marilyn Monroe), what is noticeably absent is any sense of social renewal or return of social order. On the contrary, the subversive potential of Osgood Fielding III's (Joe E. Brown) acceptance that Jerry/Daphne (Jack Lemmon) is a man reasserts their extraordinary status. Furthermore, having witnessed a second massacre, Joe and Jerry are again on the run from gangsters. The ideological conflicts set in motion by *Some Like It Hot* cannot be contained by The End.

Local conventions

Neither dual-focus narrative nor the happy ending are exclusive to Hollywood romantic comedy. Few genre conventions are exclusive in this way, but the patterns in which they coagulate can create a better sense of the generic corpus. Douglas Pye recognises generic differences as emerging from the 'combination of these basic [narrative] tendencies and the more local conventions' (1975: 33). Such conventions are determined by various recurring conditions, such as themes, tropes, diegetic worlds (conventions of time and space), iconography, plot structures, and character types. 'Each of these contains a wide range of possibilities – in combination, the possibilities are enormously multiplied [. . .]. Seen in this way, a genre will be capable of taking an enormously wide range of emphasis' (Pye 1975: 34).

Romantic comedy's interest in the couple inevitably leads to some conventional themes and tropes. Themes include the nature of love, courtship rituals and marriage, identity, liberation, transformation, renewal, and the relationships between individuals and society. Identity is very often mistaken in comic genres, and frequently involves disguises and deception. Such masquerades usually involve inversions of social status, most usually of class (a poor person pretending to be rich, or vice versa), but sometimes of gender as well (a woman passing as a man or, more rarely, vice versa). Critics have often linked these inversions to Bakhtin's ideas of the 'carnivalesque' – that is, a festive liberation from social norms, in which conventional hierarchies are temporarily suspended. Mistaken identity and inversion function as generic tropes, working at a secondary symbolic (and ideological) level in addition to their literal meaning. Other tropes include weddings, remarriage and journeys.

Diegetically, Hollywood romantic comedy is a flexible genre, virtually unlimited by time or space. It can be set in the past or the present (but I have never seen one set in the future), in any country, in cities, small towns, the country, or travelling between these spaces. Neither does it involve specific iconography (such as sheriffs and saloons in the western). Despite these possibilities, the vast majority of Hollywood romantic comedies are set in the present time, in the US, in a middle- to upper-class urban milieu. They also tend to be thoroughly bourgeois in their outlook: white, heterosexual and (ultimately) middle-class.

There is a tendency for one half of the couple to be extraordinary in some way (a screwball, a virgin, an aristocrat), while the other half is relatively ordinary and predictable. It is far more common for the woman to be the extraordinary figure, but not essential. Usually, at least one half of the couple is already involved with – or even engaged to – someone else; this person is quickly marked as 'wrong' for them (they are too boring or too attached to their mother or, occasionally, untrustworthy). A variation on this convention is for one half of the couple to have a best friend who acts as a sounding board, usually providing wise-cracking advice. In some circumstances (most notably some sex comedies) the 'Wrong Man' can also be the hero's best friend, but the 'Wrong Woman' is rarely likeable. The best friend, whether male or female, tends to be unmarried or much married, and is frequently coded as camp or queer.

There are some common types of Hollywood romantic comedy plot (most of which can be found in the broader genre as well). The 'Cinderella' plot can involve love at first sight, and the obstacles to union are created by external social forces (family, class, peer pressure); it has become a standard feature of teen romantic comedy, and often also involves the 'magical' transformation of the heroine (the 'Cinderfella' variation is still surprisingly rare). A variation is the 'odd couple' plot, which combines internal and external conflicts, raising issues around social conformity, particularly in relation to hierarchies of class or (more recently) racial difference. The 'comedy of remarriage' plot involves the reunion of a couple: usually, they have been separated, and possibly divorced, but discover they still love each other (see Cavell 1981); obviously, this plot is predominantly concerned with the meanings of marriage (and divorce). The most common Hollywood romantic comedy plot involves the 'battle of the sexes': the hero and heroine are in competition, initially disliking or even hating each other, but move from antagonism to compromise, often through a process of reversal. This plot invariably raises questions around gender and equality.

These local conventions can occur in various combinations. Within individual cycles of films, these conventions become still more localised and tend to form specific patterns. Before these specific forms are detailed, another dynamic factor in genre development needs to be acknowledged: industrial processes.

Commercial production

Transhistorical approaches also mask the economic imperatives and institutional regimes affecting genre production. Genre was one of the ways in which the Hollywood studio system standardised film production to meet demand. It enabled the studio to re-use sets, costumes, stars and crews to create an easily recognisable product that could be produced on a cost-effective, regular basis. In other words, the conventions of Hollywood romantic comedy were affected not only by genre and narrative, but also by the very processes of production, certainly in terms of the kinds of plots, sets, decor and costumes used. The vertically integrated parts of the Hollywood industry also meant that the major studios could guarantee markets for their films, through block-booking distribution and through their own first-run theatres. This perhaps explains why the majors continued producing screwball comedy, even though the cycle's popularity quickly dwindled.

The industrial process is more dynamic than this initially suggests. Hollywood could not afford to repeat itself *ad infinitum*; it could guarantee distribution, but it could not guarantee a paying audience. Some degree of novelty was also required. Thus, as Richard Maltby notes, 'like that of other fashion industries, Hollywood production was cyclical, always seeking to replicate its recent commercial successes' (2003: 78). Cycles usually capitalise on the (often unexpected) success of a film that offers a new twist on an old genre (for example, the proliferation of ensemble romantic comedies made in the wake of *Four Weddings and a Funeral* (1994)). Subsequent films are marketed by comparison to earlier successes, and sequels are a common ploy. Romantic comedies do not usually provide fertile ground for spawning sequels, however; successful stars and directors are instead repackaged in new vehicles (e.g. *Notting Hill* (1999) and *Love Actually* (2004) reunite Hugh Grant and Richard Curtis, while *Runaway Bride* (1999) reunites the stars and director of *Pretty Woman* (1990)).

Economic factors are not sufficient explanation for the development of a cycle, since they do not account for the original success of key films. Such cycles of popularity (both in production and consumption) are influenced by the specific cultural situation – a moment at which a genre's tropes seem particularly resonant. For example, the revival of 'old-fashioned' romantic comedy in the 1980s is hardly coincidental in a decade noted for its reactionary cultural and sexual politics (a situation exacerbated by the emergence of AIDS in 1981). To neglect the cultural and historical specificity of genre films is to miss the point.

As far as Hollywood romantic comedy is concerned, part of this specificity involves the 1930 Production Code and its administration. Rather than face federal censorship, the studios willingly signed up to a system of self-regulation, because this allowed them to maintain ultimate control of production and exhibition. The studios' main priority was to maximise profits by maintaining an inclusive approach to audiences (they rejected the option of a ratings system). The Code outlined various contentious subjects that should be avoided, and stated as a general principle that 'correct standards of life, subject only to the requirements of drama and entertainment, shall be presented' ('The Production Code' 1996: 139). The emphasis on 'correct' standards immediately signals the moral tone of the Code (and its ideological functions), but the qualification of the requirements of drama and entertainment also suggests a process of negotiation, rather than rigid enforcement (see Vasey 1997). As the Production Code Administration (PCA) files amply demonstrate, the process of negotiation involved devising a system of representation that allowed 'sophisticated' viewers to draw conclusions that were unavailable to 'innocent' viewers (see Maltby 2003: 472–5). For example, under 'Particular Applications II – Sex', the Code makes the following stipulations: 'the sanctity of the institution of marriage and the home shall be upheld. [. . .] *Adultery*, sometimes necessary plot material, must not be explicitly treated or justified or presented attractively' ('The Production Code' 1996: 139). Within this logic, it is fine to treat adultery implicitly: for example, phallic symbols signal to the 'sophisticated' viewer that Rick Blaine (Humphrey Bogart) and Ilsa Lund (Ingrid Bergman) commit adultery in *Casablanca* (1942), but all we actually see is a kiss, a tower, a dissolve, and Rick smoking a cigarette some time later.

The administration of the Production Code in the 1930s and 1940s affects Hollywood romantic comedy in two ways. Most obviously, it restricts the kinds of relationships which can be represented, insisting that the 'correct' standards are marriage, heterosexuality and racial purity (sex 'perversion' and miscegenation are both forbidden). However, by simultaneously encouraging a system of ambiguity – meanings which can be read in different ways by different viewers – the Code paradoxically also enabled a range of queer possibilities. The Code encouraged negotiated meanings at both the levels of production and reception.

The meanings of Hollywood romantic comedy are far from stable, therefore, and certainly contingent upon industrial, historical and cultural processes. By comparing various concurrent and subsequent cycles of Hollywood romantic comedy, a much more complex understanding of the genre can emerge. As Jonathan Munby emphasises, 'the term "cycle" [. . .] does justice to the idea that while these films shared generic conventions, they were also part of a socially volatile formula in flux' (1999: 4).[8] In direct contrast to a transhistorical approach, then, analysis of distinct cycles elucidates shifts in generic meanings and functions, as well as the relationships between genre, industry and culture.

The rest of this chapter outlines the screwball comedy, career woman comedy and sex comedy cycles. Although the cycles are treated chronologically, this does not involve a comprehensive history of Hollywood romantic comedy; these cycles are not intended as the limits of the genre during the period, or as exclusive groupings. A genre may produce more than one cycle at a time, and these cycles may overlap. *His Girl Friday* (1940) may be referred to as a screwball comedy, a career woman comedy, or a comedy of remarriage, depending on the context. My aim in describing these cycles is not categorisation, therefore, but affiliation: *His Girl Friday* has things in common with both the screwball comedy *Bringing Up Baby* and the career woman comedy *June Bride*; but *Bringing Up Baby* and *June Bride* have relatively little in common, beyond the generic label romantic comedy. Rather than treat these cycles as discrete entities, the following sections aim to delineate various production trends, emphasising the generic processes of repetition and difference through comparison and contrast.

Fresh starts

On 3 February 1934, *It Happened One Night* was quietly released. Reviews were favourable, but unremarkable: the *New York Times* described the film as a 'merry romance' (Hall 1970: 1035) while *Variety* qualified the unpromising sound of 'another long-distance bus story' with such phrases as 'intangible quality of charm' and 'a happy accident' (27 February 1934).[9] Neither hinted at the possibility that the film presented a definitive break with tradition. However, once the film became a sensational success, such a claim was soon common, as the *Variety* review of *She Married Her Boss* (1935) reveals: the 'essence of the picture's likable qualities is in the treatment. [. . .] A couple of years ago the same story would probably have been handled as a heavy, tragic domestic treatise with everything sour until the sweet ending. But "It Happened One Night" and "The Thin Man" [1934] have changed a lot of things and smashed numerous precedents' (2 October 1935). From being the tail end of an extremely limited cycle of bus movies, *It Happened One Night* was retrospectively recognised as a starting point for a whole new way of telling stories.[10] However, this change is described not in terms of genre, but in terms of 'treatment' – a style which could be applied to a variety of plots, from romance and comedy to murder mysteries and musicals.

This breezy new style was not quite as original as it seemed; it was rather the combination of effects that appeared so refreshing. In the early 1930s, romantic comedy had been dominated by two discrete, distinctly class-bound, strands: sophisticated comedy and 'tough comedy' (Harvey's term 1998: 83). Like the operetta and the backstage musical cycles, sophisticated comedy tended to be produced by the 'classier' MGM and Paramount, while Warner Bros and Columbia stuck to a (lower-budget) working-class milieu. Sophisticated comedy (as epitomised by the work of Ernst Lubitsch) often relied on theatrical sources, and although films such as *Private Lives* (1931), *The Guardsman* (1931) and *Design for Living* (1933) focused on marital and sexual entanglements, it was from an immaculately 'civilised' and peculiarly European perspective. At the other end of the class scale, the tough comedy was typically home-grown in its rough urban setting. However, perhaps because of the milieu, these films often mixed snappy dialogue with melodramatic situations, sometimes switching tone with surprising bluntness (as in *Me and My Gal* (1932) and *Advice to the Lovelorn* (1933)). Frank Capra's *Platinum Blonde* (1931) is a particularly useful example, since, as Harvey observes, it 'has almost all the elements of screwball comedy – the characters, the settings, the "madcap" stunts [. . .]. It has almost everything but the élan' (1998: 118). The film's journalist hero, Stew Smith (Robert Williams) marries society girl, Ann Schuyler (Jean Harlow), suggesting a template for *It Happened One Night*; however, the marriage is a disaster, and Stew ends up with his newspaper sidekick, Gallagher (Loretta Young). *Platinum Blonde* is typical of early-thirties comedy in this respect: attempts to cross class lines prove futile.

It Happened One Night and *The Thin Man* took these two extremes of sophistication and toughness and mixed the glamorous, pleasure-filled lifestyle of the former with the wise-cracking sexual tension of the latter (see p. 7). This new treatment maintained a more consistently comic tone than the tough comedy. It also, by its very nature, endorsed a more mobile class structure, infused with a distinctly American sensibility. The alien mores of 'civilised' European sophistication were effectively slapped into an American frame of reference. Andrew Sarris credits *Twentieth Century* (released 11 May 1934) with being 'the first comedy in which sexually attractive, sophisticated stars indulged in their own slapstick instead of delegating it to their inferiors' (1962: 23). What distinguished the new comic treatment – and screwball comedy in particular – was the positioning of the couple as the centre of the comic spectacle.

Indeed, screwball comedy was the apotheosis of the new style. As Otis Ferguson noted in 1940, 'With *My Man Godfrey* in the middle of 1936, the discovery of the word screwball by those who had to have some words to say helped build the thesis of an absolutely new style in comedy' (1971: 24). *Variety*'s review is a good example: 'Miss Lombard has played screwball dames before, but none so screwy as this one' (23 September 1936). Similarly, Lewis Jacobs, writing in 1939, refers to films such as *It Happened One Night* and *My Man Godfrey* as 'daffy' comedies (1969: 535), but explicitly associates them with 'new hero and heroine types. Among the women Carole Lombard is the most outstanding in her "screw-ball" activity' (1969: 536). As this suggests, it is initially the central characters who are labelled 'screwballs', not the films. In fact, the films were described with a variety of terms. For example, in a review of *Easy Living* (1937), *Variety* asserts that 'slapstick farce, incredible and without rhyme or reason, is Paramount's contribution to the cycle of goofy pictures which started and, from a box-office standpoint, practically ended with "My Man Godfrey"' (7 July 1937). Similarly, *Double Wedding* (1937) is described as 'another of those madcap comedies' and as 'the latest starter in the goofy sweepstakes which got under way last year with "My Man Godfrey"' (*Variety*, 22 September 1937). The profusion of terms does not obscure the fact that these reviewers recognised a distinct cycle, with *My Man Godfrey* taken as the yardstick against which all others could be measured. By the following year, the term 'screwball comedy' had entered the reviewers' vocabulary, with Bosley Crowther calling *Three Loves Has Nancy* (1938) 'another of those screwball comedies' (1970a: 1527), and *Variety* calling *Say It in French* (1938) the 'latest in the apparently unending string of romantic screwball comedies' (30 November 1938). Thus, while the new style affected most comic films of the period, at the core of this activity existed a distinctive cycle, united by local conventions of character, themes and structure. It is this core to which I apply the label 'screwball comedy'.

Screwball comedy

'Screwball comedy' is a notoriously troublesome term in this respect: some critics use it to refer to *any* romantic comedy made in Hollywood between 1934 and the early 1940s, and others use it to refer to any comedy (irrespective of date) with irresponsible or 'crazy' characters and slapstick tendencies. I am not disputing these uses, as such, but wish to maintain a distinction between the cultural specificity of the original cycle of films, and the broader meanings the term has accrued over time. By using the term 'screwball comedy' too loosely, the typical structures and meanings of the cycle become misrepresented. For example, many critics include Frank Capra's populist trilogy – *Mr Deeds Goes to Town* (1936), *Mr Smith Goes to Washington* (1939) and *Meet John Doe* (1941) – within their discussions of screwball comedy, misrepresenting the role of the screwball heroine in the process. In Capra's trilogy, the heroine is scarred by cynicism and worldly experience; she plays an integral part in the public humiliation of the hero, who, like Christ, rises again, 'saving' her in the process. Considering this narrative focus on the idealised male, it is worth noting that Capra favoured such all-American stars as James Stewart and Gary Cooper; screwball comedy, on the other hand, prefers the more urbane and sexually ambiguous personalities of Cary Grant, Melvyn Douglas and William Powell.

Further confusions arise in Steve Neale and Frank Krutnik's (1990) influential discussion of the 'comedy of the sexes'. They focus on 1930s and 1940s romantic comedy, but treat the term 'screwball comedy' as a synonym for the genre (1990: 138). They identify 'the desires of the woman as the major obstruction to union, and hence as the principal object of the comic transformation' (1990: 142). However, much of their argument refers to *Tom, Dick and Harry* (1941), a film which bears little relation to screwball comedy tropes and conventions. It more rightly belongs to the concurrent 'Cinderella' cycle, which involved 'a wistful or determined heroine dreaming of and finding (if only temporarily) a life steeped in luxury on the arm of her Prince'

(Sennett 1973: 24); such desires are revealed to be misguided, and the heroines typically realise their mistake, finding 'true' love with an average Joe instead, as in *Hands across the Table* (1935), *The Gilded Lily* (1935) and *Tom, Dick and Harry*.

'Cinderella' may seem a misnomer, since the heroine rarely gets the prince (if she does, she was not looking for one in the first place) – but 'gold-digger' is too harsh a description. These heroines are working girls, characterised more by their romantic, fairytale daydreams, than by a hard-edged mercenary ambition. It is precisely this romantic daydreaming which distinguishes the Cinderella cycle from screwball comedy. Although the two cycles can overlap, as in *Midnight* (1939) and *The Palm Beach Story*, screwball heroines pursue rich men for purely practical reasons. This romantic/practical distinction can be pushed further to reveal a more crucial difference between the Cinderella and screwball comedy cycles: 'Cinderella' discovers 'real' life is better than fantasy; the screwball heroine tends to have her cake and eat it, getting the wealthy 'prince' after converting him to *her* way of thinking (*If You Could Only Cook* (1935), *Easy Living*, *Woman Chases Man* (1937), *Fifth Avenue Girl* (1939), *The Lady Eve* (1941)). Both plot trajectories are obviously born of the Depression, but their ideological negotiations diverge; while screwball comedy embraces liberation and change, the 'Cinderella' cycle functions to romanticise the everyday and the status quo. Invariably, it is the hero who represents these everyday values, and Cinderella (like Capra's heroine) recognises the error of her ways. The cycle certainly corroborates Neale and Krutnik's arguments about the reaffirmation of patriarchy through the 'conversion' of the female to the male's 'correct values' (1990: 144), but the narrative structure and meanings of screwball comedy are distorted as a consequence.

Far from affirming the everyday, screwball comedy embraces chaos. As Ed Sikov notes, 'by the early 1930s [the word] "screwball" successfully brought together a number of connotations in a single slang and streetwise term: lunacy, speed, unpredictability, unconventionality, giddiness, drunkenness, flight, and adversarial sport' (1989: 19). Thus, the word connotes both physical and mental instability. Above all else, perhaps, it is this sense of instability and inversion – a world turned upside down – that epitomises screwball comedy.

The screwball world is upper-class and urban, peopled by café society types in black tie and dazzling evening dress, guzzling champagne; the narrative often involves a journey, usually to the green world of Connecticut. The screwball couple seem to have little in common and may come from different social backgrounds: eccentric, runaway heiresses mingle with journalists, professors and detectives. This difference in social potency, frequently connoted by wealth, is often a source of antagonism, but it also enables the displacement of the power inequalities of gender. The heroine usually has (or appears to have) more social power than the hero; alternatively, the hero pretends to have less social power than he really does. In most cases, there is no question of '*boy* getting girl'. Rather, autonomous and desiring women take action, while men learn that they are not all-powerful, and not always right. The norms of male-dominated courtship are repeatedly inverted, and films such as *My Man Godfrey*, *Theodora Goes Wild*, *Breakfast for Two* (1937), *Woman Chases Man*, *Bringing Up Baby*, *The Lady Eve* and *Ball of Fire* (1941) blur traditional assumptions of active and passive gender roles.

Unconventional courtship also acts as a catalyst for much-needed, revitalising change. Usually, one (occasionally both) of the couple is in a position of entrapment, confined by social institutions of wealth, class and/or family. In *It Happened One Night*, Ellie Andrews (Claudette Colbert) is literally captive on board her father's yacht, but more commonly this entrapment is signalled by a sense of stagnation: for example, Richard Barclay's (Melvyn Douglas) gloomy house in *She Married Her Boss*; Margit Agnew's (Myrna Loy) strict breakfast menus in *Double Wedding*; or David Huxley's (Cary Grant) obsession with dinosaurs in *Bringing Up Baby*. Although a few other screwball comedy women are stuck in a rut, it is more common for the men to suffer from this condition. In many cases, it is the hero's stagnating complacency which requires Neale and Krutnik's 'comic transformation' (1990: 142) and – far from 'obstructing' the union – it is the active desires of the female which tend to initiate this change.

Unstable energy is essential to the screwball process of liberation, and typically involves three related motifs: spontaneity, inebriation and play. Cosmo Topper (Roland Young) neatly expresses the process to the ghostly George Kerby (Cary Grant) in *Topper* (1937): 'Look – I think I could learn how to live after all, you know? – I . . . I can drink all right . . . and I can dance fine. Now, about singing, hmm? . . . Let's sing a little, eh?' As Henderson notes, spontaneity 'reigns supreme in thirties romantic comedy, where it stands in for and includes wit, intelligence, genuine feeling vs. conventional response, adaptable moral response, vitality, life' (2001: 313). Spontaneity is often linked to improvisation as well, particularly in relation to the adoption of alternative personae: for example, Julia Scott's (Claudette Colbert) drunken escapade in a store window with Lennie Rogers (Michael Bartlett) in *She Married Her Boss*; Lucy Warriner's (Irene Dunne) masquerade as her husband's (Cary Grant) socially unacceptable sister, Lola; or Susan Vance's (Katharine Hepburn) 'Swingin' Door Susie' *alter ego* in *Bringing Up Baby*. Above all else, such performances are playful shifts in identity which lightly mock conventional definitions of gender and class behaviour.

Screwball improvisation and play also involve a resurgence of childlike vitality through the liberating properties of fun and laughter. This can involve a contest, but it also offers the couple an opportunity to put aside their own differences, to act together and share the joke. This emphasis on play involves a rejection of romance (see Chapter 2), but also the displacement of sex. Screwball comedy is fascinated by sex, but cannot explicitly mention its interest, owing to the restrictions of the Production Code; sexual tension is instead displaced on to slapstick violence and energetic play. However, the cycle is a prime exponent of 'sophisticated' meanings, able to imply far more than it actually shows, and occasionally even drawing attention to its ironic compliance with the Code. *It Happened One Night* set the standard, with the famous blanket Walls of Jericho allowing the unmarried couple to share a room: as Ellie puts it, '*That*, I suppose, makes everything quite all right?' The couple's childlike innocence gives further licence to wit: despite the prevalence of *double entendre* and *risqué* situations, screwball comedy is rarely lewd or blatant, primarily because the couple remain oblivious to the implications of their actions and words. Even when David talks of 'losing his bone' in *Bringing Up Baby*, it is said with such an ingenuous lack of innuendo, that any double meaning seems (almost) accidental.

Working girls

By the early 1940s, screwball comedy begins to lose this innocence, as the headstrong heiress is superseded by the sharp-witted con artist. In screwball comedies such as *Midnight* and *Ball of Fire*, sex is becoming a female weapon again, wielded with as much deadly accuracy as the apple Jean Harrington (Barbara Stanwyck) drops on Charles Pike's (Henry Fonda) head in *The Lady Eve*. Indeed, as Lori Landay has pointed out, these female confidence tricksters prefigure the duplicitous *femmes fatales* of *films noirs* (1998: 146), transforming the liberating energies of screwball comedy into a potentially destructive force.

Gender inversion in screwball comedy is usually intended to level the playing field, disrupting the binary hierarchy of masculine/feminine to allow the couple to form an equal relationship. This balance is disrupted in *Ball of Fire* and *The Lady Eve*: the woman's power becomes more obviously exploitative, and the couple's wits seem much less evenly matched. On the one hand, characters such as Jean Harrington and Sugarpuss O'Shea (Stanwyck again, in *Ball of Fire*) are logical developments of screwball comedy's interest in strong-minded, independent women; on the other, their deceptions are premeditated (rather than spontaneously improvised) and criminally (rather than ideologically) transgressive. Partly for these reasons, the female confidence trickster's power tends to backfire: rather than securing the couple's reunion (as in *Bringing Up Baby* or *The Awful Truth*), her actions threaten to destroy her own happiness as well as the hero's.

The figure of the female confidence trickster recurs in a cluster of early 1940s' romantic comedies. As the convention develops, however, it breaks completely with the structures of screwball comedy, forming a small cycle in its own right. In both *Rings on Her Fingers* (1942) and *Slightly Dangerous* (1943), for example, the heroine is originally a working girl (a shop assistant and soda jerk, respectively); dissatisfied with her job, she masquerades as an upper-class lady for financial gain, but lives to regret the success of her trickery. In both films, the heroine is relatively powerless compared to the screwball comedy heroine, and the confidence scheme is soon out of her control. Despite her transgressions, there is little sense of gender inversion, and the happy ending is brought about by the actions of the hero. The later confidence trickster films are also more conventionally romantic than screwball comedy, with love being the main cause of the scheme's failure.

Sentiments of war

The generic process of repetition and difference is still clearer when *Once Upon a Honeymoon* (1942) is considered. Here, too, a working-class girl masquerades as an upper-class lady, but this time in order to catch a wealthy husband. The standard gold-digging plot is complicated, however, when we discover that the object of her 'affection' is Hitler's *agent provocateur*. Unlike most gold-diggers, Katie O'Hara/Katherine Butte-Smith (Ginger Rogers) actually marries Baron Von Luba (Walter Slezak). Consequently, the conventional romantic triangle – with O'Toole (Cary Grant) as its third point – rapidly becomes more dramatic than comic, and ends with the Baron's death. *Once Upon a Honeymoon* attempts to combine occasional screwball situations with more serious issues (including a scene in a Jewish internment camp) but the result is generally awkward and inconsistent. The shift in sensibilities is apparent in the obligatory 'drunk' scene, in which Katie (in upper-class 'Katherine' mode) explains her life view:

> KATIE: I agree with Browning [. . .]: 'The lark's on the wing, The snail's on the thorn, God's in his heaven, All's right with the world.'
> O'TOOLE: That is a truly remarkable bit of philosophy, Baroness, coming at a time like this, when the whole world's going behind a cloud.

Rather than embracing screwball comedy's fun-loving way of life, Katie's optimism is characterised as misplaced and even inappropriate in the current climate. The narrative trajectory of *Once Upon a Honeymoon* involves not the liberation from social stagnation, therefore, but the acceptance of national duty, as Katie accepts the responsibility of spying on her husband.

As this example suggests, America's entry into World War II (December 1941) entailed a dramatic shift in cultural attitudes. The innocence and irresponsibility so vital to the screwball comedy sensibility simply could not survive in this atmosphere of patriotic duty. Romantic comedy went into decline, in terms of quantity and quality. Where screwball comedy had been irreverent and even cynical about American society, film comedy was now quickly engulfed by complacency, sentiment and nostalgia. Treading a fine line between entertainment and propaganda, Hollywood turned its attention to celebrating traditional American values. Period and domestic comedy burgeoned, offering a comforting picture of middle-America to those fighting overseas, at the same time as reassuring those on the home front that life could, and would, return to 'normal'. This generic shift may partly have been in response to institutional factors as well: as Michael Renov points out, 'the loss of male personnel within the studios [. . .] necessitated a greater frequency of pictures starring women, children and animals' (1988: 54).

Career woman comedy

To an extent, the career woman comedy cycle proves an exception to the above characterisation of Hollywood's wartime production. The cycle began in the late 1930s, with films like *Double Wedding* and *Honeymoon in Bali* (1939), and peaked in 1941 and 1942; although production declined between 1942 and 1945, the end of the war heralded a revival of interest (see Appendix). Unlike the concurrent cycle of home front comedies, such as *Government Girl* (1943) and *The Doughgirls* (1944), which invariably required their working girl heroines to contribute to the war effort, only a few career woman comedies refer directly to the war. Instead, the cycle was primarily concerned with the changing role of women in the public sphere – a concern that was exacerbated by the unprecedented influx of women into the labour force during the war. Like the female confidence trickster, the career woman's characterisation reflects the increasingly misogynistic tenor of American culture, transforming female power into a problem.

It is worth clarifying the distinction being made here between 'working girl' and 'career woman'. The primary difference is between wage labour and a salaried profession. Working girls in romantic comedy tend to be secretaries, shop assistants and waitresses. These jobs not only lack authority and public power, they are also conventionally 'feminine' roles, providing support, service, food and care. Although the job titles may have changed during the war crisis, the working girl's function as assistant remains essentially the same. Implicitly, this kind of employment is understood as an acceptable substitute for wifely duties, and it is assumed that the job will be put aside once the girl's real work (marriage) begins. In the career woman comedy, however, the heroine's career tends to take precedence over all other aspects of her life, partly because her occupation is more usually understood as 'men's' work. She is the managing executive, not the secretary; the magazine editor, not the model; the political correspondent, not the gossip columnist;

the doctor, not the nurse. The gender distinction is two-fold, therefore, placing the heroine in a 'male' profession and giving her a position of authority (rather than a 'feminine' supporting role).

The career woman's power depends upon this 'masculine' positioning, and the films often begin with the comic revelation of the heroine's sex. For example, in *They All Kissed the Bride*, a group of middle-aged executives march into a boardroom to the beat of a military drum. When the corporation head, M. J. Drew (Joan Crawford), enters the room, one of the men stands up; she sternly berates him for treating her like a woman. In this respect, it is particularly significant that the career woman comedy re-establishes a male-dominated courtship pattern, with the hero pursuing the heroine. This pattern functions in part as a corrective to the woman's masculine activity in the workplace, and some of these films end with the woman deliberately adopting a passive position as a method of acknowledging the error of her ways. Thus, while inversion in screwball comedy revealed the inadequacy of conventional notions of active/masculine, passive/feminine to describe 'male' and 'female', here such notions are reaffirmed by treating inversion as 'unnatural' and the cause of conflict.

Indeed, the very phrase 'career woman' often appears to be partly understood as a contradiction in terms. A similarly oxymoronic effect is found in Ted Sennett's alternative label for the cycle: 'boss-ladies' (1973: 197). Sennett takes the description directly from *Lady in the Dark*, in which fashion editor, Liza Elliot (Ginger Rogers), is contemptuously addressed as 'boss-lady' by her advertising director, Charley Johnson (Ray Milland). As this suggests, there is something implicitly derogatory in the phrase, which is one reason why I have followed later critics in describing the cycle as career woman comedy (Walsh 1984: 137 and Harvey 1998: 414). Neither term seems to have been used at the time, however, and contemporary reviews generally refer to the relevant films simply as 'romantic comedy', 'comedy' or 'farce'. *Variety* provides one exception, describing *They All Kissed the Bride* as 'another in the current Hollywood cycle of girl-immersed-in-biz vs. irresponsible male' (3 June 1942); despite the lack of a pithy label, the review at least confirms that a cycle was seen to exist.

As 'girl-immersed-in-biz vs. irresponsible male' suggests, the basic structure of the career woman comedy involves a conventional battle of the sexes. The source of conflict is not simply the woman's career, but also the disproportionate energy and time which she devotes to it. Thus, although the heroine may hold a powerful, public position of authority, the films usually suggest that her success in this man's world comes at a cost: no social life and *No Time for Love* (1943). Into her life comes a man with less public power, either literally working for her, or representing a more creative, 'carefree' way of life (a writer, journalist or footloose bohemian type). The exact dynamics of this power relationship vary. In some cases, the man resents her power, possibly even wanting her job (*Lady in the Dark*); in others, he converts her to his way of living (*They All Kissed the Bride*). Either way, it is the woman who is the problem and the problem is solved by the man.

Effectively, this structure reverses the screwball pattern: now it is the woman who is stuck in a rut, and the man who must teach her how to live. In theory, such a reversal need not be reactionary; in practice, however, the exposition reveals a conservative logic. As Harvey notes, 'it was no longer the witty heroine who had the edge but the feet-on-the-ground hero' (1998: 409). As the cycle develops, the hero's values are increasingly naturalised as common sense, rather than celebrated as eccentric. Most importantly, he does not teach the career woman how to be a better human being, but how to be a better woman. The narrative process of change primarily involves the transformation of the heroine, therefore, and often involves her public and/or private humiliation.

While this begins to suggest intransigent levels of sexism and misogyny, the narrative logic tends to be more confused and contradictory, particularly with regard to 'natural' and performative gender. The career woman's assumption of a 'male' position is usually accompanied by the 'masculinisation' of her personality: she is *too* practical and efficient (supposedly masculine traits). Again, *They All Kissed the Bride* offers a useful example. In addition to the androgynous initials (a common strategy), M. J.'s appearance is stern and masculinised. She wears a plain-coloured suit with shoulder pads, relatively unadorned, and her hairstyle is quite severe. The heroine's masculine appearance and behaviour is understood as 'unnatural' and must be replaced with 'natural' femininity, but this process is often equated with *appearing* more feminine, primarily by dressing more glamorously and wearing more cosmetics. This physical appearance is then extended to include behaviour, ending with the woman deliberately adopting a subordinate position. The heroine performs femininity, but paradoxically is somehow more 'natural' because of it.

This contradiction is often 'explained' by reference to (vulgar) psychoanalysis. Psychiatrists and doctors are stock characters in the career woman comedy; indeed, the career woman may be one herself, as in *She Wouldn't Say Yes* (1945) and *Let's Live a Little* (1948). Usually, the woman's 'masculine' behaviour and appearance is translated into her repression of her 'natural' femininity. By this logic, the career woman comedy psychopathologises gender essentialism: practicality is naturally masculine in a man; in a woman, it is a sign of her repressed emotions and frigidity. Masculine rationality becomes feminine irrationality. The theme of repression is often elaborated through the use of fantasy sequences. *Lady in the Dark* takes this furthest, with Liza's spectacular dreams being explained by her psychiatrist as symptoms of her neurosis.

While screwball comedy was *Love Crazy*, the career woman comedy treats love as the key to sanity. As the tagline for *They All Kissed the Bride* declares, 'There's Never Anything Wrong With A Woman That A Man's Lips Won't Cure.' The hero's pursuit of the heroine unleashes her repressed femininity and re-establishes 'normal' relations. Often the career woman is highly resistant to love and relinquishes self-control only at the last moment. Indeed, a secondary plot structure found in a number of career woman comedies places 'love' in direct opposition to the career woman's plan of action. For example, in *This Thing Called Love* (1941), insurance agent, Ann Winters (Rosalind Russell) marries Tice Collins (Melvyn Douglas) with the proviso that for the first three months the marriage should remain unconsummated. Her intention is ostensibly pragmatic: she has written a pamphlet entitled 'A Practical Solution to the Marriage Problem', intended to reduce the number of divorces (presumably by replacing them with annulments) and her own marriage is a test case. Her 'practical' approach is rendered absurd, and dismissed by Tice's lawyer (Allyn Joslyn) as one of those 'silly ideas females have every now and then'. In fact, Ann's motivation is explained in relation to her own parents' divorce when she was six, again psychopathologising the heroine's problem. A wooden fertility god features in the narrative. In the final shot, the figure opens its eyes, literally overseeing the consummation of the marriage. In the same way that Maggie starts daydreaming about babies in *They All Kissed the Bride*, love and sex are identified with procreation, reasserting woman's biological function as paramount.

To sum up, the career woman comedy replaces screwball reversals with gender contradiction, and eccentricity with neurosis. Love is a cure for the career woman's illness and is both more romantic and sexual (particularly in relation to reproduction) than in screwball comedy. Play has been replaced with a more aggressive competition for power – a competition which the woman inevitably loses.

Recycling and rejuvenation

By the 1950s, the 'problem' of the career woman no longer excited such anxiety. As the feminine mystique took hold, women seemed happy to fulfil their 'natural' career as homemakers. Hollywood's production of romantic comedy lacked inspiration: a spate of insipid remakes reworked pre-war plots, often with musical numbers and Technicolor production values. In addition to the remake of *My Man Godfrey*, *The Awful Truth* was remade as *Let's Do It Again* (1953), and *The Birds and the Bees* (1956) recycled *The Lady Eve*.

You Can't Run Away from It (1956), *Silk Stockings* (1957) and *The Girl Most Likely* (1957) were musical versions of *It Happened One Night*, *Ninotchka*, and *Tom, Dick and Harry*, respectively. Perhaps most bizarre were the reworkings of *Nothing Sacred* (1937), *The Major and the Minor* (1942) and *The Miracle of Morgan's Creek* (1944) as the Jerry Lewis and Dean Martin vehicles *Living It Up* (1954), *You're Never Too Young* (1955) and *Rock-a-Bye Baby* (1958, without Martin). In each case, Lewis is cast in the role originally played by a woman (respectively, Carole Lombard, Ginger Rogers and Betty Hutton).

This erasure of strong female leads by an infantile male speaks volumes about the representation of women in the fifties. Instead of the intelligent sophistication of Claudette Colbert or Irene Dunne, romantic comedy was dominated by dumb blondes (Judy Holliday, Marilyn Monroe, Jayne Mansfield) and spunky girl-next-door types (June Allyson, Shirley MacLaine, Debbie Reynolds). The older male stars, however, were still claiming romantic abilities, resulting in a cycle of May–September romantic comedies, such as *Sabrina* (1954, Audrey Hepburn choosing Humphrey Bogart over William Holden), *Susan Slept Here* (1954, Dick Powell and Debbie Reynolds), *Love in the Afternoon* (1957, Gary Cooper and Audrey Hepburn), *But Not for Me* (1959, Clark Gable choosing ex-wife Lilli Palmer rather than Carroll Baker) and *The Moon Is Blue* (Maggie McNamara resisting David Niven's charms in favour of William Holden).

The particular notoriety of *The Moon Is Blue* lies in its defiance of the Production Code. Based on a Broadway play, the film openly referred to virgins, pregnancy, seduction, and mistresses, and alluded to prostitution as well. The PCA refused to grant the film a seal of approval, but United Artists released it anyway. This was one of the first public challenges to the code, and the film's success proved a watershed. This shift towards a more 'adult' cinema undoubtedly reflected the commercial challenge posed by the more family-oriented medium of television – but the 1953 release of *The Moon Is Blue* also coincided with the launch of *Playboy* magazine and the publication of Alfred Kinsey's second report, *Sexual Behaviour in the Human Female* (which spent several months on the *New York Times* best-seller list). America was evidently obsessed with sex.

Sex comedy

Broadly speaking, the majority of Hollywood romantic comedies can be described as sex comedies, given that sex is usually an issue, albeit an implicit one. However, 'sex comedy' is more commonly used to describe a type of Hollywood comedy produced during the late 1950s and early 1960s. The term 'sex comedy' was rarely applied at the time and contemporary reviews tend to combine a variety of suggestive adjectives ('adult', 'sexy', 'racy', '*risqué*') with more generic nouns such as 'comedy' and 'farce'.[11] The *Variety* review of *Pillow Talk* demonstrates that a cycle was certainly recognised: 'a sleekly sophisticated production that deals chiefly with S-E-X. [. . .] follows the current trend in romantic comedies of being about as broad as the traffic allows these days' (12 August 1959). Their review of *Strange Bedfellows* (1964) is still more telling: 'Story line differs enough so that it isn't [a] simple carbon copy of all the [Rock] Hudson–Tony Randall–Doris Day comedies that have come before' (16 December 1964). The same issue describes *Kiss Me, Stupid* (1964) as both a 'sex comedy' and a 'sexploitation comedy'.

In an important sense, 'sexploitation comedy' is a more accurate description, since a key theme of the cycle is the connection between sex and money – or more specifically sexual desire and consumerism. For example, in *Ask Any Girl*, Meg Wheeler (Shirley MacLaine) asks market research expert Miles Doughton (David Niven) to help market her as the ideal wife/object of desire for his playboy brother, Evan (Gig Young). Having discovered what Evan finds attractive in each of his numerous girlfriends – from hair colour to cooking – she imitates each and every unique trait and finally succeeds in getting him to propose. By this point, though, she has realised she actually loves Miles.

The cycle frequently makes such use of consumer industries and products as plot material. For example, *Will Success Spoil Rock Hunter?* (1957), *I Married a Woman* (1958) and *Lover Come Back* all deal with advertising; *Pillow Talk* makes use of interior design; and *It Started with a Kiss*, *Pillow Talk* and *That Touch of Mink* use specific consumer objects as narrative devices. The films' glossy *mise-en-scène* embodies these narrative interests, but it also relates more directly to consumerism through the extratextual importance of spectacular *haute couture* costumes, widescreen formats and colour processing. Thus, while the Day–Hudson comedies have been recognised by most reviewers and critics as central to the cycle, a more important connection between *Pillow Talk*, *Lover Come Back* and other sex comedies is their visual style – the 'sleekly sophisticated' production values noted by the *Variety* reviewer. Similar comments are made about *The Tender Trap*: 'the picture has been given a plushy look [. . .] through slick settings and the CinemaScope–Eastman Color lensing' (*Variety*, 26 October 1955). Another review notes that, 'like "Pillow Talk" and other recent-vintage comedies, "Lover Come Back" has its girls beautifully gowned and its sets handsomely dressed' (*Variety*, 12 December 1961). As this glossy style implies, the diegetic world of the sex comedy is entirely metropolitan and most of the films are set in Manhattan. Key sites include glamorous apartments, swanky bars and restaurants, and corporate offices.

The sex comedy plot repeatedly centres on the twin themes of virginity and seduction. Most commonly, a virginal career girl and a bachelor playboy meet: she wants love (and marriage), he wants sex (without commitment). Courtship patterns are confused: in most cases, the woman thinks she is taking the lead, but only because the playboy has resorted to devious methods of seduction, including masquerading as someone else. These deceptions are inevitably found out (just) before the virgin gives in to his charms. In the meantime, the playboy has fallen in love with the heroine, usually because she is marked out as 'different' from other women: her virginal status functions to signify her 'worth' and the rate of sexual exchange is marriage.

This shift to outright seduction is one of the most overt developments between the cycles. According to the Production Code, seduction is 'never the proper subject for comedy' ('The Production Code' 1996: 140); this is apparently no longer considered the case by the late 1950s. Few of the later sex comedies are as frank about sex as *The Moon Is Blue*, but the characters are far more self-conscious of innuendo than the blithely innocent screwball couple were. The sex comedy also makes full use of the cinematic rhetoric of romance: passionate kisses, soft-focus close-ups, and emotion-enforcing music are entirely typical. However, this rhetoric is not necessarily used sincerely and, more often than not, romance is associated with the artifice of seduction, in opposition to the 'naturalness' of 'true' love. Seduction and romance are revealed to be based upon manipulation and commodification.

In this respect, the cycle's glossy visual style is symptomatic of a wider thematic interest in image and identity. While adopting an alternative persona in screwball comedy involved a playful shift in identity, and masquerade in the career woman comedy involved a corrective performance of feminine subordination, in the sex comedy such masquerades are deliberately intended to manipulate and mislead. The implicit opposition between artificial image and 'authentic' identity is not always resolved decisively, however, and on occasion the cycle demonstrates a postmodern awareness of the social construction of gender and sexual identities. Moreover (unlike screwball comedy, in which the heroine assumes an identity) it is usually the identity of the hero which is in question. In *Teacher's Pet* (1958), *Pillow Talk*, *Lover Come Back* and *Sex and the Single Girl*, the hero literally pretends to be someone else in order to seduce the heroine, but the level of deception is not always this extreme. For example, in *Sunday in New York* (1963), Mike Mitchell (Rod Taylor) and Adam Tyler (Cliff Robertson) have to pretend to be each other, in order to protect the 'honour' of Adam's sister, Eileen (Jane Fonda). To add to the confusion, Adam and Mike then rehearse Eileen's explanation to her fiancé, Russ Wilson (Robert Culp): in the middle of a Japanese restaurant, Adam and Mike dance with each other, pretending to be Eileen and Russ, respectively.

The resulting destabilisation of male identity is an integral facet of the sex comedy's representation of cultural anxiety about masculinity. As Chapter 6 elucidates, the playboy's heterosexual virility is seriously compromised by such masquerades. This instability is partly displaced on to the neurotic side-kick, who may also be the Wrong Man. Often played by Gig Young or Tony Randall, this figure is presented as comparatively inadequate, neurotic and emasculated. He is also the hero's friend. As Neale notes, the neurotic side-kick was 'frequently undergoing analysis' and 'became the site of all that was suppressed in the figure of the hero – insecurity, failure, sexual uncertainty, a lack of control, an inability to cope with the demands and pressures of modern life, and so on' (1992a: 292). This 'sexual uncertainty' means that the sidekick may also function as the heroine's potential love rival: there is often some confusion about the sidekick's sexuality, which can also involve confusion about his identity. For example, in *That Touch of Mink*, the heroine's friends repeatedly mistake the neurotic sidekick, Roger (Gig Young), for the playboy hero, Philip Shayne (Cary Grant); but he is also mistaken for a 'homosexual' by his analyst, Dr Gruber (Alan Hewitt). This error is only compounded by the film's coda sequence, in which Roger proudly shows the doctor 'his' baby.

This kind of coda sequence is quite common in sex comedies and often functions to destabilise the 'normative' resolution of heterosexual union. In particular, sexual consummation tends to be elided with reproduction as well as marriage. Thus, *Sunday in New York* ends with Adam walking in on Eileen and Mike about to have premarital sex. Rather than prevent this happening (as he would have earlier in the film), Adam discreetly leaves the apartment and throws away the key, at the same time as his voice-over tells us, 'And so they were married. And went to Japan for their honeymoon, and had three lovely daughters, who grew up and were lectured by their father and, of course, me, their uncle, on the nice things that can happen to a girl if she remains virtuous, even on a rainy Sunday in New York.' In one sense, this voiceover functions as a safety-valve, reassuring the conservative spectator that they lived normatively ever after. In another sense, the entirely unprecedented voice-over draws attention to the film's manipulation of time and space to achieve a conventionally happy ending. As Sikov notes, 'voice-over narration specifically addressed the fact of form throughout the era' (1994: 195) and typically 'present[ed] the audience with versions of reality that declare[d] themselves by their very nature to be mediated, structured, and controlled' (1994: 195–6). Perhaps most importantly, as far as the sex comedy is concerned, Adam's voiceover also completely elides sexual pleasure with its consequences: (consumer) desire can only lead to (mass) reproduction.

Some initial conclusions

Even a brief survey of Hollywood romantic comedy between 1934 and 1965 demonstrates that the various cycles embody quite different versions of the heterosexual couple. While the structures of romantic comedy have remained relatively stable – mistaken identities, deceptions, gender inversion, and happy endings – the functions of these structures have differed dramatically. The stock characters and conventions of each cycle are similarly distinct, and figures such as the runaway heiress, the career woman, the bachelor playboy and the neurotic sidekick reflect culturally specific discourses and anxieties. But these conventions are only the most easily recognised elements of generic repetition and difference. A more complex understanding of the representation of the heterosexual couple will involve analysing the key themes of marriage, equality and desire, and their shifting importance from cycle to cycle.

Notes

1 A distinction needs to be made, though, between romantic comedies which aim for laughter, and romantic melodramas which are (or have become) laughable. For example, the melodramatic excess of a film like *All that Heaven Allows* (1955) may now cause audiences to burst into laughter more often than tears, but this does not make the film a romantic comedy. Music is a good indicator of the intended mood.

2 Some romantic comedies involve multiple couples, but star pecking order usually means a central couple still dominates, while the other couples provide additional thematic facets.

3 New Comedy was 'new' in comparison to the Old Comedy of Aristophanes (fifth century BC). Old Comedy was a form of satire, while New Comedy was more a comedy of manners.

4 For example, Horton (1991: 10), and Karnick and Jenkins (1995: 73 and 165). Although Shakespeare makes use of various New Comedy devices (such as twins), 'it is only in Jonson and the Restoration writers that English comedy can be called a form of New Comedy' (Frye 1984: 79).

5 The carnivalesque has its roots in medieval festivals and the Roman Saturnalia – a festival in which slaves and masters changed clothes and roles for a day (see Bakhtin 1984). 'Liminality' refers to the temporary possibilities of threshold spaces: such spaces are associated with social transitions (e.g. the bride being carried across the threshold), but have also been theorised as spaces of ambiguity and contradiction existing on the margins of social norms (see Rowe 1995: 8).

6 Indeed, making such a claim would create a false sense of continuity, since it would involve renaming Shakespearean comedy 'romantic'. The adjective 'romantic' ('like a romance') did not even exist until the mid-seventeenth century, precisely at that moment when Renaissance romance poetry began to fall from favour. The OED appears to date 'romantic comedy' from 1872, quoting George Eliot's *Middlemarch*: 'they looked like a couple dropped out of a romantic comedy'. However, if this quotation is put into context (Eliot 1988: 406), it is revealed that the couple in question are the young Ladislaw and old Miss Noble: the line is

spoken by Lydgate who is poking fun at Ladislaw, comparing him to Daphnis, the mythological shepherd who invented pastoral poetry (presumably implying Miss Noble is a sheep). At this point, then, 'romantic comedy' refers to the kind of pastoral romance Shakespeare mocks in *As You Like It*.

7 Bordwell (1982: 4) does recognise that genre may provide adequate motivation to justify the happy ending, and that, in genres like comedy and melodrama, coincidence can supersede causal motivation; however, he does not seem to consider these genres significant enough to problematise the dominance of the classical narrative model.

8 'Cycle' thus refers to moments in a genre's history, but not necessarily to a predictable pattern of development. The term is certainly not intended to evoke 'life cycle' or evolutionary models of genre development (see Altman 1999: 21–2).

9 All quotations from *Variety* are taken from the collected volumes of *'Variety's' Film Reviews* (1983), which list reviews in chronological order by date of publication; no authors or original page numbers are given.

10 For other examples of how contemporary reviewers constructed *It Happened One Night* as the progenitor of a new type of romantic comedy, see *Variety*'s reviews of *The Bride Comes Home* (1935; reviewed 1 March 1936) and *The Bride Walks Out* (15 July 1936).

11 For example, see the *Variety* reviews of *The Moon Is Blue* (3 June 1953), *The Tunnel of Love* (15 October 1958), *It Started with a Kiss* (19 August 1959), *Happy Anniversary* (4 November 1959) and *Lover Come Back* (13 December 1961).

Part II

Marriage

Private conversation: Myrna Loy and William Powell in *The Thin Man* (1934).
Courtesy of Turner Entertainment.

2

The same, but different: marriage, remarriage and screwball comedy

There is a moment early in *The Awful Truth* when Lucy Warriner (Irene Dunne), having decided to divorce her husband, Jerry (Cary Grant), telephones their lawyer. Rather than cutting to the interior of a suitable office, the scene cuts to a large but gloomy drawing-room, filled with old-fashioned lumps of furniture. The telephone is answered by a man with silvery-grey hair and a moustache. Discovering the reason for Lucy's call, the lawyer's jovial tone turns to benevolent concern, and he attempts to lecture Lucy on how 'marriage is a beautiful thing'. As he speaks, his own wife enters the room; she too is rather gloomy and old-fashioned, and hovers in the background of the frame, repeatedly interrupting him.

> LAWYER: As I was saying, Lucy [*smiling and sincere*] marriage is a beautiful thing, and when you've been married as long as I have, you'll appreciate it too.
> WIFE: [*stepping forward and speaking quite crossly*] Your food is getting ice cold. You're always complaining about your food. How do you expect me –
> LAWYER: [*interrupting angrily*] Will you shut your big mouth! I'll eat when I get good and ready and if you don't like it you know what you can do! So – shut up! [*Turns away again*] Lucy, darling [*soft and gentle*], marriage is a beautiful thing!

The couple's age and stiff appearance and their outdated decor evoke a past era. The Victorian myth of domestic bliss is casually ripped to shreds, even as the voice of its authority – the lawyer/patriarch – attempts to reassert its virtue. Patriarchal authority is undermined further by the fact that Lucy clearly does not take his advice: the next shot is of the chancery court, and, while the lawyer is present at the divorce hearing, he does not say a word.

The awful truth

Bearing this sequence in mind, there is an evident tension between the diegetic representation of marriage and the screwball narrative's drive to unite the couple. Marriage is never a 'beautiful thing' in screwball comedy; it is always a problem. No one simply falls in love, gets married and lives happily ever after. Instead, the central couple pretend to be married (*If You Could Only Cook*, *Midnight*), pretend they are not married (*The Palm Beach Story*), think they are married (*Mr and Mrs Smith* (1941)) or get divorced (*His Girl Friday*). Engagements are made to be broken (*My Man Godfrey*, *Bringing Up Baby*, *Holiday*), implied adultery abounds (*She Married Her Boss*, *The Awful Truth*, *Topper*) and bigamy seems almost inevitable (*Libeled Lady*, *My Favorite Wife* (1940)). Every variation on the themes of marital duplicity and infidelity appears in screwball comedy. Indeed, there are hardly any happily married characters: it is a world peopled with widowed fathers, maiden aunts, bachelor butlers and maids. Thus, although the central couple is inevitably united at the end of the film, the exact status and conditions of this relationship should not be too hastily or unequivocally identified with the traditional institution of 'marriage', let alone with the convention of 'living happily ever after'.

This chapter reviews the tension between the union of the couple and the representation of marriage in screwball comedy. If marriage is not a beautiful thing, the question remains – what is it? A closer look at *It Happened One Night* clarifies the cycle's attitude. Ellie Andrews (Claudette Colbert) is already married to King Westley (Jameson Thomas) but according to her father (Walter Connolly) she will 'never [. . .] live under the same roof with him'.[1] 'Living under the same roof' functions euphemistically for the sexual consummation of the marriage (thereby presumably also confirming Ellie's virginity), but it proves to mean much more, since Ellie *does* live under the same roof with Peter Warne (Clark Gable) while pretending to be his wife. Is 'marriage' constituted by the social and legal fact of the wedding ceremony, or by the personal and physical act of 'living under the same roof'? Further questions develop when Ellie and Peter convince two detectives that they are married by quarrelling loudly: he accuses her of butting in, and the argument quickly turns towards issues of protection, possession and jealousy. Ellie pretends to cry while Peter shouts at her to 'quit bawling', even threatening to hit her; she cowers in her seat in the lower left corner of the frame, while Peter looms over her, oppressively pacing back and forth. This wretched excuse for a relationship convinces not only the detectives, but the camp manager as well: 'I told you they were a perfectly nice married couple.'

Marriage is commonly understood in the screwball world to involve misery, oppression and confinement; it is 'nice' because it is legal and, therefore, respectable. At the same time, marriage no longer necessarily involves a lifetime commitment: the narrative demands that Ellie should have one marriage annulled in order to marry the man to whom she is pretending to be married. Schatz claims the film's 'false marriages [. . .] prepare us for the "real" marriage at the end' (1981: 154), but it seems more logical to read the two 'false' marriages as undercutting the status of the legal and social institution – especially considering the words of the auto-camp manager's wife (Maidel Turner) at the end of the film: 'If you ask me, I don't believe they're married.' The paradox that Ellie and Peter are now less convincing as a 'perfectly nice married couple' is clearly related to the film's earlier representation of the institution as a battleground of misery, not a playground of fun and games and toy trumpets (Peter has requested such an item from the camp manager (Harry Holman), and it is used to signal the symbolic fall of the blanket walls of Jericho). Ellie and Peter's 'difference' is repeatedly coded as eccentric craziness – the antithesis of the social stability normally associated with marriage. For example, when Mr Andrews asks Peter if he loves Ellie, Peter evades the question: 'A normal human being couldn't live under the same roof with her without going nutty.' When pushed to answer more directly, Peter yells, '*Yes*! But don't hold that against me – I'm a little screwy myself!' Apparently, the question of living under the same roof has been answered, and it has as much to do with being institutionalised for insanity, as with the institution of marriage.[2]

Schatz goes on to make the conventional argument about the romantic comedy resolution: 'their personal union serves to celebrate integration into the community at large, into a social environment where cultural conflicts and contradictions have been magically reconciled' (1981: 155). However, the couple's reunion – the 'real' marriage – is not even seen; our last view of Ellie is of her running *away* from the altar, having decided not to officially marry King after all. The distance placed between the couple and society (including the spectator) seems to indicate a withdrawal from the public sphere and, therefore, quite the reverse of the traditional 'social integration'. Even on those occasions when the narrative does culminate in a wedding, the effect is usually far from affirmative and only serves to undermine the status of the institution further. The end (and beginning) of *The Palm Beach Story* is a key example, in which the myth of marital bliss is undercut by the use of transparent framed titles: the first declares 'and they lived happily ever after', but the second asks 'or did they?'. The qualification certainly seems justified if a closer look is taken at the final ceremony. Although the New Comedy conceit of twin siblings manipulates the possibility of a happy ending for all, the actual ceremony belies that possibility: while J. D. Hackensacker III (Rudy Vallee) is smiling at his bride, she peers round at her sister, Gerry Jeffers (Claudette Colbert), as if to ask, 'What have I got myself into?' before forcing a sickly grin; meanwhile, Tom Jeffer's brother (Joel McCrea) does a double-take of his bride, Princess Centimilla (Mary Astor), as if to say, 'How did I get here?' The presence of the Princess's pet admirer, Toto (Sig Arno), at the end of the line-up (as Best Man?) is the final taunt to the 'sanctity' of marriage and the 'happiness' of endings. Other examples of less than affirmative weddings include *Double Wedding* and *Four's a Crowd* (1938). In the former, the ceremony almost takes place in a caravan, but a riot ensues, leaving the couple unconscious and unmarried. In the latter, two couples swap partners at the very last moment, causing the *New York Times* reviewer to comment on the film's 'unblushingly superficial attitude toward romance (you never care who's going to marry who)' (quoted by Jacobs 1969: 534).

Despite this remorseless attitude to 'beautiful marriage', many critics still assume that the union of the couple in screwball comedy is ultimately conservative (see Sklar 1978: 187–8, Schatz 1981: 171, Neale and Krutnik 1990: 155–6). Wes D. Gehring is typical:

> The game still has the most conservative of goals: the heroine's madcap maneuvers are often used to capture a male and break him – or save him – from [. . .] anti-social rigidity. This is best summed up with the term marriage, or the promise of marriage, which ends the screwball comedy, reaffirming one of the most traditional institutions in Western society. (1986: 154–5)

The couple's intimate relationship is automatically and inevitably tied to traditional marriage and reaffirmation of the status quo – irrespective of the thematic and narrative content of the film. It is unclear, for example, how the 'heroine's madcap maneuvers' can be equated quite so easily with 'traditional' marriage, since traditionally marriage is controlled by patriarchy. Part of the problem is the critical tendency to collapse the union of a heterosexual couple with the social and ideological institution of marriage: the screwball ending tends, as Gehring so imprecisely puts it, to be '*summed up* with the term marriage' (my emphasis). However, not all screwball comedies end with a proposal, let alone a wedding; there is no mention of marriage at the end of *Holiday* or *Bringing Up Baby*, for example. While marriage may well be implied (or assumed), this is not the same thing as conservative reaffirmation. It would be literally impossible for a 1930s' Hollywood film, made under the moral guardianship of the Production Code, to explicitly reject marriage as the framework for a heterosexual relationship – but this does not necessarily mean that the film endorses that framework. The awful truth for screwball comedy is that there is no alternative to marriage.

The very term 'marriage' can be a source of confusion, depending on whether it is being used to refer to the legal institution, or a more general 'summing up' of the heterosexual relationship. For example, David R. Shumway argues that screwball comedy is conservative because it mystifies the state of marriage, 'portraying it as the goal – but not the end – of romance' (1991: 7); he presumes marriage is constituted by the final union and the legal fact. Stanley Cavell, on the other hand, takes a more philosophical approach, disconnecting the concept of marriage from the necessity of a legal contract. He argues that, in *It Happened One Night*, 'what we have been shown in the previous auto camps is something like their [Ellie and Peter's] marriage. We know of course that they have not been legally, actually married, but we also know that those things do not always constitute marriage, and we may freely wonder what does' (1981: 85). In their own ways, both Shumway and Cavell are right: the films do tend to mystify the institutional state of marriage by postponing the legal fact until the end of the film; but we are also meant to understand the central couple's relationship as questioning the constitution of that marriage and proposing an alternative model. For if Ellie and Peter's playful relationship seems 'something like a marriage' to Cavell, it is certainly characterised as something like a 'not-marriage' by the conventions of the diegetic world. Cavell's use of the term 'marriage' confuses the issue: the collapse of any distinction between an ideal heterosexual relationship and 'marriage' reabsorbs the potential space for resistance to the institutional status quo.[3] To avoid further confusion, the use of the term 'marriage' is hereafter restricted to the legal fact.

A further problem arises from the critical tendency to treat marriage ahistorically as 'one of the most traditional institutions in Western society' (Gehring 1986: 155), rather than as a culturally determined convention, whose specific meanings and functions alter over time. However, as Cavell recognises, the cycle's emphasis on *re*marriage suggests that 'marriage, which was to be a ratification, is itself in need of ratification' (1981: 31). Although he does not explicitly place this need for 'ratification' within a material context, his discussion does at least suggest that a specific cultural moment has prompted this narrative interest in the state and constitution of marriage.

Something old, something new

The fact of marriage may not have changed, but the modern era brought a shift in the popular meanings and expectations of love and marriage in America.[4] There was a sense of crisis as marriage rates dropped and divorce rates continued to rise; birth rates reached an all-time low in 1935 and the size of the middle-class family shrank, from an average of six children to two or three.[5] Liberal reformers and social commentators considered marriage to be in a state of transition, and frequently contrasted an outmoded 'Victorian' patriarchal model to a modern egalitarian concept of love companionship. For example, J. P. Lichtenberger claimed, 'the ancient economic–patriarchal form of the family has fulfilled its function and is becoming obsolete. [. . .] Masculine lordship is now being replaced by mutuality or mergence [*sic*] of wills in domestic affairs' (1931: 285; cf. Groves 1928, Lindsey and Evans 1928: 32, and Seidman 1991: 72–8). The patriarchal model was widely understood to be founded upon economic considerations and gender inequality, with arranged marriages and the strict separation of male/public and female/domestic spheres. Victorians considered sexual desire and sensuality to be base and egotistical, threatening both the spiritual nature of love and the social 'responsibility' of procreation. Sexual desire was a distinctly male prerogative, and the double standard prevailed: while the beastly husband struggled to contain his vile passions, the 'cult of true womanhood' placed the morally and sexually pure wife on a pedestal.

This understanding of Victorian sexuality and marriage is simplistic and problematic.[6] Nonetheless, these stereotypes played a key part in discourses around marriage in the 1920s and 1930s, helping create a common-sense understanding of the ways in which marriage had 'changed' – and masking the ways in which it had not.[7] Top of the list of 'changes' was an emphasis on love: according to Ludwig Lewisjohn, marriage 'should be held to be created by love and sustained by love', but that love should also involve a 'precise blending of passion and spiritual harmony and solid friendship' (1925: 200; cf. Groves 1928: 90, Lichtenberger 1931: 341, Dell 1973: 209). While Victorian love was based on spiritual affinity, modern love incorporated sexual fulfilment and companionship.

Judge Ben B. Lindsey defined the modern form of marriage quite specifically: 'Companionate Marriage is legal marriage, with legalized Birth Control, and with the right to divorce by mutual consent for childless couples, usually without payment of alimony' (Lindsey and Evans 1928: v). He recognised companionate marriage as a co-existing alternative to the traditional 'Family' marriage; indeed, should a companionate couple have a child, then the marriage would automatically revert to the traditional concept (1928: 139). Moreover, barring the legal aspects, Lindsey repeatedly asserted that companionate marriage was not an innovation, but a reality (1928: v, 139, 175) – at least for those middle-class couples with enough education and wealth to employ birth control methods and lawyers.

Companionate marriage, in Lindsey's sense, required a specific institutional system, but it was popularly understood to redefine marriage in more egalitarian terms, reflecting the increased independence of women. The traditional stereotypes of female sexuality (passive, indifferent, uninterested) were being undermined by the actions of the 'New Woman' and the flapper: the recorded incidence of female premarital intercourse rose significantly for those coming of age in the 1920s (D'Emilio and Freedman 1997: 256–7). It was commonplace to attribute the 'changing morality' to the demands of the emancipated woman (see Kirchwey 1925: viii and Groves 1928: 216) and, for the first time, mutual sexual satisfaction was becoming an expectation within marriage. Contemporary advice manuals, such as Margaret Sanger's *Happiness in Marriage* aimed to educate the couple in sex techniques to promote reciprocal satisfaction – including a wider variety of positions and more sensual behaviour. This potentially radical acknowledgement of female sexuality was usually qualified, however, by the reiteration of conventional gender traits: the woman was generally still cast as the more passive and sensitive partner, with the man in control of the situation (see Sanger 1927: 66, 128). As women were becoming more overtly sexual, sex was also becoming divorced from its procreative function. Victorian marriage (and marital sex) had been predicated upon procreation; modern couples were actively avoiding having children, despite the legal prohibitions on contraception (D'Emilio and Freedman 1997: 243–5). Birth control was seen as playing a major part in the changing ideology of marriage: indeed, according to Judge Ben B. Lindsey, birth control 'brought the Companionate [marriage] into existence' (Lindsey and Evans 1928: v).

Companionate marriage also became conflated with the more general sense of 'love companionship', emphasising emotional compatibility and mutual interests. Consequently, modern love extended not only into the bedroom, but also into the public domain of shared leisure activities. It is no coincidence that the increased emphasis on personal happiness and on enjoying pursuits together corresponded with the rise of consumerism.

Personal consumption nearly tripled between 1909 and 1929, with leisure pursuits and personal appearance becoming the key areas of expenditure (May 1980: 51). Consumerism certainly shaped the personal realm of courtship, not least in the rise of dating, which had 'almost completely replaced the old system of calling by the mid-1920s' (Bailey 1989: 13). While calling took place in the privacy of the girl's home, dating took place in the public sphere of cinemas, diners, and dance halls. By its very nature, dating necessitated consumption, quickly becoming a 'system of exchange' (Bailey 1989: 22) in which the boy's money played the most powerful role. The distribution of power between the sexes thereby shifted, from the girl who took the initiative in the calling system, to the boy who asked her for a date (see Chapter 6).

The amount of leisure time available expanded, owing to increased mechanisation and the effects of the Depression, culminating in the five-day working-week and the invention of the weekend as a distinct period of leisure time. As Foster Rhea Dulles noted, 'the "challenge of the new leisure" became a vital issue. Under such circumstances recreation could no longer be dismissed as a waste of time or harmless diversion. [. . .] It became for perhaps the first time in American history something which was represented as a possible good in itself' (1952: 367). While Victorian habits had emphasised economy and self-restraint, modern consumerism and leisure demanded that people *enjoy* spending money. This entailed a fundamental shift in the American consciousness, succinctly described by Martha Wolfenstein as the emergence of 'fun morality': 'fun, from having been suspect, if not taboo, has tended to become obligatory. Instead of feeling guilty for having too much fun, one is inclined to feel ashamed if one does not have enough' (1955: 168).

The potential effects of love companionship, consumerism and fun morality upon marriage should be apparent. In *The Marriage Crisis*, Ernest Groves argued that the personal expectation of pleasure was part of the reason for rising divorce rates: 'having entered marriage only for the sake of adding to their happiness, they may feel they have a right to break off their associations, since its returns in pleasure are running low' (1928: 36). Elaine Tyler May's analysis of contemporaneous divorce cases would seem to support his claim. Her evidence suggests that during the late nineteenth century, 'marriage was based on duties and sacrifices, not personal satisfaction' (1980: 47); divorce was sanctioned only in circumstances where this duty was perceived to have been flagrantly violated, in (for example) cases of desertion, brutality and adultery. By the 1920s, divorce cases predominantly featured 'conflicts involving personal appearance and youthfulness' (1980: 77), questions of incompatibility and general dissatisfaction. Thus, as May confirms, the rising divorce rate 'did not indicate a rejection of marriage; rather, it reflected the increased personal desires that matrimony was expected to satisfy' (1980: 162).

By 1939, it was clear to James Harwood Barnett that 'the social conception of the nature of marriage has greatly altered and that modern marriage is increasingly regarded, by the middle classes especially, as a highly personal relationship, rather than as an institutional, social relationship' (1968: 32). This new form of marriage involved fundamental shifts, from duty to pleasure, from spirituality to sexuality and from social responsibility to personal satisfaction. Most importantly, the basic unit of this marriage was no longer the family. It was the companionate couple.

These shifts undoubtedly involved the hegemonic struggle to reaffirm marriage in the light of substantial changes in economic conditions and social mores. Many of the changes involved conflicting pressures: for example, the progressive desires of first-wave feminism, although certainly bound up with the emergence of consumerism, cannot be equated politically with the aims of capitalism. The ideological repercussions of these changes were still being negotiated. During the thirties, the companionate marriage would become increasingly conventionalised and naturalised, ultimately achieving cultural dominance (see Chapter 3). In the meantime, marriage was in a state of transition and screwball comedy capitalised on the confusion.

The same, but different

It is worth spelling out some of the implications these cultural issues have for screwball comedy. Most importantly, the patriarchal 'Victorian' marriage was seen as outmoded: it was sexually repressed, rooted in gender inequality, tied down with responsibility, and absolutely no fun. The screwball relationship is rooted in having fun (which, by the power of the Production Code, also means sex), with the couple eschewing family responsibilities to behave like children (in screwball comedy, 'babies' are leopards and dogs). This kind of fun is often specifically formulated in terms of revitalising marriage (e.g. *She Married Her Boss*, *I Love You Again* (1940), *Two-Faced Woman* (1941)). If this process of revitalisation is seen as a metaphor (rather than just reactionary reaffirmation), then 'remarriage' can involve replacing the old model with the new: the same, but different.

The Awful Truth provides a well-defined exposition of this metaphorical transition. The lawyer–patriarch's concept of 'beautiful' marriage is visually associated with the outmoded Victorian model of separate spheres and domestic bliss. Jerry and Lucy's divorce, however, complies with Lindsey's sense of companionate marriage: divorce by mutual consent for a (wealthy) childless couple, with no payment of alimony (Jerry later inquires, 'You've never asked for money, and . . . well, do you need any?' The answer is no). It is as if this divorce is an intermediate stage, however, since it is initiated through the collapse of Jerry's double standard. The opening sequence reveals that he has spent two weeks pretending to be in Florida, but he claims, 'What wives don't know won't hurt them.' However, when he returns home, he is disconcerted to discover that Lucy is not dutifully awaiting him – especially when she finally does appear in dazzling evening dress, closely followed by a handsome Frenchman, Armand Duvalle (Alexander D'Arcy). It is clearly indicated to the spectator (through a combination of performance style, convention and cliché) that Lucy is telling the truth about her overnight adventure (the car broke down), and the question must then be asked: why is Jerry so quick to seek a divorce? The issue at stake is not so much Lucy's innocence or guilt (and even less so Jerry's), but Jerry's discovery that Lucy is not dependent on his presence, and that what husbands don't know won't hurt them either. It is the shock of discovering her autonomy that proves too hard to bear.

The turning point in Lucy and Jerry's separation comes after he gatecrashes her singing recital at Armand's apartment. Jerry stumbles in uninvited, still determined to believe that Lucy is having an affair with Armand, but Lucy displays no anger at Jerry's own impromptu slapstick performance, only amusement. As he finally rights himself, hair in his eyes and a drawer in his hand, Jerry looks at Lucy and raises his eyebrows; her answer turns the final notes of her song into vibrato laughter, and she is still laughing when the dissolve brings up the next scene. It is this fiasco which forces Lucy to admit, 'I'm still in love with that crazy lunatic and there's nothing I can do about it.' She is compelled to remember the 'grand laughs' that she and Jerry used to share – laughter they still share. It is this sense of having fun together that becomes all important, and the laughter of the recital is later reversed and reinforced when Lucy takes her turn to gatecrash. Jerry has become engaged to socialite Barbara Vance (Molly Lamont), whose parents are holding a very stuffy party; Lucy turns up, uninvited, posing as Jerry's socially unacceptable sister, Lola. Lucy demonstrates an equal willingness to appear ridiculous, and Jerry is the only one who appreciates her act; while the Vances shudder, he simply cannot help laughing.

Lucy's active pursuit of Jerry raises the issue of gender roles in screwball comedy. Whereas social convention was still rooted in essentialist gender traits and the idea of 'complementary' gender roles, screwball comedy takes gender one step further, inverting convention to further disrupt patriarchy. *The Awful Truth* begins by placing the spectator in a highly privileged position, aligned with Jerry's point of view: we are privy to an overtly masculine world (the inner sanctums of the Gotham Athletic Club) and to a male conspiracy of silence ('What wives don't know . . .'). In this masculine world, Jerry is incredibly self-confident, certain of his ability to deceive, and thereby control, his wife. The rest of the film systematically disrupts this initial state of masculine omnipotence, undermining Jerry's complacency (and our confidence in his authority) before realigning our sympathies with Lucy (around whom most of the plot action revolves). Ultimately, it is Lucy who orchestrates their reconciliation, through a liberating process of masquerade, social and legal transgression, and flirtation.

It is Jerry who must change his attitudes, therefore, and his re-education is made all but explicit at the Vances' party.

> JERRY: [*somewhat pompously*] Oh, Barbara – you can't have a happy married life if you're always suspicious. No – there can't be any doubts in marriage; marriage is based on faith, and if you've lost that, you've lost everything.

Although Jerry claims, 'I think I read it in a book or something', this little speech in fact repeats Lucy's words almost verbatim ('There can't be any doubts in marriage: the whole thing's built on faith. If you've lost that – well, you've lost everything'). His pomposity in repeating her words only serves to emphasise his self-delusion, and his pride prepares the spectator to expect another fall (promptly provided by Lucy's masquerade). It is not until the final scene of the film that Jerry can fully acknowledge his error.

> JERRY: You're wrong about things being different because they're not the same. Things are different, except in a different way. [. . .] You're still the same – only I've been a fool. But I'm not now.
> LUCY: [*murmurs*] Oh!
> JERRY: As long as I'm different, don't you think that, well, maybe things could be the same again – only a little different, huh?

The confusion of terms in this speech (which again echo words spoken by Lucy, in the preceding sequence) encapsulates the process by which their relationship has been transformed: things are the same, because they will continue to be married; but things are different, because the constitution of that marriage has changed.

Lecturing men

The 'marriage is based on faith' speech raises some vital questions about Cavell's understanding of the comedies of remarriage: he mistakenly attributes both versions of this speech to Jerry (1981: 234, 244), thereby misrepresenting the process of re-education. This feeds into one of Cavell's most influential arguments: 'the man's lecturing indicates that an essential goal of the narrative is the education of the woman, where her education turns out to mean her acknowledgment of her desire, and this in turn will be conceived of as her creation, her emergence, at any rate, as an autonomous human being' (1981: 84; cf. 55–6). Quite apart from the implication that the hero 'creates' the woman (to which I will return), this neglects the fact that the man's lecturing is usually mocked or proven unsound. For example, Cavell cites Peter's lectures in *It Happened One Night* as key evidence: the correlation of correctly dunking doughnuts with becoming autonomous is odd enough, but forgetting that Ellie succeeds when Peter's hitch-hiking demonstration fails is remiss. Elsewhere, 'lectures' are given by David Huxley (Cary Grant) in *Bringing Up Baby*, Walter Burns (Cary Grant) in *His Girl Friday*, and Charles 'Hopsie' Pike (Henry Fonda) in *The Lady Eve*: but David is constantly ignored; Walter is a proven liar, cheat and manipulator; and even Cavell acknowledges Charles is treated to a relentless 'exposure of pompous self-ignorance' (1981: 56). Nonetheless, Cavell apparently still believes the lessons worth learning.

A level of patriarchal assumption underpins not only Cavell's argument, but also the general critical tendency to posit the woman as the 'problem' in screwball comedy (for example, see Neale and Krutnik 1990: 142, 148 and Shumway 1991: 15). The hero's desires can prove just as problematic as the heroine's and the majority of screwball comedies involve a certain amount of mutual re-education. For example, the dual-focus narrative of *Theodora Goes Wild* first centres upon Michael Grant's (Melvyn Douglas) education of Theodora Lynn/'Caroline Adams' (Irene Dunne): he likens her life in Lynnfield to jail and lectures her to 'Break loose, be yourself and tell Lynnfield "Go take a jump." [. . .] It's the only way you'll ever be a happy, free soul.' Once Theodora has told Lynnfield where to go – declaring her love for Michael in the process – Michael disappears; she follows him only to discover that he is trapped in a loveless marriage to please his father. Theodora returns the favour by liberating Michael: 'You're living in a jail too – you can't call your soul your own!' What is particularly striking about their respective family 'jails' is their overt gender determination, reinforced by domestic/public and rural/urban conflicts. Theodora lives with two maiden aunts in a small town named after her family (Lynnfield), while a black-sheep uncle lives in the city; her behaviour is restricted by small-town values and conventional feminine domesticity (including gossip). Michael's father is Lieutenant Governor and a city banker, and it is the patriarch's public dignity which must be protected at all costs; Michael's divorce must be postponed until his father's retirement from office. In both cases, liberation entails breaking free from the constraints imposed by family and social mores, and declaring 'independence'.

Like Theodora, most screwball heroines acknowledge their own desire before the heroes acknowledge *any* desire (*She Married Her Boss*, *My Man Godfrey*, *Bringing Up Baby*). It is the man who must learn to acknowledge the woman's desire and the education that takes place does not necessarily demand the woman's 'emergence' as an autonomous being, but the man's recognition of her (existing) autonomy. For example, in *It Happened One Night*, Peter describes his ideal love: 'If I could ever meet the right sort of girl [. . .] somebody that's real, somebody that's alive – they don't come that way anymore.' The camera closes in on Peter's face as he settles back against his pillow and daydreams: 'She'd have to be the sort of a girl who'd, well, jump in the surf with me, and love it as much as I did. . . . You know, nights when you'n'the moon'n'the water all become one, and you feel you're part of something big and marvellous. [. . .] Boy, if I could ever find a girl who was hungry for those things!' Visibly moved, Ellie takes action, breaches the blanket-boundary and acknowledges her desire, declaring, 'Take me with you, Peter. [. . .] I love you. Nothing else matters.' Peter's initial reaction is rejection. Ironically, Cavell expresses Peter's problem well: 'what surprises him is her reality. To acknowledge her as this woman [of his dream] would be to acknowledge that she is "somebody that's real, somebody that's alive," flesh and blood, someone separate from his dream [. . .] and this feels to him to be a threat to the dream, and hence a threat to him' (1981: 100). It is precisely a question of recognising her autonomy and desire that is at stake here and Peter's misrecognition is emphasised by the fact that what did happen one night was exactly the stuff of his dream: he and Ellie have already frolicked in the water, under the stars and moon, while crossing the river. Peter also has a lesson to learn, therefore, but – unlike Ellie who displays an admirable flexibility and willingness to learn – he stubbornly clings to his stagnant rules, claiming an authority which he cannot prove, let alone maintain. It would seem that the man's lecturing has far more to do with clinging to his own threatened power than with educating the woman.

Patriarchs and procreation

Cavell's argument that the autonomous woman is 'created' through an education bestowed by the man seems inconsistent and based on patriarchal fantasy. It naturalises the autonomy and identity of the male, while assuming the subordination of the female. Part of his argument involves the equation of 'educator' not only with 'man', but also with 'father', and he particularly privileges the father–daughter relationship. In writing about *The Lady Eve*, Cavell asserts, 'Eve will say to Charles on the train, "I knew you would be both husband and father to me." She says it to deflate him for his insincerity and hypocrisy, but what she says is true, and it is the expression of a workable passion' (1981: 57). The fact that Eve is actually Jean (Barbara Stanwyck), lying through her teeth and deliberately mocking Charles's pretensions to such a role, is apparently irrelevant; her active intentions are swept aside by Cavell, and replaced with the conventional Oedipal fantasy. However – like most screwball comedies – the film's real fathers hardly justify such faith in patriarchy: Jean's father, Colonel Harrington (Charles Coburn) is a cardsharp operating outside the law; Eve's mythic progenitor is in doubt; and Mr Pike (Eugene Pallette) is kind and wealthy, but ultimately powerless (he cannot even get breakfast in his own home). Consequently, while Mr Pike's pro-Eve opinion has little effect upon his son, the couple's reconciliation is effected by Jean.

Cavell's reasoning partly stems from the 'notable absence of the woman's mother in these comedies. [. . .] Mythically, the absence of the mother continues the idea that the creation of the woman is the business of men' (1981: 57). This misrepresents the situation, however, since it is not just the woman's mother who is absent; the hero rarely has one either. Moreover, of the five screwball comedies Cavell discusses, only two heroines have fathers (and no mothers), but the other three have mother-figures (and no fathers). This absence of parents is a common feature of screwball comedy: of the selected cycle of thirty-eight films (see Appendix), seventeen have no parent characters at all, signalling a clear rejection of the patriarchal family romance.[8]

If the corresponding absence of children is taken into account, there is a more obvious reason for this general absence of the mother (and father): procreation is not the point; it is the autonomous individual which is at stake. The absence of procreation in these films directly relates to the cultural transition from the family-based patriarchal marriage to the couple-oriented companionate marriage. The absence of the mother could also signal the diminished influence of the domestic sphere, allowing the heroine into the public domain beyond the conventional space of gender destiny. In this respect, *My Favorite Wife* proves revealing: Ellen Arden (Irene Dunne) has two children and a mother-in-law. Presumed lost at sea, Ellen has been declared dead, and her husband, Nick (Cary Grant), has remarried; in fact she has spent seven years living on a desert island with Stephen Burkett (Randolph Scott), playing 'Eve' to his 'Adam'. Her return initiates the plot, which involves the reformation of the original couple. What is particularly striking, however, is that this wife with two infant children left home in the first place. Her decision to take part in the three-month anthropological expedition, as photographer, is explained by Nick: 'She needed a change . . . she had a tough time with the children – teething.' In other words, there is more to Ellen's life than domesticity, but ultimately her only punishment for this 'transgression' is seven years in Eden.

Family affairs

The general absence of parents also functions to emphasise the screwball couple's exceptional relationship to society. The heroine and hero are not bound by the social pressures of family, money or morality; if they are, then the narrative deals with their escape from such restrictions (*She Married Her Boss*, *Theodora Goes Wild*, *Topper*, *Joy of Living* (1938)). Strikingly, those screwball films which centre on the family are particularly concerned with financial issues, constructing the family as parasitic (*Joy of Living*), spendthrift (*My Man Godfrey*) or repressive (the hero's family in *You Can't Take It with You* (1938)). The corner-stone of patriarchal capitalism is repeatedly represented as corrupt and crumbling.

Holiday is a key example, quite explicitly articulating the couple's union as an escape from a literally patriarchal family: the mother is dead. Nonetheless, Mrs Seton plays an integral thematic role in the film. As her alcoholic son, Ned (Lew Ayres), explains:

> Father wanted a big family, you know, so mother had Linda straight off to oblige him. But Linda was a girl, so she promptly had Julia. [. . .] The next year she had me, and there was much joy in the land. It was a boy and the fair name of Seton would flourish. It must have been a great consolation to father; he must have been very grateful to mother. Drink to Mother, Johnny. She tried to be a Seton for a while, then gave up and died.

The stability and value of traditional marriage are totally discredited; the pressures of procreation and heritage crush the mother – and the son. The film then sets up an opposition between the patriarchal family and an implicitly egalitarian collective: 'the Johnny, Nick and Susan Club'.[9] Nick and Susan Potter (Edward Everett Horton and Jean Dixon) are Johnny Case's (Cary Grant) good friends, with a hint of parent (his own are dead); they are an affable, companionable and happy couple. Initially, it seems that Johnny is about to be integrated into the high society of the Setons, by marrying Julia (Doris Nolan); finally, however, it is Julia's sister, Linda (Katharine Hepburn) who joins Johnny's club. This reversal is closely linked to the contrast between the two sisters and specifically the different kinds of relationship they have with Johnny and with their father.

Julia is repeatedly identified with her father (Henry Kolker), but Linda is associated with their dead mother. In an exemplary analysis, Andrew Britton (1995) analyses this contrast in some depth, initially focusing his argument on the scene in which Julia convinces her father to let her marry Johnny. Mr Seton draws an analogy to his cigar: 'I know the quality of the tobacco in it because I happen to own the plantation where it was grown. And I know, therefore, that it will burn smoothly and pleasantly. And I know, above all else, that it will never explode in my face.' Julia speaks the same symbolic language as her father: she not only appreciates the meaning of the analogy ('And you're afraid that Johnny might?'), but also sustains the metaphor by reassuring him that Johnny will burn 'calmly, steadily, pleasantly'. He is a commodity to be incorporated into the Seton brand. Mr Seton and Julia's collusion includes dealing with Linda (they know how to 'take care of' her unconventional ideas), implicitly acknowledging both her difference and their repressive influence. Consequently, while Julia is her father's daughter, Linda's exuberance is chastised by Mr Seton: 'Will you be careful [. . .] you'll put out my cigar!' Linda's nonconformity is clear, and is further underlined by her invocation of her mother: turning to Mrs Seton's portrait, Linda declares, 'Mother, you'd love him!'

As Britton points out, the phallic cigar is simultaneously a sexual and economic symbol, and 'the metaphor dramatises with great succinctness the agreement between father and daughter on the requisite place of women in patriarchal–capitalist relations' (1995: 119). More specifically, it corresponds with the 'Victorian' conception of marriage as an economic investment, in which the female is an object of exchange to be given by the father. Indeed, Mr Seton has described his own marriage in precisely Victorian terms: 'In marrying me, your mother and her family took not the slightest risk, either financially or, if I may say so, spiritually.' Consequently, Mr Seton's cigar carries another connotation: stagnation through rigid tradition; he has smoked the same brand for thirty-five years, like his father before him.

Johnny arrives into this atmosphere of stale cigar smoke, according to Linda, 'like spring [. . .] like a breath of fresh air'. He too is associated with Linda's mother, primarily through his appreciation of the playroom. While the Seton mansion has made him distinctly uncomfortable (he calls it a museum), he is pleasantly surprised upon entering the playroom:

JOHNNY: This is quite different. From the rest of the house, I mean.
LINDA: This was Mother's idea. She thought there ought to be one room in the house where people could come and have some fun. [. . .] I think it was a kind of escape for her. She was marvellous.

The playroom is a space for creativity, fun and spontaneous energy – all the things repressed by the patriarchal family. Indeed, Mr Seton expressly acknowledges that he does not know 'what special virtue this room has'.

There seem to be two key aspects to consider in relation to the 'special virtue' of play: the emphasis on friendship, rather than romance (to which I will return, more than once); and the resurgence of childhood energies. Play is repeatedly linked in screwball comedy to spontaneity, improvisation and role-playing, transgressing the norms of accepted (and acceptable) patriarchal identities (hence Mr Seton's discomfort in the playroom). From a psychoanalytical point of view, the haunting presence of Mrs Seton suggests a positive 'return of the repressed' – the pre-Oedipal energies of polymorphous sexuality. For the pre-Oedipal child, masculine and feminine do not exist; the opposition comes only with the Oedipal crisis and submission to the Law of the Father. The resurgence of pre-Oedipal energies and childlike play in screwball comedy work with gender role reversal, signalling a further breakdown in the binary hierarchy of masculine/feminine. Far from implying that 'the creation of the woman is the business of men' (Cavell 1981: 57), the absent mother in *Holiday* foregrounds resistance to patriarchal control.

While Linda and Johnny's appreciation of the playroom metaphorically binds them to the 'pre-Oedipal' energies of the lost mother, Julia's presence in the playroom tends to be antagonistic and it is the site of her first argument with Johnny. Johnny and Julia's relationship is couched in the conventions of whirlwind courtship, including 'love at first sight', idealisation and repeated, passionate kissing. For example, Johnny's explanation to Nick and Susan is a cliché of starry-eyed romantic love:

JOHNNY: It's love, fellas! I've met the girl. She's . . . well, I can't describe her – but the first thing you notice is those dimples when she smiles.
SUSAN: Oh! [*laughing*] Why didn't you say so in the first place?
NICK: Of course, that's going to make her the perfect wife.

Dimples are hardly the basis for a lasting relationship, but they are typical of the feminine beauty on which Julia is repeatedly judged. Significantly, only two objects in the playroom represent Julia: a doll and a photograph of her and Linda as children – both icons to her beauty. While the presence of musical instruments and an unfinished painting symbolise the patriarchal repression of Linda and Ned's creative energies, Julia appears to have no such energies in the first place; as Ned points out, Julia is 'a very dull girl'.

The film judges a relationship based on physical appearance (love at first sight) to be inadequate. It rejects patriarchal sexuality and romance, offering the companionate fun and friendship of the playroom in its place. In true screwball style, it is Johnny and Linda who speak the same language, share a sense of humour, and play the same games. Consequently, the central metaphor for their relationship is their acrobatic performance for Nick, Susan and Ned; it is an image of support and co-operation, but also of fun, vitality and physical intimacy. However, embracing the pre-Oedipal energies of the maternal space of the playroom means there is no place for Linda and Johnny in patriarchal society. The Johnny, Linda, Nick and Susan Club must leave the old, stagnant and repressive society behind, bound for some utopian place called France.[10]

Isn't it romantic?

Holiday ends by reinvoking the metaphor of play: as Johnny belly-flops at Linda's feet, she inquires, 'Is this where the club meets?' Johnny pulls her down to his level to embrace her, but the image abruptly fades to black the moment they kiss. Since Johnny and Julia are often seen kissing, this perfunctory treatment of the final embrace is more than mere prudery, or even ironic compliance with Production Code demands; it is a formal decision, subordinating the conventions of romance. Neither is it an isolated example. Gestures of love and romance are conspicuously absent from screwball comedy, and those films which do include conventional signifiers of romance usually treat them ironically. Thus, Mr Seton lectures on 'true love' (his words may sound familiar: 'For love, true love, is a very rare and beautiful thing'); Dan Leeson (Ralph Bellamy) recites an awful love poem in *The Awful Truth*; in *The Palm Beach Story*, J. D. Hackensacker serenades Gerry with 'Goodnight, Sweetheart', but it is her husband she kisses good-night; and the Lady Eve orders the long-stemmed roses sent by Charles to be put in the umbrella stand. Similarly, the earlier sequence in which Charles selects and fits a new pair of evening slippers for Jean is clearly intended to suggest Cinderella, but the scene has more to do with lust than romance. Having told Charles (whom she nicknames Hopsie) to kneel at her feet, Jean flashes her shapely leg in his face; evidently under the influence of her intoxicating presence and perfume, Charles can barely control himself. His 'cockeyed' state is even visualised: a point-of-view shot of Jean's face is blurred and distorted. This little exercise in foot fetishism is accompanied by the familiar tune of 'Isn't it romantic?' – to which the ironic answer is 'No.' It is a part of Jean's con, a seduction routine culminating in Charles's attempt to kiss her; lightly brushing him off, she wryly declares, 'Why, Hopsie! You ought to be kept in a cage.'[11]

The Lady Eve is perhaps the most revealing screwball attack on romance, primarily because it simultaneously exposes and embraces the fiction. The key distinction is the perception of the con: the con-artist enjoys the fiction, but the sucker thinks it is real. The film's intention to expose the construction of romance is signalled by the motif of story-telling: Jean consciously scripts the famous mirror sequence and the second proposal scene, not to mention the wedding night revelations; she asks her father to tell her fortune; and 'Sir Alfred' (Eric Blore) explains the Lady Eve's existence by telling Charles the plot of '*Cecilia, or, The Coachman's Daughter* – a gaslight melodrama'. There are also the allusions to the archetypal narratives of Adam and Eve, and Cinderella. Even Charles acknowledges that his own romantic fantasy is as 'dull as a drugstore novel'. In this context, the second proposal scene demands attention, since it completely demystifies the conventionally romantic first proposal, not least because Charles repeats his fantasy, despite proposing to a 'different' woman. The scene is introduced by Jean's voice; she is telling Pearlie/Sir Alfred how she is going to trap Charles into marriage. As she weaves her story, the image begins to dissolve, and her words are seen to come true. Now in voice-over, she describes a conventionally romantic excursion: riding in the scenic hills and stopping to admire the beautiful sunset. 'And as I stand there against the glory of Mother Nature, my horse will steal up behind me and nuzzle my hair – and so will Charles, the heel.' Jean has written this romance, and she knows exactly what will happen next. Indeed, echoing Hopsie's earlier shipboard speech, she feeds Charles his lines:

> 'EVE': I – I feel I've known you always.
> CHARLES: That's the way I feel about you [*title theme is reintroduced, echoing the first proposal scene*]. I don't just see you here, in front of the sunset, but you seem to go way back. I see you here, and at the same time further away and still further away, and way, way back in a long place like a –
> 'EVE': Like a forest glade?
> CHARLES: That's right. How d'you guess?

The imagery is no less trite than it was the first time, but now it is ruthlessly acknowledged as a fantasy. Even the romance of the situation is not allowed to maintain any power, as Eve/Jean's horse (as if directed by her voice-over) insists on intruding on the intimate moment, making a laughing stock of Charles and a mockery of romance.

Charles certainly is a sucker for his romantic fantasy, but then so was Jean. She was initially prepared to live up to his ideal expectations: 'I'd give a lot to be . . . well, I mean, I, I'm *going* to be exactly the way he thinks I am – the way he'd like me to be.' While Jean is cured of romance by Charles's rejection, Charles still believes in the ideal. As Rowe puts it, 'he still wants a "virgin," a woman without a past, whose only history is in his imagination'

(1995: 166). Once again, the obstruction to union is caused by the man's romantic and patriarchal desires – just as Peter had to recognise what was right before his eyes in *It Happened One Night*, and Jerry had to acknowledge his wife's autonomy in *The Awful Truth*. Consequently, the ideal must be proven false before Charles can accept Jean for who she is, and it is for this reason that the Lady must prove to be the tramp, shattering the virgin/whore dichotomy. As Jean tried to tell him, 'The best ones [girls] aren't as good as you probably think they are, and the bad ones aren't as bad. Not nearly as bad.'

By the end of the film, Charles has learnt his lesson and is relieved to refind Jean. The film's Adam and Eve motif plays with patriarchal expectations of knowledge, experience and guilt. Jean is repeatedly presented as the one with all the worldly wisdom, while Charles's knowledge is initially hypothetical: the book he reads in the ship's dining room is entitled *Are Snakes Necessary?*[12] Once he has discovered the answer, however, he rejects the male privilege of knowledge altogether: 'I don't want to understand . . . I don't want to know. Whatever it is, keep it to yourself.' The Fall of this Man results in a guiltless embrace of female sexual experience and adultery; of course, we – and the PCA – know they are married, but Charles thinks Jean is *not* his wife. As the couple retreat into Jean's room, at the end of the film, their intentions are clear: they happily kiss in public, but behind closed doors they are going to do more than just kiss.

Embracing space

Although Charles and Jean spend most of their reunion in each other's arms, screwball comedy's anti-romantic tendencies usually go one step further: the conventional final embrace is treated as incidental (as in *Holiday*) or denied altogether. For example, in *The Awful Truth*, Lucy's last word is a laughing 'good-night'. The couple's reconciliation – and its sexual consummation – is left implicit: as the cuckoo clock strikes quarter to midnight (fifteen minutes before their divorce becomes final) the boy figurine (Grant) skips around to follow the girl figurine (Dunne) back through her door. The couple also retreat behind closed doors at the end of *It Happened One Night*, while the final embrace in *Mr and Mrs Smith* occurs just out of frame. In each case, as in *The Lady Eve*, it is sex – not romance – that is implied. Thus, the visual exclusion of the spectator is partly a consequence of screwball comedy's productive relationship with the Production Code: the knowing suggestions of sex are far more titillating (and amusing) than the controlled passion of a three-second kiss.

At the same time, the exclusion of the spectator coincides with the cycle's thematic interest in publicity and privacy, which is most often connoted by the newspaper trope (*It Happened One Night*, *Four's a Crowd*, *His Girl Friday*). This trope will be explored in more detail in the next chapter's discussion of *Libeled Lady*, but *Nothing Sacred* provides an initial example. Hazel Flagg (Carole Lombard) is raised to the dizzy heights of celebrity by newspaperman, Wally Cook (Frederic March), because he thinks she is dying of radium poisoning. The film repeatedly juxtaposes public hype with private intimacy. For example, when Hazel and Wally first meet, the camera draws attention to the voyeuristic gaze by refusing to reframe the couple: they remain in medium shot, with their faces completely hidden by a tree branch for more than ten seconds. Later, when Wally wants to talk privately, they take shelter inside an empty shipping crate. The camera remains outside this private space, first showing only their ankles sticking out (we hear them kiss), and then circling around to the other side of the crate to peer through slats (we hear Wally propose). Once again, our voyeurism is acknowledged – and teased – as we can almost see what is going on in the gaps; the effect is reinforced by the use of shadow and backlighting, with an intermittent searchlight briefly revealing their kiss. The couple's final embrace is similarly treated: they are now literally in hiding (both wearing dark glasses and hats) and although the kiss is shown in close-up, their faces are in total shadow, so nothing can be seen.

As this begins to suggest, even those screwball comedies which do include an embrace usually do not treat it in a conventionally romantic way. According to Virginia Wright Wexman, 'the movie kiss represents a privileged moment of romantic bonding [. . .]. Customarily this moment is designed to highlight the expression of romantic fulfillment on the face of the woman, who is foregrounded by a key light while her male partner remains in the shadows' (1993: 18). Anyone familiar with Hollywood film will recognise this image, but it is not one found in screwball comedy. As Wexman's description emphasises, the conventional romantic embrace focuses attention upon the woman: she is 'to be looked at' in the sense of Mulvey's 'male gaze' (1989: 19), while the overpowering hero/spectator in the shadows fulfils her passive desire. Romantic intensity is conveyed by the use of (extreme) close-up, while the camera is angled and placed obliquely to the couple in order to centre the object of desire – the woman's carefully lit, soft-focus face (for example, see the ends of *Love Affair* (1939) and *Random Harvest* (1942)). This close-up is the climax to a shot/reverse shot articulation of looks, enclosing the spectator within the space of their embrace, and matched by the romantic rhetoric of swelling violins. The frame space is blocked diagonally, often to emphasise the height and power of the man, as he enfolds the heroine in his arms, possessively incorporating her into his body. Such embraces conform with conventional binary structures of active/passive, male/female and subject/object. Romance is rooted in gender inequality: from

Petrarch to Freud, romantic love has traditionally been the privilege of the male subject; the woman can only desire to be desired, waiting to be swept off her feet by a tall, dark stranger.

Screwball comedy offers quite a different spatial representation of the embrace (whether at the film's climax, or during the plot).[13] In accordance with the narrative trope of gender role reversal, the heroine often makes the first move, acting upon her own desire. This is not visually represented as a simple power reversal, however, with the woman physically dominating the man. Instead, the screwball embrace emphasises the equality of the couple. The couple face each other, not the camera, creating a balanced division of frame space; indeed, they are often seated, de-emphasising the man's height, so that the couple's heads are relatively level. The shot/reverse shot articulation of looks is noticeably absent from these sequences: the couple remain together in the 'democratic' two-shot while the spectator (male or female) remains outside the space of their embrace. The camera also maintains its distance, and the screwball embrace is rarely seen in anything closer than a medium shot. Finally, the style remains strictly unromantic: lighting remains high-key and even; focus remains clear; and non-diegetic music is usually absent (unless this is the final shot of the film, in which case the closing theme is introduced).

The final embrace in *Bringing Up Baby* offers a clear illustration of this argument. Certainly there is nothing romantic about Susan (Katharine Hepburn) and David's courtship, which is spent changing identities as often as clothes, chasing dogs and leopards, and systematically destroying property. Even the film's potentially romantic theme, 'I can't give you anything but love, Baby', is used unconventionally to 'serenade' the leopard, Baby, and Susan initially takes the bass part while David sings the higher harmony. It is a key moment of improvisational creative play, not romance. Ultimately, their relationship is ratified by David's words: 'I've just discovered that was the best day of my whole life. [. . .] I never had a better time!' David translates this anarchic fun into 'I love you, I think', and his qualification applies as much to the appropriateness of the word 'love' to their relationship, as to its stability. As the final vestige of patriarchal society – the dinosaur – collapses at their feet, David hoists Susan up to his platform (an aerial display not dissimilar in effect to *Holiday*'s acrobatics). The couple sit facing each other, symmetrically sharing the frame space and shown in medium long shot; even as they embrace, the spectator is excluded, since they turn their heads away from the camera. Of course, Susan acts first, embracing David while telling him how he feels, to which David can only sigh, 'Oh dear! Oh my!' before relinquishing all control and returning her embrace. At this point, the film's theme returns, and the image cuts to an extreme long shot of the couple on the scaffold before fading to black.

And they lived happily ever after . . . or did they?

Cavell describes this embrace as 'notably awkward' (1981: 120), but, in the circumstances, how could it be anything else? A conventional romantic close-up would be incongruous. Cavell feels that the dinosaur's collapse casts a shadow over the happiness of this ending, and has trouble accepting that David should still want to embrace Susan, as his work lies in ruins (1981: 121). This seems to miss the point: the internal logic of the film demands the collapse of the dinosaur, as the symbol of all that is wrong with David's world of rational order: stagnation, repression, capitalism and patriarchal sexuality (Britton 1986: 41). The film does not ask us to imagine what comes next; the couple are literally left in mid-air, in a moment of chaos. Cavell recognises the 'ambivalence or instability' (1981: 124) of this couple's mode of sexuality, but rather depressingly insists on pointing out that 'the situation between this pair cannot remain as it is' (1981: 124). The couple cannot really escape patriarchal society. Their triumph is both symbolic and fleeting; it is a utopian moment, not utopia.

Whether the couple retreat behind closed doors, set sail for distant utopias, or just sit in mid-air, the screwball ending typically places the couple in limbo. As Britton argues, 'it is an essential characteristic of the couples created at the end of these films that they cannot exist in established bourgeois society' (1986: 39). Consequently, the screwball ending is distinctly anti-social: the couple's withdrawal or escape from society, and their visual privacy, is clearly at odds with the genre's traditional 'social integration'. Screwball comedy maintains a precarious balance between total anarchy and stable resolution.

While I consider the couple's privacy to coincide with their progressive potential, Shumway reasserts a conservative meaning: 'since these are thoroughly bourgeois comedies, there is no sense of festival accompanying the marriage. Marriage is a private matter [. . .]. The ending leaves the couple isolated in their own bliss [. . .]. It is in this illusory eternity that marriage is rendered mystical, in spite of whichever of its realities the film has indulged earlier' (1991: 16–17). The contemporary discourses around companionate marriage as a 'highly personal relationship' would seem to corroborate Shumway's point, and to the extent that screwball comedy assumes the importance of such personal relationships, his argument is right. These films 'solve' the problems of one extraordinary couple; they do not change the social system or challenge the material realities of inequality. However, the films themselves acknowledge both the ideal status of the couple and the ambivalence of the resolution: the same, but different.

It is this sense of flux that most clearly informs the cycle's conception of *re*marriage: screwball comedy insists that the couple must keep on playing, keep on reinventing themselves, and keep on learning to love each other. The 'illusory eternity' of just living happily ever after is wholeheartedly demystified.

Notes

1 This is a significant change in the screenplay's adaptation of Samuel Hopkins Adams's short story 'Night bus'; in the story, Elspeth Andrews only pretends to be married (to her third or fourth cousin, Corcoran Andrews), in the hope that Peter will treat her with more respect (1979: 45).

2 This link can also be found in *Bluebeard's Eighth Wife* (1938), which ends with Michael Brandon (Gary Cooper) in a straitjacket, and *Love Crazy*, in which Steve Ireland (William Powell) is institutionalised, but is only pretending to be crazy.

3 For this reason, the title of this chapter ('The same, but different') is deliberately intended to echo the title of Cavell's chapter on *The Awful Truth* ('The same and different'). The slight change is integral to my navigation of Cavell's arguments, since 'but' opens a space for negotiation, while 'and' collapses this space.

4 This analysis relies on white, middle-class discourses, which predominate both in contemporary discussions and in screwball's representation of marriage. For details of working-class and immigrant attitudes and practices see D'Emilio and Freedman (1997).

5 Divorce rates in the US had been rising steadily since the 1860s, but between 1910 and 1920 there was a significant jump, from 83,045 divorces in 1910 (a rate of 4.5 per 1,000 marriages) to 167,105 in 1920 (a rate of 7.7 per 1,000); by 1940 it had risen further, to 8.7 per 1,000 (figures from May 1980: 167). In 1920, the crude birth rate stood at 27.7 live births per 1,000 of the total population (compared to 55.2 in 1820); by 1935, the rate dropped further to a low of 18.7 (figures from US Department of Commerce, Bureau of the Census 1975: 49, Series B-5).

6 Historians have since revised these stereotypes of Victorian marriage and sexuality, revealing a much more complex picture. For example, see Seidman (1991: 16–17) and May (1980).

7 Marriage is essentially a property relation: the myth of marrying for love romanticises the realities of the legal institution. The fact that marriage is still a patriarchal institution is indicated by the number of brides who automatically expect their fathers to give them away.

8 Of the thirty-eight films, only three heroines have both a mother and a father; eight more just have fathers, but only two just have a mother. For heroes, the ratio is more balanced, but still relatively low: five with both parents; one with just a mother; and one with just a father. In the same sample of films, nine heroines and five heroes have a mother-figure (usually a maiden aunt); four heroines and five heroes have a father-figure (usually an uncle, grandfather or boss).

9 The opposition between the Setons and the Club is also economic and political, most explicitly in relation to the Setons' cousins, Laura and Seton Cram (Binnie Barnes and Henry Daniell), who are greeted with a mock Nazi salute when they enter the playroom (see Mirza 1990).

10 A more common destination is Latin America (*She Married Her Boss*, *Nothing Sacred*, *The Lady Eve*); in *Joy of Living*, it is a private island called Paradise somewhere in the South Seas.
11 Our perception of the 'romance' of this scene is a distinctly modern one, presuming that romance has something to do with sexual chemistry. *The Lady Eve* could mark a turning point in this respect: when Jean suggests, 'Don't you think we ought to go to bed?' Charles is clearly taken aback by the suggestion and grins nervously; according to *The Cassell Dictionary of Slang* (1998), the sexual euphemism 'bed' entered into slang usage in the forties.
12 I like to think that the title deliberately echoes James Thurber and E. B. White's best-selling *Is Sex Necessary?*, originally published in 1929, which defines love as 'the pleasant confusion we know exists' and loving as 'being confused by, or confusing someone' (1960: 132).
13 Examples of the screwball embrace can be found in *My Man Godfrey* (*c.* 34 mins); *Theodora Goes Wild* (*c.* 55 mins); the end of *Four's a Crowd*; and the final kiss in *The Lady Eve*. This kind of embrace is not unique to screwball comedy, but it is usually only found in films in which heterosexual coupling is a subordinate plotline.

3

Making marriage fun: Myrna Loy and William Powell

> There had been romantic couples before, but Loy and Powell were something new and original. They actually made marital comedy palatable. (George Cukor, quoted by Kotsilibas-Davis and Loy 1988: 69)

When people remember Myrna Loy and William Powell, they inevitably think of their roles as Nick and Nora Charles in *The Thin Man* films.[1] Cukor's reaction to the pairing is typical. Jacobs felt *The Thin Man* highlighted the 'intimacy and companionship of married life' (1969: 534) and Loy believed the film 'virtually introduced modern marriage to the screen' (Kotsilibas-Davis and Loy 1988: 91). Loy and Powell's star personae were remodelled to build on the film's success. Indeed, star and character quickly became mutually dependent, and anecdotes abound in which members of the public assumed the couple were really married. This immediately suggests questions about the status of identity in relation to celebrity – questions which also form part of screwball comedy's fascination with publicity.

The Thin Man was one of the films of 1934 that marked the emergence of the new comic style.[2] Although Nick and Nora display screwball traits, the film's plot revolves around a murder mystery, rather than unconventional courtship. *Libeled Lady*, on the other hand, is a clear-cut screwball comedy: as well as offering one of the few representations of the formation of the Loy/Powell couple, it also enables further exploration of some of the screwball themes touched on in previous chapters – specifically identity, privacy, publicity, play and the green world. This leads on to more detailed analysis of the Loy/Powell couple's star persona, culminating in discussion of the process by which the 'Nick and Nora' blueprint for a fun, companionate marriage becomes conventionalised and eventually domesticated. At the levels of both text and context, Loy and Powell provide a valuable site for investigating the popular media's articulation of love and marriage in the thirties.

A little *too* married

In *Libeled Lady*, Connie Allenbury (Loy) sues the New York *Evening Star* for five million dollars after a libellous front-page story calls her a 'husband stealer'. The newspaper's editor, Warren Haggerty (Spencer Tracy), hires Bill Chandler (Powell) to negate the libel suit by framing Connie as a 'real' adulterer; in order to do so, Bill marries Warren's fiancée, Gladys Benton (Jean Harlow). Unfortunately, Bill ends up charming both ladies, but falling for Connie, leading to additional deceptions and confusions. Bill finally marries Connie, only to discover that he is still married to Gladys. Although Warren and Gladys reconcile, the film nonetheless ends in this state of bigamy.

The film is more conventionally romantic (and less concerned with sex) than most screwball comedies, partly because it was produced by the upmarket MGM. As a consequence, some of the standard screwball patterns are relatively muted, but one aspect that retains its force is the film's attitude towards marriage. The only legal ceremony is Bill and Gladys's (the wrong couple) and it is a fake marriage of convenience. Conversely, the 'real' wedding – Bill and Connie's – is only briefly seen and proves to be unlawful. Once again, the diegetic representation of the institution of marriage is far from positive. In his first scene, while dressing for his wedding, Warren compares marriage to a death sentence: 'I promised I'd meet her at the altar at the stroke of twelve – and there'll be no reprieve from the governor this time!' The scene represents marriage as castrating, and the anxiety is magnified by the presence of Warren's valet, Ching (Otto Yamaoka), who is characterised in a typically racist manner as dim-witted and effeminate:

> CHING: Velly pleetty.
> WARREN: Pretty! I'm supposed to be the groom, not the bride.

Warren's hostility is clearly bound up with his fear of emasculation. His fear is manifested visually: he is dressed in shirt and sock suspenders; having put on his hat and morning coat, he almost leaves without his trousers.

Warren's premarital fears are counterbalanced by Gladys's post-marital experiences. Having married Bill, the scheme's success depends on her passing as the dutiful wife. Since she cannot be seen in public with her fiancé (Warren), and her husband (Bill) has more important things to do, Warren suggests she should stay in the hotel suite: 'You can . . . sew and sleep and play the radio. [. . .] You've got to look married.' The passive, domestic imagery encapsulates the boredom of being a housewife. The fate of the married woman is further satirised when Gladys suggests that she and Bill share breakfast, again because it will 'look married'. As they sit at the breakfast table, Bill is almost totally hidden behind a newspaper; Gladys, playing wife, offers him coffee, but he only grunts a negative. She is forced to observe, 'Well, this certainly looks married. A little *too* married to suit me!'

The film uses Warren and Gladys to set up the conventional stereotype of marriage as entrapment, but the emphasis on *looking* married also raises questions about appearance and identity. The adoption of disguise and the mistaking of identity are traditional tropes of dramatic comedy, and usually involve a period of transgression and confusion; the narrative resolution then requires the discovery (and acceptance) of true identity, often including the discovery of a new social identity through marriage (see Frye 1965: 76–82). Broadly speaking, this pattern remains true of *Libeled Lady*, but it is complicated because legal marriage is part of the mistaken identity, and the final discovery does not resolve the social situation. Moreover, the marriage is faked for a very specific reason – to create a public scandal. Shumway is right to claim that 'marriage is a private matter' (1991: 16) in these films, but the situation is more complex than he allows; it stems not only from bourgeois privacy, but also from a culturally specific anxiety about publicity.

Public affairs

This anxiety is commonly manifested by the newspaper trope, which recurs across a variety of Hollywood genres and cycles during the period, but is particularly common in screwball comedy. While the function of this trope varies, its presence is not just happy coincidence or convention. It denotes a cultural trend: scandal journalism.

This new kind of yellow journalism emerged in the twenties through the growth of the tabloid newspaper. The tabloid was 'an essentially urban journalistic phenomenon' (Murphy 1984: 57) and was from the outset more concerned with entertainment than factual news. An emphasis on personal interest stories and gossip columns was integral to these changes, but the readers were not interested in the private lives of just anybody; they wanted to know gossip about people they recognised. 'In place of village gossip that had drawn everyone into its net, urban gossip of necessity concentrated on the lives of a few – the important, the infamous, the attractive, the highly visible' (Murphy 1984: 65).

To satisfy the demand, a new class of celebrities developed. While film stars were certainly of growing interest, the New York tabloids needed local celebrities as well. As Richard Schickel argues, the tabloids turned 'giddy heiresses and nitwit playboys into public figures' (1985: 33) well before screwball comedy immortalised and idealised them. This social elite were known as café society, because they frequented such exclusive 'cafés' as El Morocco and The Stork Club. As Neal Gabler notes, 'it wasn't just that high society had gone public. Café society included people whom the Old Guard of high society would never have countenanced privately or publicly' (1996: 184) – namely, the Broadway crowd of show-business professionals and gossip columnists like Walter Winchell. Where high society had once maintained its power through exclusivity, café society gained its status through publicity; as Winchell put it, 'social position is now more a matter of press than prestige' (quoted by Gabler 1996: 185). In other words, café society provides screwball comedy with an environment of public celebrity, not just wealth and leisure.

By the mid-thirties, celebrity culture had shifted from Broadway to Hollywood, where the role of gossip proved quite different. Hollywood gossip was controlled by the studios. Even the famous Hedda Hopper and Louella Parsons had to submit copy to the studios for approval, or risk losing movie advertising for their newspaper or magazine (Gabler 1996: 254). Hollywood fan magazines also reached the height of their popularity during the thirties, offering another medium for disseminating the right kind of information about stars. Of course, publicity in this sense is no longer scandalous; it is marketing. For example, in 1933, Loy starred in *The Barbarian* with Ramon Novarro. According to Loy, 'we became friends on that film, but the studio exploited it. I picked up a newspaper and discovered the intimate details of our "torrid romance," which apparently was common knowledge to everyone but the participants' (Kotsilibas-Davis and Loy 1988: 80). Novarro was gay, but his star persona was built on the Latin lover image; the publicity was clearly aimed to revive the fiction at a point when his career was on the decline. At the same time, the gossip about Loy and Arthur Hornblow Jr (who was estranged from his wife) would have caused a scandal: 'the columnists could have had a field day with our relationship, but we managed to keep it out of the public eye during four years of courting or living together. Everybody did it, but nobody talked about it' (1988: 78). In other words, Hollywood gossip was carefully managed to divert attention from real scandal, by maximising attention on the desired star persona and the rumour of romance.

The line between public fiction and private fact became increasingly blurred. For example, in a *Modern Screen* article entitled 'What's wrong with Hollywood love?', Katherine Albert mixed an exposé of Hollywood 'publicity romances' with accounts of 'real' romances, in an attempt to explain why stars were apparently falling in and out of love so rapidly. She notes, 'there have been publicity romances – so Hollywood is skeptical of young love' (1970: 62), but then extols Loy and Novarro as 'one of the loveliest romances in Hollywood at the present time [. . .]. Those who saw the meeting said it was love at first sight' (1970: 183). Albert blames the rapid demise of 'genuine' romances on the couple's lack of privacy, claiming, 'real love thrives on romantic secrecy. [. . .] If you're a star and hold hands with another star under the table there's a photographer lurking somewhere to record the event' (1970: 61). Most obviously, this suggests anxiety about the mass media's invasion of privacy, but it also implies anxiety about acceptable forms of public intimacy in the era of dating.

The tension between privacy and publicity is not just about the celebrity and the masses, or even the individual and society. It is also about the very processes of mass communication: what is fact and what is fiction? As the opening titlecards in *Nothing Sacred* puts it, 'Truth, crushed to earth, rises again more phony than a glass eye.' From *The Front Page* (1931) to *Citizen Kane* (1941), the newspaper trope frequently signals the impossibility of *knowing* anything in a sceptical, cynical, and increasingly public world. The problem is usually displaced, however, on to the specific question of identity: films such as *Mr Deeds Goes to Town*, *Nothing Sacred* and *Meet John Doe* all emphasise the disjunction between publicity and truth by exposing the fabrication of celebrity identity. Similarly, in *Libeled Lady*, the confusion of identity involves not only the deceit surrounding Bill and Gladys's fake marriage, but also the celebrity of Connie Allenbury.

Who was that lady I saw you with last night?

The film opens with the offending article rolling off the newspaper presses. The front-page story includes a photograph of Myrna Loy and the headline 'Peer's Wife Routs Rich Playgirl! Calls Connie Allenbury Husband Stealer'. Six minutes of screen time pass before we see Connie/Loy 'in the flesh', but we have already been led to form an opinion of her, based on this dubious article and the journalists' responses to the potential situation. Most importantly, this opening defines her as a celebrity (both diegetically and extra-diegetically); the public (and audience) know who she is and want to know more.

The libellous inaccuracy of the headline story raises questions about Connie, primarily about where the truth ends and the libel starts: is it just this specific instance which is fabricated (has she stolen other husbands?) or is the entire 'playgirl' image erroneous? Our first encounter with the character seems deliberately inconclusive. We are teased with images which hide her face for as long as possible: a tennis racquet protruding into a medium shot of her father, J. B. Allenbury (Walter Connolly); her back to the camera in long shot; and a medium close-up of her sweater being roughly pulled over her head – finally revealing her face, framed by somewhat dishevelled hair. Her actions are similarly playful. She sits on the edge of her father's desk, kicking her legs against the side, bouncing a ball on her tennis racquet. Her father catches the ball, so she starts playing with his ear instead. The scene seems to be taking that word 'playgirl' literally.

If we are still not sure exactly what kind of girl Connie is, Bill claims to be an authority on the subject: 'I know all about her. Title-crazy, with a fat-headed old father to buy her in and out. America's international playgirl – that's her rep!' In other words, he knows only what the newspapers have told him, her reputation as a celebrity. He must learn that you cannot believe everything you read and, concomitantly, that he does not know everything. His belief that Connie's status depends upon her father's wealth motivates an otherwise inexplicable plan – posing as a fly-fishing expert to ingratiate himself with Mr Allenbury, rather than Connie. Bill manipulates an introduction by 'rescuing' Connie from some English reporters on the dockside (reporters he has paid to make a scene). Even this set-up betrays Bill's patriarchal assumptions, since saving a damsel in distress will impress her protective father, as much as win her gratitude. This mistaken interest in the father echoes an earlier assumption that the lawsuit is more about Allenbury than Connie. We are initially led to believe that the crux of the matter is Allenbury's rivalry with the owner of the *Evening Star*, Mr Bane (Charley Grapewin), but the patriarchal power struggle is abruptly abandoned as a source of conflict. It is never revealed why the men hate each other, let alone whose side deserves a moral victory. Patriarchal power is a red herring.

The initial success of Bill's charade is equivocal, then, since he seems to win Mr Allenbury's favour at the expense of alienating Connie. Having insinuated himself into their company, Bill proceeds to delight J. B. with fishing yarns throughout dinner; Connie is not only bored, but unconvinced. Even when Bill turns on the charm, she sees through his manoeuvres:

BILL: [*chuckling*] I'm afraid dancing isn't exactly my line.
CONNIE: I should say it was part of your line.

Her insight undermines Bill's confidence; his attempts to charm her become increasingly inept, as she challenges his originality, second-guesses his compliments and leans away from him with delicate distaste, as if he even smells slightly fishy. It is quite a different Bill Chandler (and William Powell) we see on the dance floor, as he stumbles over his words and his feet, chuckling uneasily. Connie wins every round of this first encounter, ultimately complementing her allusion to his 'line' by acknowledging her recognition of his charade: 'I should say Mr Chandler is *quite* an angler!'

During their last night onboard ship, Connie finally begins to show some interest, but only when Bill stops flattering her, and tells her what he really thinks: '"Who is this marvel?" I said. "Florence Nightingale? Jean d'Arc? What has she done to earn such a precious reputation?"' Significantly, Bill is still talking about reputation and famous women. Connie tries to explain, but Bill persists in his sarcasm, declaring that she should be 'kept under glass' as a precious object to be touched only by royalty (echoing his earlier characterisation of her as title-crazy). Cavell would undoubtedly describe this speech as the 'man's lecturing', but my point is that Bill still thinks – mistakenly – that he knows all about Connie.

The turning point in Bill's attitude comes when he escapes the influence of publicity and mass communications, during his visit to the green world of the Allenbury estate. Here, Connie tells him, 'There are many sides to my nature, depths you'd never dream of!' Although she is partly joking (referring to her unexpected ability to make flapjacks), Bill's response indicates his growing realisation that he does not know everything after all: 'I'll make a study.' His lesson begins with a moonlight swim to a floating summerhouse. This scene is pivotal, and there are a number of interrelated aspects to consider: conversation, play and the green world. All three have a bearing on the screwball couple's privacy.

Private conversations

First and foremost, the scene is *Libeled Lady*'s moment of screwball escape from society – the equivalent of the cabin in *The Awful Truth*, the playroom in *Holiday* or the forest in *Bringing Up Baby*. Perhaps most directly, it echoes Peter and Ellie's crossing of the moonlit river. Warren Susman posits an illuminating explanation for this escape, arguing that *It Happened One Night* 'exemplifies in a nearly archetypical [*sic*] twentieth-century American way the inability of individuals to communicate privately in the world of such awesome, constant, universal public communications. Adrift in a world of communications, where every private act (especially of the rich and famous) is public property, our hero and heroine can communicate only when they leave that world totally' (1984: 266). The one night when 'it' happened is the one night spent 'removed from the world of mechanical communications' (1984: 265) – the night spent crossing the river into the pastoral field. This argument also provides another motivation for Peter and Ellie's withdrawal at the end of the film. While Ellie and King Westley's excessively public wedding is going to be filmed by conspicuous newsreel cameras, Ellie and Peter's union requires the absence of the camera.

Similar principles apply to *Libeled Lady*. Connie, like Ellie, is a headline-hitting heiress (they even share Walter Connolly as a father). Bill, like Peter, is associated with the press, and both men must get to know the woman behind the celebrity image. Both films extend their interest in publicity to include the processes of mass communication: ample use is made of newspapers, photographs, telegrams, cables, long-distance telephone calls, radio, and various modes of transport. Significantly, *Libeled Lady* demonstrates the failure of mass communications, most obviously with the libellous story, but also with Warren's international search for Bill, which ends with the accidental discovery, via the humble newsboy, that he lives around the corner. In a sense, the movie includes itself in this joke. An intricate montage of telegraph wires, international operators and ticker-tape messages reflexively draws attention to the film's part in the processes of mass communication.

The impossibility of authentic public communication adds another dimension to the escape to the green world: 'here in a limited, unpretentious world

[. . .] they can find out who they are and at last be themselves in face-to-face communication' (Susman 1984: 266). *Libeled Lady*'s summerhouse (with its cushions, towelling robes, cigarettes and wireless) is more luxurious than *It Happened One Night*'s field, but few places could be more limited: floating in the middle of a lake, in the middle of nowhere, in the middle of the night. Within moments of arriving, Bill is declaring, 'You know, you're a funny kid. And that's what you seem like up here – a kid. Very different from the girl I met on the boat.' He is disarmed by Connie's frankness, as she confesses that she 'misjudged' him: 'Well, I said it first on the boat: "Just another fortune hunter chasing fifty million dollars on the hoof." [. . .] And then you told me off for being fragile, but I still said, "He's got something up his sleeve he wants to sell [. . .]." And, would you believe – I even bet you didn't fish!' As the conversation continues, the framing signals the process of Bill's re-education. A medium two-shot is intercut with three medium close-ups of Bill (the only close-ups in the scene). The first shows Bill frowning as Connie concludes her speech. His discomfort is understandable, given that her first instincts were correct; but the frown also indicates his confusion, as he is forced to reconcile this new information with his 'title-crazy' stereotype. In the second medium close-up, he still looks serious and consequently we believe him when, in reply to Connie's hope that they can be friends, he says, 'That's about the nicest thing that's been said to me this lifetime.' In the final medium close-up, this new sincerity takes hold, in an oblique acknowledgement of his deceit: 'Don't apologise for suspecting people, Connie, keep right on.' The film cuts back to the medium shot, and Bill stands up, clearly having decided not to go through with the planned scandal. Although Connie still does not know the whole truth about Bill's identity, both have rejected their preconceived stereotypes (fortune hunter and title-crazy playgirl). The symbolic change is unmistakable. Now, each emphasises the uniqueness of the other. Connie says the 'nicest thing' to Bill that he's heard this 'lifetime'; and Bill is the 'first person in years' to whom Connie has wanted to talk.

Both lines correlate private conversation with time as an expression of the extraordinary. Susman's idea of 'face-to-face communication' echoes Cavell: 'the films in question recapture the full weight of the concept of conversation, [. . .] talking together is fully and plainly being together, a mode of association, a form of life, and I would like to say that in these films the central pair are learning to speak the same language' (1981: 87–8). Cavell expressly acknowledges this language is a private one. For example, at the end of *The Awful Truth*, the couple's dialogue bounces back and forth in a process of repetition and difference which only they fully comprehend. I take this kind of reciprocal exchange to be at the heart of the 'mode of association' which Cavell calls conversation, and it involves more than just words. For example, Lucy's earlier performance as Lola relies upon a shared visual language as well, conveying a pointed message to Jerry about his previous girlfriend, Dixie Belle Lee (Joyce Compton); this kind of private joke is typical of the screwball couple and depends upon their shared past. At a formal level, screwball comedy's reliance on the two-shot also feeds into this idea of reciprocal conversation, visually balancing the couple's banter with their proxemic relationship.

Powell and Loy excel at this kind of conversation. Kay Young analyses their first scene in *The Thin Man*, noting how their words play off each other, transforming the other's meaning to make a joke. They 'construct a kind of song out of their bantering in which gaining information is not the object of their speech. Rather, it is the pleasure which each takes in knowing how to respond and in hearing the other's response that drives the conversation' (1994: 266). Nick and Nora face each other and the straight-on visual framing offers the couple as symmetrical images, as they mirror each other's movements (see p. 39). The symmetry is completed by Nora's request for five more martinis, to match Nick's consumption. Their verbal and physical conversation epitomises their egalitarian, companionate 'mode of association'.

In *Libeled Lady*, Connie and Bill must learn how to communicate in this way. Although most of their conversations take place face-to-face, in medium shot (with the occasional insertion of a close-up reaction shot), they do not always 'speak the same language'. When they first meet, the dialogue is witty, but Bill is unsure how to respond, and the joke is almost always at his expense. At the summerhouse, the conversation tends to be at cross-purposes, but nonetheless signals a growing intimacy, emphasised by framing and blocking. They are framed in medium shot, but their blocking prevents eye contact: she is lying on her front facing the camera, while he sits slightly behind her, looking at the back of her head. Despite the fact that she cannot see him from this position, Connie (or more correctly, Loy) casts wry glances in Bill's direction, particularly at those moments when she is saying something which is loaded with double meaning for the spectator. These glances simultaneously convey Connie's willingness to communicate 'face-to-face' and the failure to do so. Although this blocking is far from systematic, the general awkwardness of their physical conversation is apparent. Consequently, those moments when they do have direct eye contact become all the more striking and intimate. Still in medium shot, they sit up in unison to face each other, just before Connie asks if they can be friends.

The green playground

Screwball comedy's emphasis on private conversation transforms the function of the green world. According to Frye, most Shakespearean comedies involve a 'rhythmic movement from normal world to green world *and back again*' (1990: 182, my emphasis), enabling the renewal of society. The normal world is characterised as a world of irrational law and parental tyranny, while the green world functions as a festive 'holiday' space in which social convention can be flouted (women dressing as men) and magical things can happen. The Shakespearean green world is itself a social world, comprising exiles from the normal world (including the couple) and permanent inhabitants with magical or 'natural' qualities (Puck, Touchstone). Frye uses 'natural' to refer to the world of abundance God intended for humankind: 'this natural society is associated with things which in the context of the ordinary world seem unnatural, but which are in fact attributes of nature as a miraculous and irresistible reviving power' (1965: 142–3). The Shakespearean green world is both idyllic and ideal, and the contrast with the normal world is one between nature and human artifice.

The green world in screwball comedy shares some of these traits, but not all. Although the screwball green world is idyllic, it is 'natural' only in the modern sense of rural and unpretentious; there are no fairies or fools here.[3] Instead, the green world derives its 'magic' from its relationship to childhood. The normal world's tyranny stems from its rigidity, which has resulted in social (and economic) stagnation; this is counteracted by a resurgence of playful irrationality, often empowered by the move into the green world. The contrast between artifice and nature remains, therefore, but is recast as a contrast between dehumanising, urban existence and liberating, pastoral play. Most importantly, the green world does not represent an alternative society; it is usually inhabited by the couple alone. Consequently, no matter how beneficial the time spent in the green world is for the screwball couple, there is little sense of *social* renewal and the couple tend to remain unreconciled with their original society.

Another look at the summerhouse sequence in *Libeled Lady* clarifies these interwoven elements, particularly as they relate to childhood and play. The scene is certainly idyllic: a lake surrounded by trees, moonlight bouncing off rippling water, a safe night spent under the stars. Connie seems transformed to Bill – a 'kid' – and she expressly links the magical change to this place: 'It's all tied up with my childhood. The trees, the air, the water, even the frogs [*croaking gets louder*]. I'm mad about frogs!' The scene definitively answers the question about Connie's status as playgirl. She ducks Bill while they swim, laughs raucously, and admits to camping out there all night. By the end of the scene, Bill is joining in the fun, challenging her to a race back to shore.

In this place, time becomes 'heavenly [. . .] every minute completely filled' (Connie's words), full of vital energy; indeed, according to Bill, the day has been 'almost *too* perfect'. The function of time is utopian and extraordinary, therefore, but also fragile: the scene is offset by our knowledge of Gladys's imminent arrival – instead of at midnight, as Bill believes. Once he has decided not to go through with the plan, the sense of time running out accelerates. The conversation turns towards 'those twisted newspaper stories' and as soon as the possibility of public scandal is raised, the world of mass communication intrudes: the music on the wireless abruptly stops as the hour is chimed, and a radio announcer's voice breaks the spell. The hour is only eleven, but the fairytale time structure is soon made explicit, as Bill insists it is time to go:

> CONNIE: And who are you? Cinderella's brother? What happens at the stroke of twelve?
> BILL: You'll never know – I hope!

The time spent on the raft is acknowledged as limited, at least in part because of its associations with childhood and play. As Johan Huizinga argues, 'play is not "ordinary" or "real" life. It is rather a stepping out of "real" life into a temporary sphere of activity with a disposition all of its own' (1970: 26). Such spheres are 'forbidden spots, isolated, hedged round, hallowed, within which special rules obtain' (1970: 29). This description is wholly appropriate to the screwball green world, and further explains its privacy. It is not a 'world' at all; it is a playground.

Conversation and play work together to establish the couple's equality, compatibility and companionship. Importantly, the green playground, although private, is emphatically not domestic; it is recreational space. The emphasis on childhood is matched by the talk of friendship, and this outweighs some of the more conventionally romantic aspects of the scene (such as moonlight and music). It is no coincidence that – rather than culminating with a romantic kiss – the friends seal their relationship with a handshake.

Private recreation

When we next see Bill and Connie together (three scenes later), their recreational play has continued. They are eating hamburgers after a morning's horse-riding, and it is clear they have seen each other a number of times in the interim.

> CONNIE: You turn me down for the horse show –
> BILL: But I ride with you every morning.
> CONNIE: You scorn my bid to a concert –
> BILL: But I strum my guitar 'neath thy window each eve.

There is a marked improvement in their style of conversation, displaying more harmonious banter and eye contact. As Bill completes Connie's sentences, the rhythmic structure of the lines emphasises their new-found empathy;

Connie seems to recognise the poetic potential of the form, incorporating suitably archaic speech that Bill immediately picks up and elaborates. They are 'learning to speak the same language' (Cavell 1981: 88).

However, the dialogue also involves a split between public events (horse shows and concerts) and private activities (horse-riding and serenading). As the scene progresses, the issue of public scandal returns and, when Connie presses Bill to explain why he will not be seen in public with her, their physical conversation founders. This time, three close-ups of Connie interrupt the medium shot as she becomes increasingly serious. Bill avoids making eye contact as he evades answering her questions and, with mention of the libel suit, Connie turns away and defensively removes herself from the frame. The scene becomes increasingly uncomfortable as Bill manipulates the situation to his own advantage by suggesting she should drop the libel suit; in the process, he falls back on the issue of her public reputation, rather than revealing the truth.

This anxiety about public intimacy is well founded, given that as soon as they *are* seen together in public at the charity bazaar, the Burns-Norvells (Cora Witherspoon and Lauri Beatty) reveal the existence of Mrs Chandler to Mr Allenbury. Connie's reaction to the news is telling; she remains calm and insists on taking care of the situation.

MR ALLENBURY: You'll ask him point blank, so he can't misunderstand?
CONNIE: Yes . . . I'll ask him so he can't misunderstand.

Connie makes a fine distinction between asking a point-blank question (are you married?) and asking a question that cannot be misunderstood (will you marry me?). This might seem a perfect opportunity for private conversation, but Connie's indirect method of questioning initially leaves Bill baffled and then speechless. Effectively she must ask him five times before he can manage an answer and even then his answer is a question: 'Well! What do you think?' Her reaction signals that she is satisfied; sighing with relief, she asks, 'When?' These lines are critical, as signalled by the use of shot/reverse shot close-ups – the only break in the otherwise static medium shot. The close-ups intensify the scene's double punch: before we can recover from the surprise of Bill accepting the proposal, a more urgent question is asked, and this urgency builds to the end of the scene.

BILL: When?
CONNIE: Now?
BILL: Now? You mean soon?
CONNIE: I mean *now*. Tonight.
BILL: Tonight!
CONNIE: Will you, Bill?
BILL: *Will* I? Is there a preacher in the house?

The repetitive structure of the dialogue begins to create a sense of private conversation; we may not understand Bill's behaviour, but the couple seem to understand each other. This is reinforced by echoes of the summerhouse scene: Bill again invokes fairytale imagery (describing Connie as the 'flying princess' who flew back to her home, the moon) and the musical theme also returns. By screwball standards, the scene is relatively romantic, ending with an embracing kiss. However, the couple quickly turn their backs to the camera, which has maintained a medium distance. More importantly, the romantic consummation is undercut by our knowledge that this cannot be The End. There is still the small matter of Mrs William Chandler to be resolved.

That was no lady . . . that was my wife

The film's treatment of Gladys is, for the most part, problematic. Set up as the archetypal dumb blonde, she is the butt of a series of jokes rooted in class and sex distinctions. Warren and Bill exploit her remorselessly and, to the extent that the film enjoys making jokes at her expense, their behaviour is largely condoned. However, as Harvey notes, *Libeled Lady* is built on a pattern of personal contests: 'everyone wins, and everyone loses, at least one crucial encounter' (1998: 171). Somehow, it is only fitting that Gladys should win the final round.

We have seen Bill and Connie being married by a Justice of the Peace without understanding how this is possible. All is revealed in the final scene. Connie, Bill, Gladys and Warren stand in medium long shot as Bill explains that Gladys was never legally divorced from her first husband, Joe Simpson, so her marriage to Bill was not legal either. Connie then reminds Bill to give Warren a letter officially dropping the libel suit. Warren reads the letter, standing in medium shot next to Gladys; as realisation transforms his face, he pushes Gladys out of the way and moves towards Bill and Connie. Gladys is visually excluded from the group – pushed aside as unimportant – and an inserted close-up reveals her anger. Her insignificant status is explicitly reiterated when Connie reminds Warren that he has forgotten something. Initially, Warren thinks she is referring to his hat, but when she explains she meant 'Mrs Simpson', Warren is still confused; when he realises she is referring to Gladys, he laughs. Having been reduced to the lowest possible level of significance (less important to her fiancé than his hat), Gladys is finally allowed her revenge. She found out her first divorce was not legal, so got a second divorce in Reno. Bill has relied too heavily on his assumption of her blonde ignorance.

Gladys's revelation provides the final discovery of identity; she really is Mrs William Chandler. Paradoxically, this discovery prevents the resolution of the social conflict, and Gladys's words acknowledge this disruption: 'You were all terribly smart, weren't you? You were all building up to a nice happy ending.' Although the two couples are finally reunited (Gladys realises she still loves Haggerty after Bill punches him), their unions remain unsanctioned: Bill is a bigamist and Gladys is married to the wrong man. We may assume that the legal technicalities will be sorted out, but for now this happy ending renders social approval beside the point. Instead of social integration, the film ends with Mr Allenbury (the supposed figure of patriarchal authority) shouting for quiet as he tries to understand the situation.

A more conventional ending would cut to a double wedding coda sequence, or at least have Gladys and Warren finally making it down the aisle. Either version would correspond with Frye's arguments about marriage as social identity, although an even better resolution in this respect would be for Gladys and Bill to discover each other and stay married. Romantic comedy usually justifies marriages of convenience in this way (e.g. *Come Live with Me* (1941), *Without Love*, *Green Card* (1990)), implying that marriage should not, and implicitly, cannot, be taken so lightly. *Libeled Lady* has no such scruples.[4] By ending in bigamy, the film is not dismissing the importance of heterosexual monogamy, but contrasting two versions of what constitutes such a union. Gladys's legal right to keep Bill as a husband is characterised as vengeful and destructive ('Nobody else is going to get you, not if it kills both of us!'). Connie, on the other hand, implicitly disconnects heterosexual union from the legal fact of marriage: 'I know, you've got him now – in name anyway. But I have his love.' The personal relationship triumphs over the social institution.

In discovering the 'truth' of the false marriage, the film also corroborates the initial newspaper story. Ironically, Connie has become a 'husband stealer' after all. However, the corroboration of the public image contrasts with our understanding that this is *not* the whole truth, because there is nothing scandalous about her behaviour. The film's interest in mass communications and private conversation indicates a discrepancy between legal facts and the complexities of personal meaning. Significantly, the film omits the conversation in which Bill tells Connie the truth about himself and his scandal-mongering marriage (it is not even clear if this happens before or after their wedding). This omission might seem inexcusable in light of the ideal of private conversation, but the absence of the camera also renders the imagined scene more private. In a sense, Connie knows all she *needs* to know when Bill agrees to marry her; his public persona is no more important than hers, since both are essentially miscommunications.

Loy and Powell as screwball couple

Bill and Connie's courtship is more romantic than most screwball couplings, and the inversion of gender roles is less conspicuous. Bill demonstrates the 'willing[ness] to suffer a certain indignity' (1981: 8) that Cavell considers a virtue of the hero, but this indignity is not directly initiated by Connie in the way that Susan rains chaos on David in *Bringing Up Baby*, or Lucy topples Jerry's pride in *The Awful Truth*. Connie does not pursue Bill, as Irene pursues her man Godfrey, but she does retain her autonomy and she does propose. This signals her active power and ability to take control of the situation. Her self-possession in the face of a potential crisis is unusual, even for a screwball heroine, but it is typical of Loy's relationship to Powell. Conversely, Bill seems a far more unstable figure, taking on different personae and adapting with lightning reflexes to each twist in the plot. His mannerisms and actions are similarly flexible, and even unexpected, as when he sits cross-legged on the edge of the city magistrate's desk, while Warren tries to convince Gladys to marry him.

This pattern of behaviour – Loy as stable, Powell as unstable – is central to their persona as a star couple. It is somewhat atypical for screwball comedy, however, since it is more usually the unstable energy of the woman that releases the man from his dull routine. *Double Wedding* exemplifies this variation, placing Margit Agnew (Loy) in the position of stagnation, while Charlie Lodge (Powell) teaches her how to live again. Margit is a control freak: in addition to running her own boutique, she also runs the lives of her sister, Irene (Florence Rice), and her sister's fiancé, Waldo (John Beal); indeed she has arranged the engagement, set the date, designed the dress and organised the honeymoon. The bohemian Charlie lives in a caravan and is planning to make a film with Irene and Waldo. As if the association with the dramatic arts were not enough, Charlie also paints and even runs to wearing a beret and a full-length fur coat. Powell's character is again involved in deceiving Loy's: Charlie pretends he wants to marry Irene, hoping this will force Margit to admit she loves him. This pattern of behaviour also involves an inversion of gender norms, since masculine identity is stereotypically assumed to be stable, while masquerade and deceit are 'feminine' arts. The pattern is repeated in all their comedies together. While Loy remains calmly self-possessed, it is Powell who suffers the identity crisis.

Who was that man?

Powell's star persona seems stable in retrospect: suave, sophisticated, well dressed, witty – the quintessential gentleman. However, throughout his partnership with Loy, and more generally in the thirties, this persona is dominated by a confusion of identity. In nine of the fourteen films he made between 1936 and 1942, his character takes on an assumed identity or is dramatically transformed; in four of the others he plays the inherently duplicitous role of detective; and the remaining film is *Double Wedding*, in which Charlie's outlandish costume and theatricality at least suggest the performance of identity. This confusion is usually compounded by a degree of chicanery, as in *My Man Godfrey*, or even criminality, as in *The Last of Mrs Cheyney* (1937). Rather than refute Warren's initial description of Bill as a 'conceited, double-crossing heel', *Libeled Lady* confirms this characterisation – and yet Bill remains a sympathetic figure.

This ability to be both heel and hero is central to Powell's appeal and stems from his silent career. Powell was a clear-cut villain in twenty-nine out of thirty-five silent roles, and a hero in only three.[5] With the coming of sound, Powell's cultivated mid-Atlantic accent came to prominence, and he began the transition to gentleman hero, via roles as detectives and lawyers. The resulting contradictions in his persona are exemplified by *I Love You Again*. Powell begins the film playing a miserly, teetotal killjoy called Larry Wilson; after a blow to the head, Larry wakes up as his real self, George Carey, a conman who lost his memory nine years earlier. The contrast between criminal past and virtuous present is clear, but the crook is the more sympathetic character. Although George does not go through with his confidence scheme to fleece the other stuffed-shirts in Larry's hometown, his new roguish personality wins back the wife (Loy) he did not know he had.

Powell's screwball characters can be usefully compared to the trickster archetype. Tricksters are 'representations of liminality, duality, subversion, and irony. [. . .] they use impersonation, disguise, theft, and deceit to expose hypocrisy and inequality, to subvert existing social systems, and to widen their sphere of power' (Landay 1998: 2). Such duality accounts for Powell's ability to be both heel and hero. Landay mentions a pertinent example of the trickster in American culture, 'the nineteenth-century confidence man, who represents the shifting border between wilderness and civilization, gentlemanly and vernacular language, and class-based and fluid ideologies' (1998: 12). Powell's shifting position in relation to villainy and heroism involves a similar expression of 'fluid ideologies', as do his transformations from blueblood to butler to self-made man in *My Man Godfrey*, and from middle-American bore to urban conman in *I Love You Again*. Such roles typically place Powell in an 'unmanly' position, as a domestic servant or a teetotal killjoy; in *Love Crazy*, Powell's character, Steve Ireland, feigns insanity and masquerades as his own spinster sister. These are precisely the kinds of role that in a supporting character would be definitively coded as effeminate (and probably camp, if played by such character actors as Franklin Pangborn or Eric Blore), and yet Powell remains decidedly masculine (and heterosexual).

His trickster abilities enable him to get away with it all, epitomising the more fluid style of urbane masculinity typically celebrated in screwball comedy.

The Thin Man is central to the development of Powell's trickster persona.[6] Nick Charles used to be a detective but, having married the wealthy, upper-class Nora, now runs the businesses left by her father (Nick's own class background remains rather shadowy, and a number of jokes are made about marrying Nora for her money).[7] The world that revolves around Nick and Nora is peopled with a fine array of lower- and upper-class types. A running joke involves Nick being greeted like a long-lost friend by an unsavoury rogue; occasionally, he has even sent the other party to jail, but grudges are never held. Although Nick has the trickster's ability to move between both worlds, his relationship to the upper classes is more strained. Significantly, the murderer is always revealed to be from the 'respectable' upper-class world. The murders are frequently motivated by the desire to maintain this illusion of difference, by killing someone who is threatening to reveal the truth (often a blackmailer). By revealing the identity of the murderer, Nick exposes the hypocrisy and inequality of class structures.

The role of Nick Charles raises one final factor in the duality of Powell's persona during this period – the extratextual confusion of identity. According to one fan magazine interview, 'on the screen, he is the epitome of the man who gets out and around. Off the screen, he is the Invisible Man' (Reid 1970: 156). The interviewer wants to know why Powell has become increasingly reclusive, to which Powell replies, 'I haven't exactly *thought* myself into privacy. [. . .] I suppose it could be traced, indirectly, to the roles I've played. [...] Nick Charles, for example. [. . .] You see, he looks like *me*. And, because of that, there are actually people who think I'm Nick, or vice versa. [. . .] You see, they don't know William Powell. They know only that fellow on the screen' (Reid 1970: 156–7). The interview repeatedly articulates the source of confusion in terms of the disjunction between the private self and the public image, and 'what can happen, if you try to be yourself and go out in public, too' (1970: 158). By distinguishing the star from the character, the interview appears to give access to the 'truth', to the 'real' William Powell. In fact, the interview is no less mediated than any other fan magazine article; the real Powell (like any star) will always be 'invisible' in the sense of being unknowable. Instead, the public persona articulates the anxiety around who this real person *might* be. Dyer argues that all star images are related to contradictions in ideology (1979: 30), but Powell's movement from villain to hero requires his persona to actually embody contradiction as a value in itself. In the process, this persona allows a more fluid notion of masculine identity. It also negotiates cultural anxiety about the instability of public identities by securing the private self as the source of true identity.

The ideal marriage

These various discourses about identity, publicity, privacy and play can be drawn together by considering the meanings of the Loy/Powell couple in relation to companionate marriage, primarily as embodied in the ideal of Nick and Nora. In *Libeled Lady*, the process of 'learning to speak the same language' was enabled by the escape to the green playground; Nick and Nora, however, can already converse, and take their playground with them. For example, in *Another Thin Man*, Nick receives a note at The West Indies Club, apparently from an ex-girlfriend, Bella Spruce; he is informed the note came from a lady on the other side of the club. The film cuts to the appropriate spot, but all we see is a crowd of men. Nick goes over and delicately moves the men aside, to reveal Nora. They exchange words in a close-up shot and reverse shot:

> NICK: Now, Mommy, you know better than to come to a place like this your first day out of bed. What if the health officers find out? They'll put you straight back in quarantine.
> NORA: [*banging her hand on the table defiantly*] I won't stay in quarantine! I don't care who catches it!

As the other men hurriedly move away, Nick sits down next to Nora. In the more usual symmetrical two-shot, he asks her how long she has been 'leading this double life'. Nora, the picture of innocence, replies, 'Just since we've been married,' and flutters her eyelashes demurely. A moment later, Nick orders a drink, then – looking towards Nora – amends his request to two; she then looks to the waiter and adds, 'The same.' Nora gives as good as she gets. They spontaneously pick up their reciprocal style of conversation, despite their public location and the presence of others.

This ability to play together privately *even in public* is essential to understanding the appeal of Nick and Nora and the ideal nature of their marriage. In terms of the companionate model, their public play represents the dissolution of 'Victorian' separate spheres and, concomitantly, the modern expectations of fun morality and mutual interests. Like Lucy and Jerry Warriner in *The Awful Truth*, Nick and Nora are wealthy, sophisticated, childless (at least initially) and own a wire-haired terrier. The same kind of dog also features in *Bringing Up Baby*, suggesting the later films want to refer to the model of Nick and Nora. Rather than representing the responsibility of a substitute child, the screwball couple's dog 'seems at once to express and to provide an occasion for a kind of childlikeness in the couple' (Britton 1986: 41). Nick and Nora's wealth also functions to aid play, particularly in the field of consumption, most conspicuously of alcohol. In the *Thin Man* films, screwball liberation has already been achieved; alcohol functions instead as a general lubricant for easier living and more flexible play. Finally, Nick and Nora's companionship not only extends into the public sphere, but into the bedroom as well, and their play is more knowingly sexual than in screwball comedy. Often, as at the West Indies Club, their banter toys with the possibility of adultery, but their pleasure lies in the frisson of flirtation, rather than the possibility of transgression. Implicitly, there is no need for Nick or Nora to commit adultery; they are completely satisfied with each other.

This contented state of affairs raises questions about the nature of love in the *Thin Man* films. According to Samuel Marx (who bought the story for MGM), 'the matrimonial combination of Powell and Loy – even that was a risk, because in those days you got married at the end of the movie, not at the beginning. Marriage wasn't supposed to be fun' (quoted by Kotsilibas-David and Loy 1988: 90). Nick and Nora's fun marriage contrasts with convention, particularly the usual narrative structuring of desire, in which satisfaction is repeatedly postponed by the intervention of obstacles. Robert Lapsley and Michael Westlake have linked this structure to psychoanalytical accounts of desire, arguing that narrative obstacles displace the impossibility of the sexual relation by keeping the object of desire at a distance, masking lack in the Other in order to maintain the illusion of its perfection (1992: 41). This model bears a striking resemblance to accounts of passionate, romantic love. For example, Milton Viederman argues that passion is mysterious and illusory and 'possession is incomplete' (1988: 7; see also de Rougemont 1983: 90). The beginning of *After the Thin Man* is revealing in this respect. Nick and Nora are on a train approaching San Francisco; Nora is packing and – having been passed an undergarment by Nick – complains about how a woman is supposed to retain any 'mystery' after three days in such a small compartment.

NICK: Darling, you don't need mystery – you've got something much better, something more alluring.
NORA: What?
NICK: *Me.*
NORA: You! [*she gently shoves him, and they kiss*]

Viederman notes that 'among the enemies of passion are: absolute understanding and knowledge of the other; familiarity; certainty; predictability and repetition; absolute trust in the other and the disarming of jealousy; and legitimisation of the relationship precluding the sense of transgression' (1988: 6). These may well be the enemies of passion and romance, but they are precisely the virtues of Nick and Nora's relationship.

According to Denis de Rougemont, 'happy love has no history' (1983: 15), but perhaps this is not because happy love cannot exist, but because it cannot be narrativised. Narratives need conflict and change. Consequently, Nick and Nora's relationship exists in juxtaposition with a conventional murder mystery plot; their happy moments do not advance the story, but function as a form of spectacle, arresting – even supplanting – the causal chain of events.

The perfect wife – and her husband

In contrast to romantic structures of desire that privilege the male lover-subject (at the expense of the female beloved-object) Nick and Nora's embodiment of companionate marriage offers a more egalitarian ideal of gender relations. However, it is worth noting that while Loy was quickly retyped as 'the perfect wife', Nick/Powell is presumably not 'the perfect husband'. What is at stake in this distinction?

Loy herself notes that Nora is 'hardly the perfect wife in the sense of being the chaste, virginal creature that seemed to be so much admired' (Kotsilibas-Davis and Loy 1988: 91). Powell's explanation of her 'perfect' status is particularly suggestive: 'when the bed rolled beneath her in the hangover scene [in *The Thin Man*] and she looked up at me with the ice bag on her head and said, "You pushed me," she became every man's dream of what a wife should be: beautiful and glamorous with a sense of humor, provocative and feminine without being saccharine or sharp, a perfect gal who never lost her temper, jumped at conclusions, or nagged a guy' (Kotsilibas-Davis and Loy 1988: 92). Much the same sentiments are expressed in the films themselves. For example, in *After the Thin Man*, when Nora asks Nick if he has 'any complaints or suggestions' for her New Year's resolutions, he claims to have a few complaints:

> NICK: Well, you don't scold, you don't nag, and you look far too pretty in the mornings.
> NORA: All right, I'll remember: must scold; must nag; mustn't be too pretty in the mornings. [*They kiss*]

Nora's perfection is ironically established, but in relation to an (implicitly misogynistic) male stereotype of wives.

Jeanine Basinger takes this male fantasy of wifely perfection as indicating the essential inequality of Nick and Nora's relationship: 'there is no argument that Powell and Loy are sensational, or that the films are delightful. But is theirs the perfect marriage? Not from the woman's point of view' (1994: 320). The main source of her complaint is the unequal division of narrative action: Nick investigates, while Nora is often tricked into staying behind; she will usually then attempt to investigate on her own, but this invariably results in a comic failure. To an extent, Basinger is right, but she only paints half the picture: Nora is less subordinated than most sidekicks (female or otherwise) and frequently does play an active part in the investigation. Certainly, few

Hollywood wives would instinctively leap to wrestle a gun from a confessed murderer to protect their husbands, as Nora does at the end of *Shadow of the Thin Man* (even if she does swoon when she realises what she has done).

This courage suggests another factor which counters the apparent inequality of Nick and Nora's narrative functions: Powell's unconventional masculinity is matched by Loy's unconventional femininity. By breaking with the stereotype of the nagging housewife, Nora provides a more positive image of, and for, women. Indeed, the elements of her 'perfection' are in contravention of a number of supposedly essential feminine traits: dependence (Nora is the wealthy one); vulnerability (*Shadow of the Thin Man* is not the only time Nora protects someone from a potential bullet); and emotionalism (Nora is generally imperturbable and never hysterical). A key example of this 'atypical' behaviour is Nora's lack of jealousy. One of the defining moments of her relationship with Nick occurs in *The Thin Man*: Nora comes into her bedroom to find Nick embracing Dorothy Wynant (Maureen O'Sullivan). The camera pans to see Nick's reaction – he pulls a face – and then pans back to see Nora; she too pulls a face and enters the room. Dorothy pulls away from Nick and apologises to Nora, but Nora tells her not to be silly and offers her a drink. This is precisely the kind of thing Powell means when he talks of Nora never jumping to conclusions, and similar moments occur in almost every film. It is also a good example of the film's development of Nick and Nora's companionate relationship. In Dashiell Hammett's original novel, only Nick makes a face (1935: 14); similarly, much of Nick's witty dialogue is taken from the book (for example, 1935: 8, 18), but Nora's reciprocal replies are new.

The dynamics of the Loy/Powell persona also contribute to the unequal division of narrative action. While Powell's unstable identity and trickster abilities place him in the centre of the narrative conflict, Loy's stable self-possession places her in a reactive, rather than active, position. At its best – as in the early *Thin Man* films and *Libeled Lady* – this position is both vivacious and energetic and, in combination with their spectacular conversation, an equal role is implied. As the structure becomes conventionalised, Loy's self-possession tends to solidify into something more passive. As Loy says of *Love Crazy*, 'my part wasn't much, really, just this stodgy woman who puts up with him' (Kotsilibas-Davis and Loy 1988: 167). While the structure of their relationship is the same in all the Loy/Powell films (except *Evelyn Prentice*), the difference in characterisation and effect could not be greater.

Domesticating the companionate couple

The same process of solidification can be found in the later *Thin Man* films. As Sikov notes, 'MGM was progressively domesticating a couple whose popularity had originally been sparked by their clean disavowal of proper family values' (1989: 201). The degree and kind of domestication which takes place is revealing, since it not only suggests changing cultural attitudes and priorities, but also the hegemonic assimilation of companionate marriage.

The first step to domestication is having a child, and *After the Thin Man* ends with Nora announcing she is pregnant. Parental responsibilities shift the dynamics of Nick and Nora's relationship considerably. Nick is increasingly aligned with Nicky Jr, a process that redefines his ambiguous morality as boyish 'naughtiness', while Nora becomes ever more matronly and authoritative. For example, in *Song of the Thin Man*, Nora insists that Nicky Jr (Dean Stockwell) must be punished for trying to skip his piano practice to play baseball; spanking is Nick's responsibility, so she stands over him making sure he goes through with it. The reluctant Nick starts seeing idyllic moments from Junior's childhood (superimposed on the seat of his pants). The final image, however, shows Nick falling off Nicky's bicycle – and Nicky laughing – enabling the humiliated father to start spanking with enthusiasm. Nick's play (riding the bicycle) is now coded as both childish (rather than childlike) and foolhardy. Concomitantly, Asta the dog's influence diminishes as he is reduced to being Nicky's pet.

Other traits of the companionate couple are similarly curbed by domestic responsibilities and family values. Loy attributes the demise of the *Thin Man* series to the drinking: 'the characters drank too much, and for a while the public didn't seem to mind all the martinis and the hangovers, but then, after a while, they did, or at least the studio maintained that was what happened' (Hurley 1982: 469). The process by which drinking is transformed from a virtue to a relative vice is interesting. In *Shadow of the Thin Man*, Nicky Jr (Dickie Hall) demands that Nick should drink milk (instead of his cocktail) and Nora gleefully concurs, with a wicked glint in her eye. Nick, with his hand over his eyes, gulps it down, while Nora can barely control her giggles. In *The Thin Man Goes Home*, Nick swears off the hard stuff altogether, because *his* father does not like it; instead, he carries a flask of cider (although Nora would still prefer a dry martini) and remains sober throughout. There is a running joke about others assuming he is drunk, because he has fallen over or been knocked unconscious, but even this suggests a gap between playful inebriation and being a drunk. Nick also remains sober in *Song of the Thin Man*, but not for want of trying: his last bottle of scotch is shot out of his hand; later, shortly after someone spills Nora's sherry (!), Nick puts his glass down without taking a sip. With the exception of the scotch, these moments barely qualify for a running joke, since they are so underplayed as to be humourless. It seems far more the case that external forces (whether MGM's conservatism or public opinion) have intervened. As Nora says at the end of the film, when Nick warns her to duck if things get rough, 'I'm practically under the table now, but not the way I'd like to be.' They have become prisoners of other people's morality.

Despite these changes in the representation of Nick and Nora's relationship, they are still understood as the companionate couple. In effect, companionate marriage has become conflated with the conventional family marriage, and has taken on some of the more stereotypical attitudes associated with the latter, albeit in a muted and relatively ironic form. Marriage is marriage once again. The same, not different.

Notes

1 Loy and Powell appeared in thirteen films together: *Manhattan Melodrama* (1934); *The Thin Man* (1934); *Evelyn Prentice* (1934); *The Great Ziegfeld* (1936); *Libeled Lady* (1936); *After the Thin Man* (1936); *Double Wedding* (1937); *Another Thin Man* (1939); *I Love You Again* (1940); *Love Crazy* (1941); *Shadow of the Thin Man* (1941); *The Thin Man Goes Home* (1944); and *Song of the Thin Man* (1947). Loy also appeared in a cameo as Powell's wife in *The Senator Was Indiscreet* (1947). *Libeled Lady* and *Double Wedding* are the only films in which we do not see the couple's married life.

2 *The Thin Man* spawned a cycle of murder mystery comedies featuring screwball couples, including *Remember Last Night?* (1935), *Star of Midnight* (1935), *The Mad Miss Manton* (1936), *The Ex-Mrs Bradford* (1936), *The Amazing Mr Williams* (1939), and *A Night to Remember* (1943). There were even attempts at two further series: *Fast Company* (1938), *Fast and Loose* (1939) and *Fast and Furious* (1939) featured 'Joel and Garda Sloane'; and *There's Always a Woman* (1938) and *There's That Woman Again* (1939) featured 'Bill and Sally Reardon'.

3 Supernatural elements do occur in *Topper*, but are not confined to the green world. *Topper* introduced a cycle of fantasy romantic comedies, including *Topper Takes a Trip* (1939), *The Invisible Woman* (1940), *Turnabout* (1940), *Here Comes Mr Jordan* (1941), *Topper Returns* (1941) and *I Married a Witch* (1942).

4 In *Easy to Wed*, the 1946 remake of *Libeled Lady*, Haggerty (Keenan Wynn) *tricks* Bill (Van Johnson) and Gladys (Lucille Ball) into getting legally married; it is a sign of the comparative conservatism of the forties that the distinction is made.

5 An additional level of confusion arises from the fact that many of these villains had ethnic backgrounds – swarthy Europeans, Arabs, and Indians. Loy's early career was similarly dominated by roles as exotic vamps, as in *The Mask of Fu Manchu* (1932). On the racial aspects of these transformations, see Winokur (1995).

6 Even the title reveals a degree of confusion about identity. It originally referred to the murder suspect/victim, Clyde Wynant (Edward Ellis), but it becomes attached to Nick himself (most definitively in *The Thin Man Goes Home*).

7 *The Thin Man Goes Home* reveals that Nick comes from a small town called Sycamore Springs. Although this middle-American, middle-class background is inevitably disappointing, it is more a reflection of the series' progressive domestication of Nick and Nora, than a necessary truth. Dashiell Hammett's novel makes ambiguous references to Nick's Greek ancestry (1935: 17, 21, 26).

Part III

Equality

A little difference: Katharine Hepburn and Spencer Tracy in *Adam's Rib* (1949). Courtesy of Turner Entertainment.

4

A little difference: equality and the career woman comedy

It may seem paradoxical to discuss the theme of equality in relation to a cycle of films that is apparently obsessed with proving sexual *difference*. Most critics have understood the career woman's final acceptance of more conventional femininity as reactionary.[1] According to Sennett, 'this was the lotus-land of Hollywood, where women must remain women, and so the "feminist" attitude was really a sham: the "liberated" lady had to discover romance before the final reel, was obliged to reveal the femininity behind her iron corset' (1973: 197). However, as the 'final reel' conversion suggests, this resolution is often far from stable. At the same time as insisting upon the 'naturalness' of conventional gender roles, the career woman comedy disrupts and even disproves the logic of gender essentialism. By examining the figure of the career woman more closely – not only at the textual level of plot, but also at the extratextual levels of cultural and star discourses – a more contradictory pattern emerges.

The final scene of *Adam's Rib* provides a strong exposition of these issues. Adam and Amanda Bonner (Spencer Tracy and Katharine Hepburn), both lawyers, have resolved their differences and are getting ready for bed. In response to Amanda's teasing suggestion that she might run against him for the County Court judgeship, Adam reveals that he would stop her by crying, explaining, 'Us boys can do it too, you know; it's just that we never think to.' At first, Amanda claims that this proves what she has been saying throughout: 'There's no difference between the sexes. Men, women, the same.' She almost immediately qualifies her words, however, acknowledging that while there may be a difference, it is only 'a little difference'. Laughing, Adam declares, 'Vive la différence!' As he translates his meaning – 'Hurray for that little difference' – he stands on the four-poster bed and draws the curtains, enclosing the couple and ending the film.

The phallic symbolism of this 'little difference' is obvious, but the implications for gender and equality are not as straightforward as they might seem.

Janet Thumim berates the film for resorting to the 'unarguable biological facts of gender difference' (1986: 80):

> from a feminist point of view the film is deeply reactionary since recognition of Amanda/Hepburn's gender *difference* is used to naturalize her position of inequality in the social order [. . .]. In terms of the power struggle between men and women, the avowed subject of the film, this endows Adam/Tracy's last words 'vive la différence' with another level of significance. It is a 'différence' which privileges *him*. (1986: 80–1)

While I agree with Thumim's assessment in principle, various elements in the final scene complicate and even contradict these 'biological facts'.

Although Adam's candidacy for the judgeship suggests his patriarchal triumph, the scene is equally concerned with re-establishing the couple's relationship as one based on 'balance, equality [and] mutual everything' (Amanda's description of marriage). The scene demonstrates that playful competition is an integral part of this balance, with both giving as good as they get. The function of the song 'Farewell, Amanda' is crucial. Originally written by Amanda's admirer, Kip Lurie (David Wayne), the song has been a bone of contention between Adam and Amanda throughout (he hates it, she likes it). Now, Adam stakes a claim to the song, singing different words to suit his intentions:

> Hello, Amanda,
> Here's a hearty welcome to you.
> Hello, Amanda,
> The battle was fun,
> But it's done, it's through.[2]

While Adam sings out of frame, Amanda is reminded of another source of conflict: the bonnet he gave her, which she then lent to Doris Attinger (Judy Holliday) to wear in court. Amanda is on the point of burning the bonnet, but changes her mind and puts it on instead – just as Adam begins singing, 'The battle was fun.' Perching on the edge of the bed, Amanda coyly asks Adam if the Democratic candidate for the judgeship has been picked yet, innocently raising her eyes to heaven. By implying that she might run against him, Amanda is responding to Adam's teasing use of the love song to signal his victory. Their play is doubly provocative, simultaneously a challenge and an invitation, intended to annoy *and* seduce. Far from 'natural' male dominance and female submission, Adam and Amanda are negotiating their positions, but at this late stage of the game – bedtime – neither wishes to renounce biological difference entirely. Within this context of dual intentions and *double entendre*, the 'unarguable biological fact' of Adam's little difference is little more than a dirty joke.

The reciprocal nature of this foreplay is confirmed when Adam, looking at Amanda's bonnet, magically produces and puts on his own hat (see p. 89). There is a curious incongruity about putting on hats before going to bed, which lends them an excess of semiotic meaning. At the same time as suggesting Adam and Amanda's equality (they both put on their hats), the hats connote difference: Amanda's flower-covered bonnet is very feminine, while Adam's fedora is conventionally masculine. Putting on their hats amounts to dressing up as part of their game, an effect which is accentuated by Adam's combination of pyjama top with normal trousers.

This 'dressing up' is one aspect of a larger system within the film that interrogates the relationships between gender, costume and performance, most obviously in the courtroom cross-dressing fantasy sequence (in which Warren Attinger (Tom Ewell) is seen wearing Amanda's bonnet). The film is supremely self-conscious in this respect, drawing attention to different levels of performance through the use of intertitles and devices such as the home movie sequence. Indeed, the four-poster bed functions as a stage upon which Adam draws the final curtain, placing their 'dressing up' games within the context of performed roles. The resulting tension between performed and biological difference is manifested by Adam's crocodile tears. By demonstrating the ability to cry at will, Adam disrupts gender stereotypes on two levels: men are not supposed to cry; they are certainly not supposed to pretend to cry to get their own way. Acknowledging that there 'ain't any of us don't have our little tricks', Adam chooses this moment to put on his manly hat. In effect, by 'putting on' the signifiers of their difference, Adam and Amanda are performing their mutual acceptance of more conventional gender roles, temporarily at least.

The scene's interest in reciprocal game-playing and performance seems to contradict Thumim's assertion of 'unarguable biological facts'. The final evocation of phallic sexuality is complicated by the couple's mutual construction of sexualised pleasure, and the apparently conservative meaning of Adam's words begins to disintegrate under the pressure of their performance. Ultimately, the meaning of the scene remains unstable, the contradictions between biology and performance unresolved. These same contradictions and instabilities are intrinsic to career woman comedies – and the culture which produced them.

Contradictions in terms

During the forties, sexual inequality in the US was repeatedly explained in terms of biology, even by groups representing women. For example, in 1944, the Women's Bureau of the Labor Department declared, 'we know that actual equality under the law for men and women is not wholly possible [. . .]

because the sexes are not equal biologically or functionally' (quoted by Chafe 1995: 16). As will become apparent, this connection between social inequality and biological difference is intimately bound up with the notion of 'functional' difference, which I take to refer to the economic function of the male breadwinner (production) and the biological function of motherhood (reproduction).

The rise of capitalism in the nineteenth century had defined wage labour as a male prerogative. The breadwinner was expected to be competitive and self-seeking, while his female counterpart was characterised as nurturing and self-sacrificing, and these differences had been naturalised as biological – even God-given – traits (Matthaei 1982: 114–15). By the forties, the social realities of female employment and changing patterns of production and consumption were increasingly challenging these 'traditional' complementary sex roles.

Women's employment was controlled by sex-typing. In 1940, 'more than 75 per cent of all women workers were in jobs that employed less than 1 per cent of all male workers' (Chafe 1977: 31). Sex-typed jobs both reflected and reinforced dominant beliefs about the 'natural' differences between men and women, seeming to prove that a woman's place was in the home, even when she was at work. Unmarried women could take on supportive, 'nurturing' roles, as teachers, nurses, servants, secretaries and assistants; factory work was also segregated by 'feminine' domestic fields such as textiles, garments and food (Chafe 1977: 31). These 'natural' differences meant that even attempting to do the work of the opposite sex was seen as potentially detrimental. As Julie A. Matthaei explains, 'If a man won a competition against a woman, it proved him [. . .] to be a sissy, a man unfit for competition against men. If a man lost a competition with a woman, if a woman performed better at his job, a man's masculinity was destroyed; he was clearly proven to be at a woman's level. The mere threat of losing such a contest made men unwilling to accept jobs with women' (1982: 194). By conforming with sex-typed wage labour, unmarried working girls could enter the workforce without threatening male pride, but the career woman's 'selfish' motives always exceeded the bounds of acceptability. Her competitiveness was considered a deliberately hostile and destructive act, robbing men of their 'natural' masculinity; moreover, 'she wished to leave the home sphere [. . .] for her own self-development and fulfillment. She was, then, putting her own needs before those of her family, breaking the essential rule of womanly behaviour' (Matthaei 1982: 265).

With America's entry into World War II, in 1941, these ingrained beliefs about 'traditional' sex roles and employment received a new challenge.[3] More than six million women took on war jobs to meet the 'manpower' shortage; nearly two-thirds were over thirty-five, and nearly three-quarters were married (Chafe 1995: 11, 13). In the thirties, over 80 per cent of Americans had opposed married women working, primarily because of the potential effect upon the male population: if a wife was winning her own bread, how was a man supposed to earn his masculinity? By 1942, 60 per cent thought wives should be employed in the war industries (only 13 per cent were opposed), and 71 per cent felt more married women should take jobs (Chafe 1991: 132). The nature of the work undertaken by many of these women involved a further challenge to accepted norms. The most high-profile jobs were in the munitions industries, and required 'male' skills, such as riveting, welding, and ship-building.

The radical potential of such 'unfeminine' economic activities was counteracted by the strategies used to encourage women to seek war work. It was first necessary to convince women they were capable of doing men's jobs. The most common strategy was to draw analogies with familiar domestic chores, re-typing the work as requiring 'feminine' skills of dexterity and patience, rather than 'masculine' strength and creativity (see Anderson 1981: 59–62 and Chafe 1991: 124, 140). Although women were paid more for doing 'men's work', re-typing also justified paying them about 35 per cent less than a man would be paid for doing the same job. This feminisation was reinforced by the glamorisation of war work, most concretely through media representations of the new woman worker, who was predominantly represented as young, white and conventionally feminine, bar her overalls. The importance of these discourses is evident from the War Production Board's decision to continue manufacturing basic cosmetics such as face powder, lipstick and rouge, because they 'were of crucial importance for civilian morale' (Renov 1988: 19). Most discourses on the 'home' front also emphasised women's patriotic duty, but this was articulated through conventional feminine traits, such as self-sacrifice and assistance. A time constraint was also implied: women were holding the fort until their men came home, and would happily relinquish their jobs when the time came.[4]

Many of these same strategies were applied more generally, particularly in relation to the career girl. As Margaret Mead noted in 1950, 'all girls working in white-collar jobs are said to have "careers", and careers are glamorous, while most men with similar skills merely have jobs' (1971: 293). Such 'careers' were often considered stepping stones to marriage. For example, in 'Woman's place in advertising', Dorothy Dignam advised her readers to look their best because they would work primarily with men: 'dress and groom yourself as carefully as though you were going on a date. You might just *get* a date that way!' (1948: 218). In addition to advice on appearance, posture and etiquette, Dignam stressed the importance of considering whether advertising was 'sufficiently rewarding in its interest and variety, apart from actual pay – because no one should grind away, day after day, *just for clothes, carfare, and milk shakes*' (1948: 203, my emphasis). A woman's 'career' may be more than just a job, but by trivialising women's economic needs, the male breadwinner ethic remains unchallenged.

While the war proved a decisive turning point in the general employment of married and middle-class women, the advances for women seeking professional employment were less significant. Dignam expressed concern about the inequality of opportunities for women within advertising, noting that women were largely confined to advertising 'feminine' products (such as domestic appliances and cosmetics) and only a handful of agencies had female vice-presidents. Such sexual discrimination was rife. For example, medical schools maintained a 5 per cent quota on female admissions, and most hospitals refused to accept female interns (Chafe 1991: 163). By 1950, women contributed 6.1 per cent of doctors (only 0.1 per cent higher than in 1910), but 98.0 per cent of nurses; similarly, the percentage of lawyers who were women had risen from 2.4 per cent in 1940 to 3.5 per cent in 1950 – but still remained at this level in 1960 (Epstein 1970: 179). Overall, 'the percentage of women in professional and managerial fields remained almost static between 1930 and 1960' (Filene 1998: 181).

The relative proliferation (and acceptance) of professional women in the career woman comedy contrasts with the realities of the forties; their fictional prominence instead highlights the growing cultural hysteria about 'natural' gender roles. For example, in their best-selling book, *Modern Woman: The Lost Sex*, Ferdinand Lundberg and Marynia F. Farnham, MD, declared, 'contemporary women in very large numbers are psychologically disordered. [. . .] As a group, and generally, they are a problem to themselves, to their children, and families, to each other, to society as a whole' (1947: v, 1). Women are called a problem five times on page one, but the only problem with men, apparently, is that they know women: 'men, standing before the bar of historical judgement, might often well begin their defense with the words: "I had a mother . . ."' (1947: 3). Lundberg and Farnham blamed juvenile delinquency on rejecting, overprotective and dominating mothers, and homosexuality on over-affectionate mothers (1947: 304–5). Similarly, in 1942, Philip Wylie coined the term 'momism' to describe the 'megaloid momworship' (1955: 198) he claimed was corrupting American manhood and society. Such mothers were considered selfish, driven by the desire for ego-satisfaction. Against these types, Lundberg and Farnham set the 'The Feminine Mother' (1947: 319), who 'accepts herself fully as a woman [. . .]. She knows [. . .] she is dependent on a man. There is no fantasy in her mind about being an "independent woman," *a contradiction in terms*' (1947: 319, my emphasis).

Modern woman is a problem for Lundberg and Farnham precisely because she denies her 'nature' and strives for independence. They regard the first wave of feminism 'as an expression of emotional sickness, of neurosis' (1947: 143) and psychopathologise feminists in terms of penis envy and masculinity complexes (1947: 452–3). The source of all these problems, they claim, is the feminist quest for equality. According to Lundberg and Farnham, 'in stressing equality Mary [Wollstonecraft] and the feminists after her were only insisting that men and women are identical. This is what equality means: identity' (1947: 147). Of course, Wollstonecraft insists nothing of the sort; Lundberg and Farnham are playing with words to suit their own ends. As far as they are concerned, there can be no such identity between man and woman: 'Women are in general a more complicated question than men [. . .]. They are endowed with a complicated reproductive system [. . .], a more elaborate nervous system and an infinitely complex psychology revolving around the reproductive function. Women, therefore, cannot be regarded as any more similar to men than a spiral is to a straight line' (1947: 3).

The oppositions of simplicity/complexity, straight/spiral and male/female reveal not only the inherent binary logic of Lundberg and Farnham's arguments, but also the ways in which this logic is used to underpin their faith in biologism – the belief that gender (whether masculinity or femininity) is biologically determined (see Moi 1997: 108). Having defined masculinity and femininity in terms of reproduction, they conclude that 'the bachelor and the spinster both represent examples of impaired masculinity and femininity' (Lundberg and Farnham 1947: 382), thereby naturalising marriage as well. The result is an extremely narrow definition of 'normal', 'healthy' gender roles – the active, masculine father and the passive, feminine mother – against which any deviation can be described as 'sick'.

As Mead observed in 1950, 'when one follows the shrill insistencies of books like *Modern Woman: The Lost Sex*, [. . .] one realizes that we are passing through a period of discrepancies in sex roles which are so conspicious [*sic*] that efforts to disguise the price that both sexes pay are increasingly unsuccessful' (1971: 274). Of course, this did not stop people from trying. In effect, as Beth L. Bailey has argued, most of these efforts focused on 'traits one could simulate, products one could buy' (1989: 106). Dating etiquette and advice columns repeatedly translated masculinity into 'dominance' and femininity into 'submission'. What is particularly striking is the degree to which these 'natural' gender traits were consciously performed during the period: 'the young man who did not assist his date from the car was not being discourteous in ignoring her need for assistance; he was "unmanly" because he was not *demonstrating* his control and protection. The woman who, on a date, opened the car door and exited unassisted [. . .] was being "aggressive" and unfeminine by preempting the male role' (Bailey 1989: 110). Other signs of such 'aggressive' female behaviour included ordering your own food or lighting your own cigarette. Women were repeatedly advised not to appear overly competent or intelligent, but to appear totally dependent upon their escort. For example, in *How to Meet Men and Marry* (1943), Juliet Farnham advised intellectual women to seek highly intelligent men, and then 'go gay, in a deep way. He'll know it's only an act. But you'll soon become the little woman to be pooh-poohed, patronized and wed' (quoted by Bailey 1989: 113). Implicitly, the logic of gender inequality must be fostered even where it does not exist. It is a strange conception of the 'natural' state of affairs.

The discourses of biologism and social function worked together to justify unequal opportunities and conditions for men and women, primarily to protect the interests of patriarchal capitalism. These discourses also happened to naturalise dominance, independence and power as essentially masculine/male traits: the man had to be boss. The 'boss lady', like the 'independent woman', was a contradiction in terms.

Who's the boss?

From a cultural perspective, it is extremely unlikely that *Adam's Rib* would reject the 'unarguable biological facts' of difference altogether. Nonetheless, although Amanda's public career presents a threat to her private marriage, the film never suggests that she should give up her profession to be a better wife (unlike some other career woman comedies). This relatively progressive position is reinforced not only by the absence of children, but by the absence of any mention of Amanda's 'natural' destiny to reproduce. What seems to be at stake in the final 'difference' between Adam and Amanda is less the 'biological fact' of this difference, than the *littleness* of this difference. Even their names and nicknames – Adam/Pinky and Amanda/Pinkie – come as close as possible to suggesting the 'identity' that Lundberg and Farnham assert is impossible. In this context, the 'littleness' of their difference can be construed as a relatively positive statement, as Adam and Amanda must constantly renegotiate an equal relationship in an impossible situation.

The same cannot be said for all career woman comedies, but even the most overtly reactionary films are riven with many of the same tensions and contradictions regarding gender and equality. Andrea S. Walsh describes *Lady in the Dark* as 'the most antifeminist film of the decade' (1984: 160) and the film overflows with dialogue about 'natural' gender roles. For example, Charley Johnson (Ray Milland) declares that Liza Elliott (Ginger Rogers) 'shouldn't try to be Top Man – she's not built for it. It's flying in the face of nature'. And yet, the film still attempts to negotiate a version of 'equality' with its final union. Having spent most of the film involved with an unattainable father-figure, Kendall Nesbitt (Warner Baxter), Liza is finally 'cured' of her neurosis and rushes into an engagement with Hollywood heart-throb, Randy

Curtis (Jon Hall), only to discover that he expects her to continue being the 'boss'. In effect, Liza has gone from one extreme to the other – from father to boy – and this polarisation is reflected in Liza's own movement from repressed 'boss-lady' to submissive 'real woman' ('I want and need someone to lean on'). Instead of accepting either extreme, however, the film offers a last-minute compromise. Rather than quitting altogether, as she had intended, Liza suggests that she and Charley should co-edit the magazine, before adding, 'After a while, I might even step aside. That is, if you don't get too drunk with power.' Power is the key word: Liza has relinquished some of her (excessive) power in favour of Charley, but the stability of the relationship depends upon him not letting this go to his head. Unlike *Adam's Rib*, however, this compromise is unconvincing. Liza's words are undercut by Charley's actions. He immediately suggests changing the format of the magazine and sits in her chair, causing her to fall on the floor in an undignified heap. This relatively unprecedented moment of slapstick marks an awkward shift in tone. On the one hand, it could be argued that this is the final humiliation of the career woman, visually reduced to her 'proper' place of subordination. On the other hand, the fall initiates the couple's recognition that they love each other, leading them to kiss. In this respect, it is significant that Liza and Charley's relationship complies with the conventions of the thirties' romantic comedy couple – antagonism leading to love, peppered with witty barbs. This type of couple implies an equality that Liza and Charley do not actually demonstrate.[5]

The formation of the couple in *Lady in the Dark* reveals an unresolvable contradiction lying at the heart of the cycle: companionate equality has become the romantic norm, but society demands the man must be the boss. As Mead noted, 'maleness in America is not absolutely defined, it has to be kept and re-earned every day, and one essential element in the definition is beating women in every game that both sexes play, in every activity in which both sexes engage' (1971: 289). Consequently, the reciprocal game-playing of screwball comedy is refigured in the career woman comedy as an aggressive competition which the man must win in order to prove his masculinity. As Charley explains to Liza, 'You've always had to be the boss and something inside me deeply resents that. [. . .] There's always been that secret battle between us [. . .] and I've always had to win because – well, because I'm me, I guess.' The fact that Charley cannot put his reasons into words reinforces the sense of his 'natural' masculine instincts. Similarly, at the height of conflict in *Adam's Rib*, Adam tells Amanda, 'I'm old-fashioned – I like two sexes. [. . .] I want a wife, not a competitor. Competitor! Competitor! If you want to be a big he-woman, go and be it – but not with me!' Thus, although Amanda wins the public court case (proving the sexist double standard of the law), it is essential to the narrative's logic that Adam should win the private argument (forcing Amanda to acknowledge that no one has the right to shoot an unfaithful spouse).

The dual-focus narrative in screwball comedy enabled the couple's re-education and the disruption of patriarchal binary logic. In the career woman comedy, there is far less emphasis on mutual re-education; it is the woman who is misguided and 'wrong', while the man ultimately tends to be proved right. By winning the battle, the man proves her 'logic' is illogical, her pragmatism impractical. A dual-focus narrative may still be used (as in *Adam's Rib*), but it is more common for the woman to be the site of transformation (as in *Lady in the Dark*).

The unnatural woman

Amanda's triumph in court is not exceptional. The career woman may be misguided, but she is always highly competent, professional and well respected (or even feared) by her peers. Rather than admitting that this disproves the logic of gender essentialism, the films tend to construct the career woman as an aberration or oddity. Time and again, her femaleness is denied, not because she is too 'masculine' to be a woman, but because her lack of 'femininity' implies she is not quite human. For example, in *They All Kissed the Bride*, Mike Holmes (Melvyn Douglas) tells M. J. Drew (Joan Crawford), 'You're a machine, not a woman. You've no right to assume any of the feminine graces.' And in *Take a Letter, Darling* (1942), G. B. Atwater (Robert Benchley) attempts to distinguish between a 'woman' and A. M. MacGregor (Rosalind Russell), before conceding, 'There's no name for you yet'.

As Robin Wood notes, 'our culture has habitually confused (in order to mystify) the terms "natural" and "normal," conflating both with "healthy"' (1989: 312). The feminisation of the career woman is closely linked by these films to biologism and human 'nature', thereby mystifying the ways in which the social construction of gender difference works to validate sexual inequality. The cycle employs a variety of strategies to represent this return to a 'natural' state and, although these are not used consistently or comprehensively, they recur frequently enough (in various combinations) to warrant further delineation.

a) Costume. Just as discourses of glamour helped to contain the threat posed by women war-workers, fashion is used in the career woman comedy to reaffirm traditional notions of femininity. The entire process can be symbolised by the function of the *haute couture* hat in *Ninotchka*, not only because Ninotchka's (Greta Garbo) desire for the hat signals her emerging 'feminine' desires, but also because the hat itself is so foolish – its pointed style contrasting with the flat practicality of Ninotchka's own beret. The 'femininity' of the hat lies in its excessive impracticality. It is entirely decorative.

In her 1941 book, *Fundamentals of Dress*, Maria Kettunen asserts that women's personalities vary from the 'extremely feminine type' to the 'definitely masculine type' (1941: 328), before going on to detail the style of clothing each type should favour. The masculine extreme 'should choose fabrics that spell simplicity, severity, and rather rough quality [. . .] adapted to the construction of simple, well-tailored garments' (1941: 328). In keeping with this simplicity, no mention is made of accessories. The feminine extreme, however, should prefer 'soft challis, sheer novelty woolens, luxurious velvets, flowing chiffons and georgettes, and sheer summer fabrics. Her accessories should be chosen accordingly – delicate but rich jewelry, appropriate laces, and other ornamental touches that make for daintiness and charm' (1941: 329). These same tendencies are frequently employed by the career woman comedy, with the heroine's simple 'man-tailored suits' (plain, dark fabrics, shoulder pads and slim-hipped skirt) and severe hairstyles gradually being softened by a new-found interest in accessories, corsages, softer colours, lacier fabrics, furs and frills.

Lady in the Dark goes furthest in developing this strategy, underlining the process with the irony that Liza's career is editor of a fashion magazine. At the outset of the film, her hair is scraped back in a severe pompadour, she wears horn-rimmed glasses and a pin-striped suit with power shoulders and no accessories (even her hats are mannish trilbies). The point is rammed home when, leaning in to feel the lapel of her jacket, Charley declares, 'Just like mine! We must go to the same tailor.' The film goes so far as to explain Liza's neurosis as being caused by the traumatic childhood experience of her father's rejection when she tried on her dead mother's blue evening dress. Her repressed femininity begins to return in the film's spectacular dream sequences as she fantasises about being beautiful: 'My jewels, my gown, my hair. Oh, how lovely!' Once 'awakened', she consciously tries to be more feminine, but again goes from one extreme to the other – a red sequinned evening gown with full-length fur skirt – before reaching a more subtle compromise. At the film's end, she is wearing a suit of muted yellows and browns, with a frilly scarf at her neck and a ribbon in her more softly styled hair. Similar transformations can be found in *They All Kissed the Bride* and *A Foreign Affair* (1948). At the very least, most career woman comedies use the conventions of 'masculine' business suits and 'feminine' evening clothes.

An interesting variation on the theme is provided by a 'B' movie, *She Couldn't Say No* (1941). Alice Hinsdale (Eve Arden) is a qualified attorney, but her fiancé, Wallace Turnbull (Roger Pryor), will not hear of her taking a case. Although she is quite content to remain his secretary until they can afford to marry, she is manoeuvred into accepting a case by their friend, Banjo Page (Cliff Edwards). Banjo convinces the client to hire a 'lady lawyer' by telling him how attractive Alice is: 'One sweet smile and they [the jury] let her do the voting.' When they enter the office, however, Alice has transformed herself into a stereotypical career woman. Her hair is pinned back quite severely, she is wearing a dark suit with a white shirt and tie, and round, black-framed glasses; she even puts on a deeper voice, and gruffly demands to know what they want. Alice thought it was 'better to look cold and businesslike', but Banjo is horrified: 'I had him all set to meet an attractive, fascinating gal.' Alice's legal talents are irrelevant; only the effect of her appearance is at stake.

b) Instincts and the body. It is often implied that the career woman's success has required the repression of her 'natural' instincts; the process of humanisation consequently involves the eruption of uncontrollable somatic reactions. For example, in *Ninotchka*, Leon d'Algout (Melvyn Douglas) wants to hear Ninotchka 'laugh from the heart', but his forced jokes have no effect on her; it is only when he accidentally falls off his chair that Ninotchka spontaneously bursts out laughing. The juxtaposition of Leon's deliberate and unintentional actions reinforces the sense of Ninotchka's 'natural' response. In *They All Kissed the Bride*, the moment when M. J. laughs at a joke is underlined by Mike's words: 'I don't believe it – you *can* smile! [. . .] It's the beginning of a new era!'

They All Kissed the Bride provides another example of somatic reactions. M. J. literally goes weak at the knees whenever Mike is around. Although M. J. claims that it must be her liver, her mother (Billie Burke) says it is a 'family characteristic' of being in love; once M. J. has realised that this is the case (at the film's end) her mother pronounces, 'You're a woman now.' As if this was not proof enough of the mechanical M. J.'s transformation into the womanly Maggie, Maggie has also been daydreaming about babies (producing a hallucinatory vision around her head). This final emergence of maternal instinct is the ultimate expression of the career woman's 'natural' bodily reactions.

Maternal instincts feature strongly in a number of films. The presence of children is not essential to the cycle, but it is certainly more common than in screwball comedy (and dogs are nowhere to be found). In *Honeymoon in Bali*, Bill Burnett (Fred MacMurray) is guardian to a small girl and Gail Allen's (Madeleine Carroll) transformation is motivated as much by her feelings for the child as for Bill. In *The Doctor Takes a Wife*, the turning point in the couple's relationship comes when Dr Timothy Sterling (Ray Milland) has to deliver a baby; June Cameron (Loretta Young) proves her 'natural' instincts are 'feminine' by assisting him and looking after the father and siblings. When Tim describes the baby as 'another career woman – kicking and screaming', the reformed June softly replies, 'She'll get over it.' Despite the rural location, they are a long way from the screwball green world.

c) Fantasy sequences. Maggie is not the only career woman to see things. For example, in *The Bachelor and the Bobby Soxer* (1947), Judge Margaret

Turner (Myrna Loy) follows the example of her younger sister, Susan (Shirley Temple), by hallucinating that Richard Nugent (Cary Grant) is a knight in shining armour. These fantasies can take the form of dreams, often making use of vulgar Freudian notions of dream imagery to reveal the career woman's repressed desires and anxieties.[6] *Lady in the Dark* takes this tendency furthest, using Liza's 'talking cure' to structure the narrative. In *No Time for Love*, Katherine Grant (Claudette Colbert) is a professional photographer who develops an obsession about tunnel digger, James Ryan (Fred MacMurray). In her dream, she fantasises about 'Superman' Ryan saving her from a melodramatic villain: Ryanman seizes a bullwhip from the villain, who then pulls out a gun, but the bullets bounce off Ryanman's chest. *Let's Live a Little* indicates the imbalance of gender power through castration imagery: Duke Crawford (Robert Cummings) and his ice-cold psychiatrist, Dr J. O. Loring (Hedy Lamarr), both dream about chopping down trees; he is crushed by the one tree he cuts down, but she cuts down *all* the trees.

d) Losing inhibitions. While somatic reactions imply 'natural' human instincts, the losing of inhibitions usually involves an external force acting upon the career woman's repressed desires. Two such forces are alcohol (*Ninotchka*, *Woman of the Year*, *They All Kissed the Bride*, *A Foreign Affair*) and medical treatment (*They All Kissed the Bride*, *Lady in the Dark*). While alcohol in screwball comedy was enabling, the career woman's consumption of alcohol tends to be accompanied by a loss of power as well as inhibitions. Thus, Ninotchka wakes up with a hangover to discover the jewels are missing and, in *They All Kissed the Bride*, the class solidarity of the drunk scene is then undercut by Maggie being blamed for the workers being sacked.

Medical treatment can take the form of sedatives (*They All Kissed the Bride*) or some form of psychoanalytical counselling; the career woman is often described as being on the verge of a nervous breakdown. The films seem to agree with Lundberg and Farnham: the career woman is not 'in sober reality, temperamentally suited to this sort of rough and tumble competition, and it damages her' (1947: 11). Unlike psychiatrists in screwball comedy, doctors in career woman comedy are invariably respected authorities – as long as they are men. According to Mary Ann Doane (who has analysed the medical discourse of the woman's film of the 1940s in some detail) the figure of the male doctor functions as 'reader or interpreter, as the site of knowledge which dominates and controls female subjectivity' (1988: 43). Within such films, the failure of the woman's body to conform to the specular logic of the erotic gaze is considered symptomatic of her disease or neurosis; the male doctor can 'see through' her bodily symptoms to the source of her problem. Doane cites *Lady in the Dark* as an example, concluding that 'the lack or impairment of a narcissism purportedly specific to femininity' (1988: 42) is one such symptom. Thus, Dr Brooks (Barry Sullivan) repeatedly decodes the manifest content of Liza's dreams in terms of her fear of competing with women for the sexual attentions of men ('Even the plain way you dress is a protective harbour'). Presumably *this* kind of competition is quite 'normal', unlike her unfeminine competition with men. When Dr Brooks finally explains Liza's neurosis, she asks him what the answer to her problem is. 'Perhaps some man who'll dominate you,' he replies. As Doane notes, 'Psychoanalysis is used very explicitly to reinforce a status quo of sexual difference' (1988: 46). By losing her inhibitions, the career woman again loses her power.

e) Subordination. Dr Brooks is not the only paternal figure to recommend that a career woman needs a man who will dominate her. In *They All Kissed the Bride*, Maggie's elderly doctor (Ivan Simpson) tells her that she will love the 'first presentable man that comes along', with one proviso: '*He* will have to dominate *you*.' One of the strangest examples of this strategy is found in *Honeymoon in Bali*. Gail's window cleaner, Tony (Akim Tamiroff) – who has already advised her on her choice of clothes – tells her she should not marry her fiancé because 'He will let you be the boss [. . .] and a woman ain't supposed to be the boss. [. . .] Your kind of boss woman needs a – you know – a boss man.'

f) Love. Ultimately, the only consistent factor in the career woman's transformation is falling in love. Love is presented as both an internal 'natural' instinct and an external force which cannot be resisted, and consequently entails a further loss of power, not only through the heroine's subordination to her 'boss man', but also through her loss of professionalism. Once she starts thinking about babies, Maggie cannot concentrate on refrigerated trucks (*They All Kissed the Bride*). In *This Thing Called Love*, a dreamy-eyed Ann Winters (Rosalind Russell) wanders out of an important business meeting after a telephone call from Tice Collins (Melvyn Douglas); and in *No Time for Love*, Katherine's photo shoot of the (male) 'Body Beautiful' is totally disrupted by Jim Ryan. Love transforms the unnaturally efficient career woman into a 'normal' irrational woman.

The power of love

For the most part, these strategies imply that a woman who lacks 'femininity' is not normal; she may even be 'sick'. In the process of 'getting well', the career woman loses her power, her professionalism and perhaps her career – but gains a man. However, this system of 'love curing all' involves a contradiction: why is the hero attracted to the aberrant career woman in the first place? With one or two exceptions (most notably *Lady in the Dark*), the hero not only finds this strange creature attractive, but actively pursues her as well. One explanation is that, despite her lack of 'femininity', the career woman is physically very striking (not least because of the potency of the star who plays her) and she invariably has more than one male admirer. A second factor is the absence of any serious alternative. Paradoxically, other women in these films are presented as less suitable mates, precisely because they are stereotypically feminine: they may have 'allure' (Tim's description of Marilyn (Gail Patrick) in *The Doctor Takes a Wife*), but they are also clinging, demanding, hysterical and/or scatter-brained. In other words, the heroine must find a happy medium by the end of the film, somewhere between unfeminine self-sufficiency and hyperfeminine dependency (June describes Marilyn as a 'barnacle'). The third – and vital – factor is the need for the hero to be in control. The alternative possibility of the career woman pursuing the man (perhaps even physically transforming herself to seem more attractive as part of the pursuit) is conceivable, but would have quite different implications for the structure of power. Instead of the career woman relinquishing her 'unnatural' power, she would entirely dominate the man.

Given this requirement for male-dominated courtship, it is striking that the rhetorical conventions of romance also make a return. Passionate kissing is quite common and is usually initiated by the man, who enfolds the woman in his arms, overpowering her. In most cases, a two-shot is used (rather than shot/reverse shot), but the camera comes much closer to the couple than in screwball comedy, and a high angle may also emphasise the man's dominance. The shot is usually blocked so that the man turns his back to the camera; when the kiss ends, it is the woman's facial reaction we see.[7]

Design for Scandal provides a particularly interesting example of these tendencies. Jeff Sherman (Walter Pidgeon) is trying to compromise the integrity of Judge Cornelia Porter (Rosalind Russell) by creating a scandal.[8] Cornelia has repeatedly pre-empted Jeff's usual 'romantic' techniques, and his girlfriend, Dotty (Jean Rogers) has indirectly informed the audience of his usual line: 'I had a dream about you . . . you were far away in sort of a rose garden.' Nonetheless, the next scene begins with him using this line on Cornelia. Cornelia remains unimpressed by his romantic rhetoric: 'Let's be honest, mm? [. . .] Let's not talk like an advertisement for Tahiti, just because there's a moon and things. I'd rather you say, "Ug," and meant it than a lot of bosh you thought the moment called for.' Cornelia's emphasis on emotional honesty is contrasted with Jeff's romantic dishonesty, but this is then complicated by the couple's discussion of more conventional gender roles.

JEFF: You're suffering from too much success as a judge [*takes her hand*]. It's made you dogmatic; you live by rules.
CORNELIA: In other words, unfeminine, eh?
JEFF: Well, you don't sound exactly like the woman's page.
CORNELIA: [*looking into his eyes*] How do other women act?

At this point the two-shot cuts from medium length to medium close-up. The increased intimacy is accompanied by Jeff coaching Cornelia in how another woman would behave in this kind of situation. First, he brings her towards him and puts his arm around her so that she is leaning against his chest. The camera tracks into close-up and non-diegetic romantic music fades in. Then, he feeds her lines and directs her performance; needless to say, her role involves doing very little, beyond prompting him to continue his romantic monologue.

JEFF: Then I kiss her.
CORNELIA: And what does she say?
JEFF: She doesn't say anything, usually, because I kiss her again.

At this point he really does kiss her. Although the shot remains in close-up throughout, the blocking of this embrace is consistent with romantic conventions. He dominates the screen space and, when they part, we have a good view of her face, gazing into his eyes. As they kiss again, she embraces him back; the music reaches a climax, and the scene fades to black.

The use of a fade (rather than a dissolve) indicates this is a decisive moment in some sense – the moment when Cornelia abandons her 'unfeminine', sensible approach to love and becomes a 'woman' – and the scene marks a turning point in their relationship. The couple's mutual recognition of the construction of romance enables their performance of 'conventional' gender roles, redistributing the imbalance of power. The paradox, here, is that by performing romance Cornelia is somehow more 'natural', while her initial preference for primitive instincts ('Ug') is displaced as 'unfeminine'.

The conventions of romantic love fit well with the binary logic of gender essentialism. Romance requires the man to take control, to pursue and seduce the woman, sweeping her off her feet. Romantic love is also constructed as entirely 'natural', a force that knows no bounds and that cannot be resisted. Ultimately, the identification of romance with femininity proves inimical to female independence. As Tom Verney (Fred MacMurray) tells A. M. MacGregor, when she runs away from love in *Take a Letter, Darling*, 'You've worked hard for your independence, and you're afraid you're going to lose it. You are.'

Boss men

In contrast, the heroes in career woman comedies tend to be fiercely independent, roaming the world and going where they like. In the later films, they are often associated with the war (*Without Reservations* (1946), *A Foreign Affair*, *June Bride*), but in the earlier films the most common occupation is – perhaps surprisingly – artist (*Double Wedding*; *Third Finger, Left Hand*;

Take a Letter, Darling; *The Bachelor and the Bobby Soxer*). What links these two types is the rejection of the conventional masculine role as breadwinner; their occupations are about more than earning a living. Because the career woman's wealth and earning power is usually in excess of the hero's, his masculinity must be secured in a different way.

In *Take a Letter, Darling*, A. M. MacGregor offers Tom a job. Tom is baffled: 'What am I?' She wants him to be her private secretary, despite his lack of secretarial skills. As if offering him a 'feminine' sex-typed job were not enough, it turns out that the main function of the role is to escort Mac to business functions, in order to keep lecherous businessmen at bay and their jealous wives happy. Although this role is meant to be 'strictly business', Mac does expect Tom to flirt with the wives so she can win the deal. Tom's initial question, 'What am I?' is repeated in various forms, all of which problematise his masculinity. His friend, Fud (Charles E. Arnt), sees him dressing for dinner and initially assumes he has got a job as a head waiter. When he finds out this is not the case, he asks, 'Hmm. What are you?' When Tom tries to explain, Fud jumps to conclusions and calls him a gigolo. Tom replies, 'I really haven't had time to think about it – I wonder what I am?' Similar questions are asked by two other male characters: 'What kind of a job is that?' and 'What kind of a man is that?' Having placed Tom in this unmanly position, the film takes pains to prove his 'natural' masculinity. As the *Variety* review put it, 'Fred MacMurray is *properly* masculine as the not-too-bright secretary' (6 May 1942, my emphasis). Firstly, he is always shown to be extremely uncomfortable in his 'secretarial' role, and explicitly comments, 'I don't feel honest – I don't even feel like a man.' Secondly, he resists being dominated by Mac, refusing to wear the kind of 'form-fitting' tuxedo and top hat she prefers, leading her to describe him (somewhat sardonically) as 'a rugged individualist'. Finally, and most importantly, his 'natural' talents as an artist enable a double triumph: he beats Mac at her own game, producing a better advertising campaign for Caldwell tobacco; and he breaks up her engagement to Jonathan Caldwell (Macdonald Carey) by sending a revealing painting of her as a wedding present. If the first half of the film focuses on the question of 'what kind of man is this?', the second half leaves no doubts. He is 'properly' masculine, and the film appears to end with the couple setting off to fulfil *his* dream – living in a caravan in Mexico, so he can earn his beans by painting.

The hero's 'proper' masculinity is further ensured by contrast with the Wrong Man and the career woman's 'inadequate' male colleagues and friends. Caldwell, for example, is an untrustworthy, slick multi-millionaire with four ex-wives; his wealth is inherited, not earned, and his Southern ancestry stereotypically connotes degeneracy. The career woman is often engaged (officially or unofficially) to someone she works with, but he is usually older and/or ineffectual and their relationship distinctly lacks passion (*The Doctor Takes a Wife*, *Lady in the Dark*, *No Time for Love*). In *They All Kissed the Bride*, one of M. J.'s executives, Marsh (Roland Young), is clearly infatuated with her, but his appearance (older, balding, mildly fastidious) and behaviour (stuttering, hesitancy) imply he is not 'man' enough for her. *No Time for Love* goes furthest, with Katherine having a posse of artistic male friends who are all but explicitly coded as gay.

Even with these precautions, the boss man still remains a problematic figure, because of the effects of star power. With the exception of Spencer Tracy, and possibly Fred MacMurray, the male stars of these films are considerably less potent than the women. The career woman comedy is usually a vehicle for a particularly strong female star – Rosalind Russell, Joan Crawford, Claudette Colbert – who is even billed above the male star (a rare occurrence in Hollywood romantic comedy). Significantly, the more conventionally feminine Colbert is paired with stronger men in particularly macho roles: Jim Ryan/Fred MacMurray is a tunnel digger (*No Time for Love*) and Rusty Thomas/John Wayne is a marine (*Without Reservations*); in both cases, their masculine power is explicitly constructed as sexual. The more 'unfeminine' career women seem to warrant less 'masculine' mates: Melvyn Douglas, Ray Milland, Brian Aherne, George Brent and John Lund are hardly the most virile stars Hollywood has produced. These are actors with weak chins and thin moustaches, and slim or stolid builds (rather than muscular physiques); they dress well and their manners are refined. They are ladies' men. Physically, they are very similar to the actors who play the wrong men and inadequate colleagues. Lee Bowman even plays both types: he is the Wrong Man in *Third Finger, Left Hand* and *Design for Scandal*, but Mr Right in *She Wouldn't Say Yes*. Given this similarity, the difference between the hero and the inadequate male must be marked through behaviour and attitude; the hero performs acceptable masculinity in a way that the other men do not.

Irreconcilable differences

The ambiguities about gender, biology and performance are not easily resolved. The career woman comedy requires the union of the couple to involve the restoration of 'normal' gender relations: the man must take control of the situation and the career woman must relinquish her power, happily taking up a subordinate role. In practice, this restoration is often unconvincing. For example, in *June Bride*, Cary Jackson (Robert Montgomery), disgusted by the behaviour of his editor (and ex-fiancée) Linda Gilman (Bette Davis), is all set to leave the country to return to his usual trade as a foreign correspondent (thereby taking control of his life and demonstrating his masculine independence). Linda convinces him that she has learnt her lesson and is happy to follow him around the world, by picking up his suitcases and standing respectfully two steps behind him. The idea of Bette Davis submitting to any man (let alone Robert Montgomery) exposes the resolution as a token gesture; female subordination is performed in order to concede male dominance, but this seems far from 'natural'.

The last reel conversion to 'normal' gender roles is further destabilised by the fact that the couple have spent so long failing to be 'properly' masculine and feminine that the final union seems improbable. They claim to love each other, but they have not spent much time alone, and there is certainly little sense of private – or even civil – conversation. This leads to some very peculiar and incoherent endings. For example, the final scene of *Take a Letter, Darling* is entirely in long shot, with no audible dialogue between the couple (beyond Tom calling Mac's name). As Mac stomps down the road, away from Caldwell's, Tom drives up in a jalopy towing a trailer. He stops to pick Mac up, but she throws rocks at him. As Tom struggles to pull Mac into the car, a train is seen approaching. The caravan is directly over the track, but Mac still resists getting into the car, until the point when a crash is imminent, when she gives in and they drive out of frame. The final shot is of the train rushing past, with a sign reading 'The End' visible behind its wheels. There is no happy reunion and no embrace, just a narrowly avoided disaster. While the privacy of the couple's final embrace in screwball comedy suggested sexual intimacy, there are no such connotations here. *Without Reservations*, on the other hand, ends with the couple's reunion taking place downstairs (out of sight, but not earshot), while the camera holds a medium close-up of Kit Madden's (Colbert) bed. This certainly implies sexual consummation, but it seems very out of place, not least because we have not seen the couple together at all for the last fourteen minutes of the film.

Given the cycle's insistence on the unnaturalness of the career woman, perhaps the most surprising aspect of these resolutions is their ambiguity. The heroine may have been transformed by love, but there is rarely any direct declaration that she will give up her career to become a wife. For all its reactionary rhetoric, even *Lady in the Dark* fails to confirm or deny Liza's intentions (or Charley's expectations). Usually, the film leaves the question of the woman's career in limbo. For example, *They All Kissed the Bride* ends with Maggie and Mike being whisked away in a truck, calling back instructions about when she will return to the office:

MAGGIE: I won't be available for two weeks.
MIKE: Make that four weeks!
MAGGIE: Make that indefinitely!

This kind of ambiguity contradicts everything the film has prepared us to expect. Within the wider sexual politics of forties' culture, this ultimate refusal to define the heroine as one thing ('feminine' wife) or the other ('masculine' career woman) might seem relatively progressive; instead, it seems like a last-minute equivocation.

The happy ending is unstable in both screwball comedy and the career woman comedy, but for quite different reasons and with quite different effects. The utopian moment of the screwball ending developed systematically from the cycle's interest in gender fluidity, privacy, play and spontaneity. Its instability suggested the im/possibility of escaping patriarchal sexuality. The resolutions of career woman comedies reflect the incoherence of the plots' representation of gender. The cycle can only offer a non-committal resolution, leaving the question of what happens next to the spectator's interpretation.

The paradox of complementary equality

The gender politics of the forties insist on sexual difference. Such discourses are strongly at odds with the ideals of companionate equality found in screwball comedy. Nonetheless, compared to the arguments of a book like *Modern Woman: The Lost Sex*, the career woman comedy is relatively 'liberal' in its attitudes to the working woman. The very prevalence of high-powered, professional (and married) women in these films can be seen as 'empowering' for the female audience (to the same extent as this can be said of the action heroines of the nineties) and the ambiguous endings enable the spectator to read against the grain. In a sense, the cycle still attempts to articulate the union of the couple in terms of equality. The career woman's transformation often involves going from one extreme to the other (from excessive and 'unnatural' power to overcompensation or hyperfeminine masquerade), before finding a 'natural' balance, matched by the hero's 'proper' (but not excessive) masculinity. This process of moderation means the couple are *relatively* more equal by the film's end, without actually being equal.

This is the paradox of complementary equality. By insisting on sexual difference and the 'natural' traits of men and women, the discourses of complementary gender construct man and woman as a balancing act, each needing the other to perform a vital role. While this 'natural' balance implies a degree of equality, the binary logic of such constructions means that the two parts can never be equal, since the 'male' position is always already identified with power.

Notes

1 For example, see Basinger (1994: 457) and Harvey (1998: 409). On *His Girl Friday*, see Gaines and Herzog (1982) and on *Lady in the Dark*, see Doane (1988: 41). A more nuanced approach is taken by Walsh, who traces the 'thematic evolution'

(1984: 139) of the cycle, finding *His Girl Friday* less reactionary than *Lady in the Dark*, but less progressive than *Adam's Rib*.

2 The original words were: 'Farewell, Amanda, | Adios, addio, adieu. | Farewell, Amanda, | It was all great fun | But it's done, it's through.'

3 It is beyond the scope of this chapter to explore every aspect of women's wartime employment; for more detailed discussion, see Anderson (1981), Honey (1984), Renov (1988), Chafe (1991 and 1995) and Dabakis (1993).

4 Policy makers 'deliberately formulated a middle-class identity for the war-worker – a hiring strategy that assumed the temporary labor of housewives who did not "need" to work for wages' (Dabakis 1993: 188). This image was largely false and, according to some surveys, as many as 75 to 80 per cent of women fully intended to continue working (Honey 1984: 23).

5 Indeed, if it were not for these conventions, *Lady in the Dark* would barely qualify as a romantic comedy. The film is more concerned with the psychodrama of Liza's neurosis than with the comic formation of the couple, and the musical dream sequences further confuse the issue.

6 Freudian imagery is a common tendency in Hollywood films of the 1940s, with *Spellbound* (1945) providing a melodramatic counterpoint to the career woman comedy. Dr Constance Peterson (Ingrid Bergman) is a psychoanalyst, but is represented as frigid and repressed; the moment John Ballantine (Gregory Peck) kisses her a succession of doors are seen opening (her mental release), simultaneously creating a long passageway (her sexual awakening).

7 Examples of such kisses can be found in *Take a Letter, Darling* (*c.* 38 mins), *No Time for Love* (*c.* 38 mins) and *Without Reservations* (*c.* 60 mins).

8 This is a good example of the ways in which studios recycled plot outlines. Both *Libeled Lady* and *Design for Scandal* were produced by MGM, but in the later film, the focus of attention has shifted from the celebrity heiress to the career woman.

5

Economy and excess: Katharine Hepburn and Spencer Tracy

> They were the oddest of odd couples, two people at opposite ends of the personality spectrum. (James Spada 1986: 89)

Katharine Hepburn and Spencer Tracy epitomise the adage 'opposites attract'. Sexual difference is not their only opposition: she is upper-class, while he is lower-class; she is liberal, he is conservative; she is Anglo-Saxon Protestant, he is Irish Catholic; she is intellectual, he has common sense. The various textual and extratextual discourses about the Hepburn/Tracy couple repeatedly work out this structural opposition through a process of moderation. For example, the press book for *Woman of the Year* 'quotes' Hepburn: 'He's the most economical actor I've ever known [. . .] and I'm the most uneconomical. [. . .] I felt that we were so different, we'd be sure to strike a happy medium' (MGM 1942: 8). Seemingly having nothing in common, Hepburn and Tracy's union symbolises the moderation of oppositional idiosyncrasies creating a stable equilibrium. The metaphor of economy and excess proves extremely useful in characterising this dynamic, but it also suggests a hidden gender essentialism: male as practical and rational, female as impractical and irrational – or the difference between a straight line and a spiral (Lundberg and Farnham 1947: 3).

It is not so much the pairing of terms that is problematic, but the implicit values attached to each term of the pair: one side is preferred, while the other is denigrated. As Hélène Cixous argues, it is 'always the same metaphor [. . .]. Thought has always worked through [. . .] dual, hierarchical oppositions. Superior/Inferior' (1997: 91). Patriarchy is shored up by defining itself positively in opposition to that which it is not, whether that is not-female, not-homosexual, not-working-class, not-black, or just not-different. Binary thought is not just about gender; it is about power. It is also about masking the contradictions embedded in patriarchal ideology. In most respects, Hepburn appears to be positioned on the side of power, since she belongs to the upper-class, educated elite of WASP society – but within the discourses of American ideology, this is part of the problem. It is not just Hepburn's femininity which is at stake; her privileged background contradicts the values of the 'democratic' American dream. Tracy, on the other hand, embodies the populist position of the average Joe.

Power is an explicit theme in almost all of Hepburn and Tracy's films together, and it is expressly articulated in terms of excess and moderation.[1] Britton describes the films as falling into two broad groupings: the melodramas, in which the man's ambition and excessive conservatism threaten the couple; and the comedies, in which the woman's ambition and excessive liberalism pose the threat (1995: 188, 200). Although this presents a somewhat simplistic reduction of the films' conflicts (and misrepresents the less well-known *Without Love* and *Desk Set*), it does provide a useful indicator of the ways in which Hepburn and Tracy function as a supremely 'democratic' couple. *State of the Union* is worth mention in this respect (not least because of the title of this book).[2] Grant Matthews (Tracy) is running as the Republican candidate for president; his campaign is co-ordinated by Jim Conover (Adolphe Menjou) and Kay Thorndyke (Angela Lansbury) who are both motivated by greed and self-interest. Grant's ambition leads him into personal and political corruption: in addition to an affair with Kay, he makes deals with various labour leaders and big-businessmen to guarantee votes. Grant's wife, Mary (Hepburn), manages to show him the error of his ways by the end of the film, restoring not only the patriarchal family, but also American democracy. Thus, Grant and Mary's reunion functions as a metonym for the normative values of a 'healthy' society.

The process of moderation embodied by the Hepburn/Tracy union is further validated by extratextual knowledge of their love affair (they had a relationship for over twenty-five years, although Tracy remained married to another woman, with whom he had a child). The textual and extratextual discourses confirm each other, authenticating the sense of their 'natural' attraction and balanced equality. Indeed, the 'real' love story seems to play out the narrative of a career woman comedy.

Taming the star

In one vital respect, the plot of the career woman comedy serves a conflicted purpose. Each film seeks to perpetuate the success of a real career woman – the female star. Hepburn is a particularly interesting case in point, exemplifying the problem of the unconventional, independent woman. As Britton has ably demonstrated, her star persona is beset by paradox: 'she renounces glamour, and yet she is glamorous; she isn't what a star should be, and yet she is a star' (1995: 22). During the 1930s, critics and publicists struggled to define Hepburn within normative categories of class, beauty and femininity, but her eccentricities always destabilised such attempts. For example, Britton quotes a review: 'that troubled, mask-like face, the high, strident, raucous, rasping voice, the straight, broad-shouldered boyish figure – perhaps they may all grate upon you, but they compel attention and they fascinate an audience' (1995: 29).[3] As Britton concludes, 'the insistence of the vocabulary is unmistakable: the fascination is reluctant, capture is offset by resistance, and this interplay of attraction and disturbance is focused on Hepburn's unsatisfactoriness as a *feminine* object' (1995: 29).

While early publicity sought to mitigate Hepburn's difference, her increasing unpopularity following a string of box-office failures (including *Bringing Up Baby*) led to more open hostility. In 1938, Harry Brandt, the president of the Independent Theater Owners of America, took a full-page advertisement in the trade press declaring that such stars as Hepburn, Marlene Dietrich, Joan Crawford and Fred Astaire were 'box-office poison' (see Spada 1986: 74 and Kanin 1972: 38). This declaration was as much about block-booking as it was about the stars, and it is hardly surprising that the androgynous, exotic and sophisticated allure of these particular stars did not go down well in rural areas, where most of the independent exhibitors were located.[4] These provincial tastes again suggest that part of Hepburn's difference is her 'alienation' from the values of populist American ideology.

Hepburn responded by buying out her contract with RKO. She made one more film (*Holiday* at Columbia) and then headed to the East coast. According to Hepburn, 'I was obsessed by my own failure and I wondered whether I could put it right' (1992: 163). When she returned to the screen in 1941, the first two films she made were carefully chosen. Both *The Philadelphia Story* and *Woman of the Year* demonstrate a conscious effort to reclaim Hepburn's star persona by assimilating her 'otherness' into patriarchy. Moreover, she never looks more glamorously feminine.[5] Considering the previous emphasis on her androgyny and unstable gender positioning, this glamorisation can itself be recognised as a strategy of recuperation.

It is worth emphasising Hepburn's active involvement in this process. Philip Barry had written the play, *The Philadelphia Story*, expressly for Hepburn; they were both involved in the funding of the play's production and Hepburn also secured the film rights. Indeed, as Andrew Sarris has observed, 'the play was about Katharine Hepburn herself, and what the American people thought about Katharine Hepburn in 1939, and what Katharine Hepburn realized that she had to do to keep her career going. *The Philadelphia Story* [. . .] is Katharine Hepburn getting her comeuppance at long last, and accepting it like the good sport she was' (1998: 451). Hepburn co-ordinated the film deal with MGM, not only choosing the director, George Cukor, but also arranging for Cary Grant to play the lead. Hepburn's collusion in her rehabilitation continued with *Woman of the Year*. She sent Ring Lardner and Michael Kanin's original treatment to Joseph Mankiewicz (who had produced *The Philadelphia Story*) and she again co-ordinated the deal with MGM. This time, she wanted George Stevens to direct, apparently explaining to her friend, Cukor, that the film 'had to be directed by a very macho director from the man's point of view and not the woman's' (Hepburn 1992: 146). She also insisted that Spencer Tracy should play the male lead.

The pairing with Tracy (both textual and extratextual) became a vital part of Hepburn's recuperation. The apocryphal tale of their first meeting almost serves as a plot summary of their comedies: when Hepburn remarked, 'I'm afraid I might be a little too tall for you, Mr Tracy,' Mankiewicz interjected, 'Don't worry, he'll soon cut you down to size' (quoted by Spada 1986: 93). James Agee applauded the film's casting: 'as a lady columnist, she's just right. As a working reporter, he is practically perfect. For once strident Katharine Hepburn is *properly subdued*' (quoted by Kanin 1972: 8, my emphasis). In a similar vein, MGM's publicity for *Without Love* proclaimed, 'Miss Hepburn is humanized in the inimitable Tracy manner' (quoted by Thumim 1986: 79). As Thumim points out, 'there is more than a hint here of a "Taming of the Shrew" response to gender politics. Hepburn *is humanized*; she is acted upon, thus subject to Tracy. He is the active party' (1986: 79, emphasis in original). Although the accuracy of describing *Without Love* in these terms is questionable (there is little of the shrew about Hepburn's character, Jamie Rowan), the main point is that Tracy's persona somehow explains – even guarantees – Hepburn's transformation. The same pattern characterises much of the discourse around the couple's 'real' love affair. For example, according to Spada's glossy tribute to Hepburn, Tracy was a 'strong man [. . .]. Their friends were continually astonished at the subservient position she happily assumed when around Spencer' (1986: 89). Hepburn seems to concur: 'I loved Spencer Tracy. He and his interests and his demands came first. [. . .] He didn't like this or that. I changed this and that. They might be qualities which I personally valued. It did not matter. I changed them' (1992: 311–12).

Hepburn's career parallels the structure of the career woman comedy: an 'unfeminine', ambitious woman is 'tamed' by (the love of) a strong man. However, as far as choice of films is concerned, this 'taming' is a masquerade orchestrated by Hepburn to save her career. Paradoxically, by acting out her subordination on screen, Hepburn regains her power off screen – she becomes a star again. The tensions between the 'real' woman's renewed success and the 'performed' woman's submission is also reflected textually by the use of masquerade to bring about resolution in all the Hepburn/Tracy comedies made in the forties (up to and including *Pat and Mike*). Ultimately, Hepburn's persona still exceeds the cultural norms of 'femininity', as closer analysis of *Woman of the Year* reveals.

When is a woman not a woman?

Tess Harding (Hepburn) and Sam Craig (Tracy) are columnists for the New York *Chronicle*; she writes about international affairs, he about national sports. After a whirlwind romance, they marry, but Tess has no idea what marriage entails and continues to put her career before all else. Tensions build, until Sam leaves. Tess has an epiphany about the meaning of marriage at the wedding of her father, William Harding (Minor Watson), and aunt, Ellen Whitcomb (Fay Bainter). Trying to make amends, she attempts to cook breakfast for Sam, but fails dismally. At the last minute, Sam changes his mind and they are reunited.

In many respects, *Woman of the Year* is an exemplary career woman comedy, utilising a number of key conventions: Tess's career is more high-powered than Sam's; Tess's secretary, Gerald (Dan Tobin) is an 'inadequate' male; Sam denies Tess's femaleness; and the film's resolution is brought about by her conversion to Sam's point of view. There is one significant difference. Visually, Tess almost never appears less than feminine. Indeed, she is looking her most glamorous at the very moment when Sam denies her femaleness: it is the evening she is to be awarded a plaque naming her 'America's Outstanding Woman of the Year', and she is dressed in a full-length, off-the-shoulder tulle gown, with long gloves, a fur coat, and diamond ear-clips. And yet, as far as Sam is concerned, 'The Outstanding Woman of the Year isn't a woman at all.'

The sequence is central to the film's project and demands closer attention. The spectator is clearly meant to agree with Sam, having been consistently aligned with his point of view. But if this feminine-looking creature is not a woman at all, what is she? And if appearance is not a guarantee, then how is 'womanliness' being defined? The sequence itself sets these questions in motion, opening with a stereotypically feminine pose: Tess is sitting at her vanity table, preening in front of the mirror. When Sam nuzzles the top of her hair, Tess ducks away; she looks at him, uttering an admonishing, 'Darling!', then turns back to check her reflection, patting her hair into place. She is more concerned with her own appearance than with Sam's affection and feelings. Sam jokingly asks if he looks like the outstanding husband of the outstanding woman of the year; after a brief glance, she perfunctorily tells him that he looks 'fine', but is already concentrating on her own image again, this time using a hand mirror. As he leaves the room to check on Chris (George Kezas) – the Greek boy whom Tess has decided to take in – Sam asks her if he will be expected to make a speech. Still preening, Tess distractedly replies, 'I don't see why.' The scene cuts to Sam, who stops in his tracks to look back in Tess's direction, before sadly turning away. Tess's vanity defines her here not as feminine, but as self-centred and egotistical, the very antithesis of femininity by the standards of the time.

Implicitly, the film suggests that a 'real' woman should put the needs of others first, and the sequence takes this implication further in relation to Chris. Sam is horrified to discover that Tess is planning to leave the boy alone in the apartment for four hours, and decides to stay with him, at least until he falls asleep. At this point, the tension which has been brewing reaches boiling point – but it is Tess who loses her temper first.

> TESS: [*symmetrical face-to-face two-shot*] You simply don't want to come to the dinner – that's why you're putting on this paternal act.
> SAM: I'm not putting on any act. We accepted a responsibility, didn't we?
> TESS: But everyone will be looking for you. What shall I say you're doing?
> SAM: Say that I'm at home minding the baby. [. . .] [*the camera pans with Tess's movement, leaving Sam out of frame*] Tell 'em anything! I don't care what you tell 'em. Tell 'em I had something important to do.
> TESS: Who would believe that *you* had anything [*walking back towards him, bringing the camera with her*] that was important enough to do to warrant –
> SAM: [*moves into symmetrical face-to-face two-shot*] You know, it's too bad I'm not covering this dinner of yours tonight, because I've got an angle that would really be sensational: [*pauses for effect*] 'The Outstanding Woman of the Year' isn't a woman at all!

In stark contrast to the typical use in screwball comedy, the symmetrical two-shot is used here precisely at those moments when the couple are most antagonistic (these are the only such shots in the sequence and they are rarely used elsewhere in the film). While Sam seems genuinely paternal (a trait he defines as accepting responsibility for the child), Tess's casual attitude and irresponsibility signal her lack of maternal instincts. The only reason she took Chris on in the first place was because 'some idiot' suggested that, as Chairman of the Greek Refugee Committee, she should do so. The sequence also reveals that Chris's toys (wholly inappropriate sports equipment) were bought by Gerald, not Tess, and she now appears ready to leave without even saying goodbye (despite being the only one who can speak a language Chris understands). This 'unnatural' state of affairs is further emphasised by Sam's line about minding the baby; Tess has placed him in a feminine position. The crux of the matter, however, is Tess's arrogant assumption that nothing Sam does could possibly be more important than attending this banquet in her honour. Her pride in her own achievement has made her insensitive to Sam's ego, dismissing his importance both to her own success (like a trophy wife, he will not be expected to make a speech) and in the world at large.

This is not the first time that Tess has slighted Sam's importance. Her career always takes precedence and she repeatedly expects him to be at her beck and call. For example, when Tess explains the difficulty of arranging their wedding to suit the schedules of three people, Sam looks surprised ('Three?'), but Tess's reply is even more of a shock: 'Pops, Aunt Ellen and myself.' Sam is then forced to move into her apartment because it is more convenient for her. Effectively, he takes the subordinate 'wifely' position and this reversal is developed further in a later scene. Despite the fact it is Sunday, Tess is working at home and twice fobs off Sam with the claim that she will be with him in two minutes. Strikingly, this is one of the very few occasions that Tess is dressed in a 'masculine' fashion. She is wearing wide-legged trousers with what looks like a smoking jacket (black velvet with smooth satin lapels, buttoning at the waist); the suit is very plain and dark, worn with a white shirt buttoned to the throat, and her shoes appear totally flat. Sam, on the other hand, is disappointed when Tess does not realise he is wearing a new hat. Stereotypically, it is the wife who sulks when her husband does not comment on her appearance. Here, Sam petulantly throws the hat down while Tess patronises him ('I said I liked it'). As far as Sam is concerned, the real problem is that he had to buy the hat himself; he hoped she would notice the new one because he had needed it for some time. Her failure to notice again signals her lack of (feminine) concern for her husband, and this lack is compounded by further inversions. Sam has to cook eggs not only for himself but for Tess and her secretary as well. He also has to answer the telephone, even though Tess is nearer (a fact underlined by the camera movement, which pans from Sam to the telephone and then to Tess). The call is, of course, for Tess. When she tells Sam she does not want to speak to the caller because he is a pest, Sam repeats her words verbatim and puts down the receiver. Finally realising she has upset him, Tess tries to make amends by feigning interest in Sam's work, but it quickly becomes apparent that she is not really listening and is reading his newspaper instead. The depth of Tess's misapprehension is signalled when it transpires that they were both in Chicago the day before. While she thinks it is '*really* funny', Sam is furious: 'The point isn't whether we could've got together, or not; the point is that you never even thought of it.'

Throughout this scene, Tess fails to live up to Sam's expectations, and her behaviour seems inconsiderate, arrogant and selfish. The various elements of the sequence can all be summed up by the final argument: she does not bother to think about him. However, while this scene undoubtedly uses gender role inversion to reveal Tess's faults and failures *as a woman*, the inversion is done in such a way as to expose the inequality of the norm as well. Tess is playing the stereotypical self-absorbed, patronising husband, Sam the neglected, servile wife. The relationship would seem no more 'ideal' if the genders were returned to their 'normal' positions. The problem is not just that Tess is emasculating Sam, but that this structure represents a genuine inequality in their relationship. To appreciate this distinction fully, it is helpful to consider what kind of marriage Sam actually wants. Does he want their current positions inverted to 'normal', or does he want something else?

The perfect marriage?

At first glance, *Woman of the Year* appears to fit Cavell's conception of the comedy of remarriage: the 'drive of its plot is not to get the central pair together, but to get them *back* together' (1981: 2). However, while Cavell describes the impetus behind this drive as internal to the institution – 'as if marriage, which was to be a ratification, is itself in need of ratification' (1981: 31) – the impetus in *Woman of the Year* is rooted in Tess's misapprehension of the institution.

After the 'Woman of the Year' argument, Sam leaves Tess, taking Chris back to the children's home on the way. The following day, when Sam refuses to talk about 'patching' things up, Tess asks what he wants her to do, 'Just throw out everything we've had, when it was so perfect?' Sam is surprised she thinks they had a perfect marriage:

SAM: I don't think it was either: perfect, or a marriage.
TESS: I don't understand.
SAM: That's just the point.

The film repeatedly emphasises this distinction: Tess does not understand what marriage means. Sam's opinion, on the other hand, is presented as authoritative. When Tess and Gerald are arranging the wedding (for the day after the proposal) Sam is anxious: 'Why do we have to do it so quick? [. . .] The whole thing seems so important for such rush.' He has always looked forward to his wedding day: 'I thought I'd do it up right, like most people. I even thought I might go for the striped pants.' In other words, Sam is old-fashioned about these things and values the ritual of the institution. Tess, on the contrary, has always sworn she would never marry, because she was frightened of being tied down; this attitude is later reconfirmed when she tells Ellen, 'I always felt that you were above marriage.' Although Sam gets his pants (and the morning coat and top hat to match), the wedding itself has to be crammed into ten minutes of Mr Harding's precious time. No sooner has the Justice of the Peace pronounced them 'man and wife' than Tess is called to the telephone, her father has to leave and her aunt goes with him; Sam is left to toast their marriage all by himself. This is quite a different attitude to the wedding ceremony to that found in screwball comedy. The farcical complications of a screwball wedding undercut the institution; here the comedy mocks the particular couple, making a travesty of their union. The rest of the film is concerned with recuperating this inauspicious start, reaffirming the sacred institution in the process.[6]

Tess learns the 'real' meaning of marriage at the wedding of her father and aunt – a union which simultaneously reaffirms the traditional family. The scene is extremely overblown and sentimentalised, but this in itself is revealing. In contrast to her own, this ceremony is overseen by a priest in a picturesque private chapel and Tess plays the wedding march on an organ as William and Ellen walk down the aisle. The only part of Tess and Sam's ceremony witnessed by the spectator was the pronouncement; now, the priest's speech is heard at length (from 'Dearly Beloved' to the opening vows). The entire scene is built around Tess's reactions, shown in tight close-up, to this speech's description of marriage.

> PRIEST: As the bride gives herself to the bridegroom, let him be, to her, father and mother, sister and brother, and – most sacred – husband [*cuts from a medium shot of William and Ellen at the altar to a close-up of Tess, whose eyes are cast down*]. As he gives himself to her, let the bride [*Tess raises her eyes*] inspire and sustain him, let her unite with him in all the experiences of life to which their paths shall lead – the great and the small. [*Tess casts her eyes down as a tear falls*]

The speech does not end here, but my main interest is the different roles accorded to the husband and wife. He becomes her entire family (effectively, her world); she must nurture him ('inspire' and 'sustain') and unite *with* him. The patriarchal tradition of the institution is reinforced not only by the fact this is her father's wedding, but also by the presence of Ellen's elderly servants. In a moment of unbridled sentiment, the scene cuts to a medium shot of the servants holding hands as the priest talks of the joys and sorrows of each being the joys and sorrows of both, before cutting back to the close-up of Tess looking in the servants' direction, with tears glistening on her cheeks. Every aspect of the *mise-en-scène* reinforces the symbolic meaning: in soft-focus, glowing close-up we see Tess discover what marriage 'really' means. Without further ado, she races back to Sam's new apartment to make amends. Having woken him with her incompetent banging around in the kitchen, she tries to convince him that she has learned her lesson. This time, she declares, she heard the words that she had only listened to before.

At the very moment the film seems to have achieved its conservative, patriarchal aim, however, Sam rebuffs Tess's submission. As she kneels at his feet, radiant and eager, he mocks her intentions: 'You mean you're going to live here with me, and kiss me goodbye in the morning, and wait for me to come home at night, loaded down with pipes and slippers and stories about what you and the girls did all day? [. . .] Cook and sew, and put on your rubber gloves and wash the dishes on the maid's day out? This is the top phoney of them all.' Tess has gone from one extreme to the other; she is overcompensating. Not only does Sam think she is incapable of performing these 'little ordinary things that any idiot can do' (Tess's words) – and will soon be proved right in his opinion – he also implies that he does not want such a wife. Instead of expecting her to give up her job to nurture him, he suggests a compromise: 'I don't want to be married to Tess Harding any more than I want you to be just Mrs Sam Craig. Why can't you be Tess Harding Craig?'

How convincingly this solution negotiates the conflicts of the film remains to be seen, but its egalitarian intentions need consideration. Confusion about Tess's maiden and married names has been a recurring motif of the film. For example, when the maid, Alma (Edith Evanson), calls Tess 'Miss Harding', Sam corrects her by saying, 'We're married now'; Alma then calls her 'Mrs Harding', and Tess corrects her again, 'Mrs Craig.' Later that night, Dr Lubeck (Ludwig Stössel) calls Sam 'Herr Harding'. Most significantly, when Tess telephones Ellen to tell her about the 'Woman of the Year' award, she asks the operator to say that 'Miss Harding' is calling. Sam's suggestion of 'Tess Harding Craig' rejects the unequal relationships implied in both other names: as Tess Harding she has too much power; as 'just' Mrs Craig, she has too little. The fact is that – no matter how conservative and patriarchal the film ultimately appears – Sam's compromise is exceptional by the standards of the period. He neither expects nor wants his wife to give up her career.

'Tess Harding Craig' may represent a relatively progressive ideal, but the ideal is still defined by the man. Rather than being a mutual process with each party conceding ground, Tess occupies both extremes, while Sam moderates in the middle-ground. It is a false compromise, rooted in the assumption that Sam knows best and has the power to rename Tess's identity. This lack of mutual responsibility for the final compromise raises other questions about the representation of the couple, particularly in relation to the key areas of communication and equality and their articulation through dual-focus narrative and framing.

Failing to communicate

For all their antagonism and oppositional attraction, Tess and Sam's courtship is relatively conventional – a whirlwind romance followed by marriage (and then sex). Their first meeting is marked by exchanges of looks, signalling their mutual attraction at first sight. The scene opens with Sam entering his editor's office and stopping dead in the doorway, looking down at something out of frame. The space has not been established well enough to cut to a point-of-view shot, but the camera's movement stands in for Sam's look, sweeping right, then tilting down to reveal what has caught his eye; a woman extends a shapely leg into the frame as she fixes her stocking in place (this is also the spectator's first view of Tess 'in the flesh'). The camera tilts up from the leg to reveal Tess's face, and she looks out of frame to where we know Sam is standing. She too glances down and then up (matching the look of the camera) and her eyes widen in pleasurable surprise. The fluidity of the single take creates a sense of connection between Sam and Tess, which would have been lost in the more usual shot/reverse shot articulation. Their initial physical attraction is then consolidated through overtly sexual flirtation and innuendo. They hold each other's gaze and smile wryly, and when the editor, Clayton (Reginald Owen), asks them to kiss and make up, Sam admits he is at least willing to kiss. When Tess leaves the office, she makes sure that Sam is following, and then lies in wait for him, positioned in such a way that he cannot avoid physically bumping into her. As they circle each other on the stairs, romantic string music accompanies their mating rituals, culminating in Sam asking Tess to attend a baseball game. A succession of dates follows, involving such conventional romantic signifiers as a gift of flowers, passionate kissing, romantic music and atmospheric lighting. For example, when Sam tells Tess he loves her, in the back of a taxi, they are framed in close-up with chiaroscuro lighting; inside her apartment, the lighting is still darker, non-diegetic string music is again heard and, as the couple kiss passionately, they are silhouetted in extreme close-up. The sexual tension is too much for Sam and he leaves without his hat.

The next day, he explains she is 'practically the only woman in the world' that he would have walked out on, because he wants to marry her. His 'gentlemanly' behaviour is presumably tempered with a patriarchal interest in her virginity (an interest which is soon confirmed by the telephone conversation in which Sam tells his mother that 'you don't ask girls a thing like that' – the punchline being his agreement to ask Tess if she is a 'good cook'). The whirlwind romance is quickly undercut, however, by the failure of their 'happily ever after'. Instead of solving the couple's conflict, the marriage merely solves the romance; their incompatibility remains the cause of antagonism.

This inherent clash of personalities is indicated from the very beginning of the film. The opening montage of newspaper headlines detailing Tess's political activities ends with two advertisements for the New York *Chronicle*: 'Tess Harding says, "Hitler will lose!"'; 'Sam Craig says, "Yankees won't lose!"' While Sam is all-American, Tess is associated with all things un-American. Indeed, her suggestion that baseball is a waste of energy and should be banned for the duration of the war, initiates a journalistic battle, before they even meet. Sam begins typing a second editorial attack declaring, 'Tess Harding is so busy telling the American people what to do, she's probably never taken the time to get out and meet some of them.' Before he can get any further, he is called to the editor's office to meet Tess, but takes the sheet of paper with him, enabling her to read the comment. Once she has agreed to attend the baseball game, Sam throws the paper away as extraneous: Tess Harding is about to meet the American people.

The initial pattern of contrast is developed more fully in the following pair of scenes, in which Tess and Sam first encounter each other's environment.

Tess readily adapts to the new environment, enjoying the game – despite Sam's confused explanation of the rules – and ultimately winning over the hostile men around her. Her enthusiasm and energy are connoted here as positive, attractive values and the scene is as close as the film comes to suggesting a screwball sense of play. The same certainly cannot be said for the following scene, which entirely undercuts these positive effects. The spectator, like Sam, assumes Tess has invited him for a private tête-à-tête, not a meeting of the 'League of Nations' (as Sam later calls it). Tess's demeanour is quite different, and she seems insincere and aloof. Even her enjoyment of the baseball game is brought into question: when told that the Yankees won, she declares, 'Everyone in Philadelphia must be so happy.' She soon leaves Sam stranded in the middle of the room, surrounded by strangers who literally do not speak his language. Although he does attempt to engage in conversation, his efforts are thwarted and he eventually leaves without saying goodbye. In combination, both scenes elaborate the American/un-American opposition in terms of class politics: Sam's world is lower-middle-class and 'democratic', while Tess's is upper-class and elitist. The metaphor of 'foreign' language is used to symbolise difference in both instances, but a distinction can be made between the attitudes of the native to the outsider. Sam at least attempts to teach Tess the jargon of baseball and thereby includes her in his world; Tess not only fails to include Sam, but also exacerbates his exclusion by speaking a variety of (untranslated) foreign languages herself (thereby further alienating the spectator). In effect, Sam's inability to adapt is displaced on to Tess's failure to look after him.

The metaphor of speaking different languages inevitably evokes the screwball theme of conversation. The morning after the soirée, Sam explicitly states that he had hoped to speak to Tess alone. When the chance comes, however, the conversation takes place not in the green playground but in the back booth of Pinkie's (William Bendix) bar and, instead of reciprocal play, the couple become competitive. Sam looks mildly perplexed when Tess downs a scotch almost as quickly as him, and he orders another; she, however, responds, 'Great idea.' As they put their glasses down, almost in unison, Sam asks for a double, but Tess says, 'Me, too.' The contrast with Nick and Nora in *The Thin Man* is striking: rather than Nora's balanced response to Nick's drinking, Sam is keen to out-distance Tess; by matching him, she is being unfeminine. When the double scotches are brought, Tess immediately starts to sip hers and the real competition begins. Sam warns Tess about the strength of the drinks, but she seems unconcerned, explaining, 'As a diplomat's daughter, I've had to match drinks with a lot of people [. . .] and I may say I've never wound up under the table.' Sam is reminded of drinking games he used to play in college: 'I used to bet on drinking, make a contest outta it – kids' stuff.' Although Tess laughs at the idea, calling it silly, the glances which she and Sam exchange function as a challenge – accepting the bet, so to speak. Far from the neat visual symmetry of Nick and Nora's exchange, here the camera moves progressively further round to Sam's side of the table, finally making a visual joke at Tess's expense: following the acceptance of the bet, the medium shot dissolves to a medium long shot showing Sam in profile, resting his head on his fist; Tess is speaking out of frame and the camera pans right while tilting down to reveal she is 'under the table' (replacing the spilled contents of her handbag). She has lost the contest.

There is very little sense in *Woman of the Year* of the couple 'learning to speak the same language' through play. For example, we cannot imagine Tess or Sam characterising their relationship in terms of sharing 'grand laughs', as Lucy Warriner characterises her relationship in *The Awful Truth*; on the contrary, the laughter evoked in the audience by *Woman of the Year* is not shared by the couple. The difference is clearly demonstrated by comparing Jerry's intrusion on Lucy's recital to Sam's intrusion on stage during Tess's speech at the Riverside Hall. Lucy's and Jerry's actions complement and enhance each other in such an unlikely way as to increase the audience's pleasure; Jerry's antics would be less effective if Lucy's singing accompaniment stopped and vice versa. Sam's intrusion is more disruptive as he replaces Tess as the focus of attention for both the diegetic and extra-diegetic audiences. Tess's speech breaks off when her audience starts laughing, drowning her out; when she hesitantly continues, she is almost entirely left out of frame, while Sam's comic spectacle takes centre stage and screen. As a result, Tess's words become little more than background noise, but close attention reveals that her subject is the test of responsibility now facing the women of the world: 'Our place is no longer only in the home; it is also in the first line of battle.' Jerry made a fool of himself because he was jealous and suspicious; Sam's comic spectacle only serves to undermine Tess's authority.

The balance of power

The dynamic of Sam and Tess's relationship is quite different to that of the screwball couple. Rather than embodying reciprocal equality and mutual autonomy, almost every aspect of the narrative is concerned with redressing the imbalance of power in Sam's favour. As in most career woman comedies, there is an inherent contradiction between Tess's deviance from feminine norms and Sam's attraction to her. The film combats this instability by alternating scenes in which Tess is entirely charming and personable with scenes in which she is arrogant, alienating and unsympathetic. Indeed, the split in her personality is explicitly acknowledged at the baseball game, when Sam – surprised at her behaviour – claims to have mixed her up with someone else; when he asks her name, Tess replies, 'Just call me, Tessie.' The baseball game and the evening soirée in no way offer a dual focus. Sam is unquestionably the protagonist of both scenes, and it his point of view with which the spectator is expected to identify.

This is not to say that the film entirely lacks a dual-focus structure. On the contrary, Sam's point of view is maintained until the night of the 'Woman of the Year' banquet, after which the narrative focuses on Tess (but this is well over halfway through the film). The switch is carefully signalled when Sam returns Chris to the Greek Children's Home. Just as the matron (Sara Haden) realises who Sam is, the award ceremony is transmitted over the wireless. As the speaker announces, 'America's Outstanding Woman of the Year [. . .] who so magnificently symbolises the full and rounded life – the glorious emancipation of womanhood in this country,' the camera cranes in for an extreme close-up of the wireless and the scene dissolves to Tess at the banquet. The irony of the announcement is made all the more bitter by the shot that follows: Tess looks to her father and aunt for their congratulations and support, but they only have eyes for each other. For the first time, Tess seems shaken and unsure.

The rest of the film consolidates and expands this uncertainty into a full-scale 'cutting down to size'. For example, prior to the switch, the newspaper office sequences always start in Sam's office and follow his movements towards Tess. After the switch, we begin in Tess's office, as she resists telephoning Sam; a dissolve to Sam shows he is doing much the same thing. The sequence dissolves back to Tess, just as she receives the telegram from Ellen inviting them to Connecticut. Using this as an excuse, Tess telephones Sam, and asks him to come up; he presumably refuses, because she then agrees, 'I'll be right down, Sam.' She only pauses long enough to check her hair – this time for the 'right' reasons – before rushing out. Tess becomes the focus of attention, not because her point of view is as valid or important as Sam's, but because the film wants the spectator to see her learn her lesson well.

The film's system of framing achieves a similar redistribution of power. As mentioned earlier, the symmetrically balanced medium two-shot is noticeably rare and tends to be used only at moments of intense emotional conflict. Instead, Sam and Tess are usually framed in medium close-up, with one of them visually dominating the other by occupying the upper diagonal of the frame. In the first part of the film, it is usually Tess who takes the upper diagonal. For example, when she organises their wedding, she is perched on the edge of her desk, while Sam sits in a lower chair, and when she feigns interest in Sam's work, she is lying on top of him, as he reclines on a *chaise-longue*. The moments when Sam dominates the frame are equally significant: when he kisses Tess goodbye at the airport; in the taxi when he tells her he loves her; and when he tells her that their relationship was neither perfect, nor a marriage. The framing repeatedly reflects the shifting balance of power.

Ultimately, the final embrace is shown in a medium close-up two-shot, revealing their 'natural' difference in height.

The chauvinistic male

These variations on the dual-focus structures of narrative and framing also raise the question of mutual re-education. Tess certainly has more than one lesson to learn, but to what extent can the same be said for Sam? As Carolyn Galerstein puts it, 'there are compromises, but they are all hers. [. . .] He goes on doing just what he did before' (1989: xv). Galerstein implies that this is an unfair situation, but the truth of the matter is that – as far as the film is concerned, at least – there is nothing wrong with what Sam was doing before. He does not need to change.

There are two related aspects to consider: the stability of Sam's (and Tracy's) masculinity and his status as an all-American regular guy. In most career woman comedies, the heroine's challenge to contemporary gender norms poses a threat to the hero's masculinity; her career places him in a subordinate (feminine) position and her 'aggressive' behaviour threatens his performance of the 'natural' masculine role. Tess repeatedly treats Sam as subordinate to her interests and her actions also tend to be quite 'aggressive', as when she competes with Sam in the consumption of scotch (a conventionally masculine drink). However, Sam wins these competitions by actively demonstrating his masculinity. For example, in the airport farewell scene, Tess fails to allow Sam to light her cigarette for her and Gerald then adds insult to injury by telling Sam to park the car. However, when Tess brazenly explains that she asked Sam to drive them because she thought he might like to kiss her goodbye, Sam takes charge of the situation. Turning his back to the camera he draws her to him; the camera moves into close-up, but the frame is filled with Sam's back, as he masterfully overpowers Tess with his kiss. Visibly moved, Tess breathlessly mutters something about sending him a wire and Sam consolidates his dominant position by telling her firmly to make sure that *she* sends it – 'Don't have the little corporal do it.' In effect, Sam's masculinity remains secure, even when challenged. Indeed, Sam seems confident enough in his own identity to absorb these challenges quite easily (even curtseying when leaving the stage at the Riverside Hall). It is, in part, Spencer Tracy's appearance and performance that guarantees Sam's masculine identity. In Hepburn's words, 'Spencer's face was [. . .] Irish and solid and strong. He was a man. He was the American man with an Irish background. It represented MAN in capital letters' (1992: 180).

Sam's masculinity is further secured by the cycle's usual displacement of emasculation on to the inadequate male colleague. Gerald not only works for a woman, but also has a 'feminine' sex-typed job. His 'unmanly' position is compounded by his behaviour and appearance. He is petty and snide, bureaucratic and officious, and he is the type of Hollywood man who wears bow ties and bowler hats. Simply displacing the threat of emasculation is not enough for *Woman of the Year*. For all the egalitarian potential of Sam's compromise ('Tess Harding Craig'), the film's resolution hinges upon Sam's expulsion of Gerald and all that he symbolises. Just as Sam seems to have solved the couple's conflict, Gerald reappears, expecting Tess to leave with him to launch a battleship. There is no question of Tess deciding what action to take; she barely moves – her only reaction a look of confused alarm. Sam takes complete charge of the situation. He escorts Gerald outside and a loud crash is heard. Sam returns alone, announcing he has just launched Gerald. Sam has proved his 'natural' masculine dominance once and for all.

The scene unquestionably carries the unpleasant marks of homophobic male aggression, but the film itself treats Sam's actions approvingly. Sam calls Gerald 'the little corporal' – a phrase more commonly applied to Hitler – thereby constructing Gerald's difference as potentially dangerous and 'un-American'. A similar bias prevails at Tess's soirée when Sam tricks one of her guests (whose only word of English is 'yes') into agreeing that he looks like a 'pretty silly-looking little jerk sitting there with that towel wrapped around [his] head.' The guest's 'foreignness' is also connoted in terms of emasculation: he is short and overweight, with mildly effeminate deportment and gestures.

The chauvinism of this moment reflects a wider tendency of the film. The ways in which (Uncle) Sam's role as all-American regular guy is contrasted with Tess's exceptional status repeatedly reinforce American ideology as 'normal' and everything else as an entirely 'foreign' aberration. A particularly telling sequence, in this respect, is Sam and Tess's conversation about her childhood (following their drinking contest). Sam expressly states that he wants to know about 'the girl *without a country* and how she grew up' (my emphasis).

> TESS: She grew by remote control. I read *Uncle Tom* in the Argentine [. . .] and I read, er, *Huckleberry Finn* going down the Yangtze.
> SAM: Did it seem like the Mississippi?
> TESS: I've never seen the Mississippi.

While it is striking that Tess should refer to two novels dealing with slavery, I think Britton is right to conclude that 'no irony beyond the obvious one is intended. [. . .] The function of *Huckleberry Finn* here is to be the exemplary *national* classic – a signifier of "Americanicity", and of Tess's estrangement from it' (1995: 205). This estrangement is reinforced by the connotations of growing by remote control. The mechanistic metaphor implies that Tess has merely accumulated information (like a computer), rather than learnt anything (like a human being). Indeed, growing by remote control connotes something entirely unnatural, once again suggesting that the career woman 'isn't a woman at all', not because she is a 'man', but because she is not human. It is *Woman of the Year*'s peculiar distinction, however, to identify not-human with not-American. Consequently, Sam explicitly connects Tess's first step to humanisation to experiencing America: when she claims to have 'come home' to America with her father, Sam interjects, 'That isn't when you came home [. . .]. It was in the ball park.' The imagery is completed by Sam's recognition of the woman in front of him as a 'little gal [he] ran into at the ball park, name of Tessie.' As if the diminutives were not enough to convince us of her childish human frailty, Sam reveals he knows Tessie by the freckles on her nose. Tess Harding is reborn, temporarily at least, as an all-American girl-next-door, but it is Sam, once again, who is given the power to redefine Tess's identity.

Woman of the Year is less interested in mutual re-education than in proving that Sam knows best. While Sam's chauvinism may seem distasteful to a 'foreign' audience, his diegetic status as voice of authority ensures that he will not be expected to change. In this respect, the question of the film's ending becomes particularly significant because Tess's domestic humiliation was not originally part of the plan. The synopsis printed in the American press book describes quite a different turn of events following the 'Outstanding Woman of the Year' argument. Having taken Chris back to the Children's Home, Sam 'goes on a drunk. He is supposed to cover a big fight at the [Madison Square] Garden and to protect him, Tess writes his column, but inadvertently makes a laughing stock of him. Later he learns that Tess wrote the column because she wants nothing more than to be his wife and helpmeet. But Sam decides that she doesn't have to give up her career. "If I can do both, why can't you?" he asks Tess. And Tess proves she can' (MGM 1942: 2). According to Hepburn, this ending 'stank' (1992: 176) – despite being her suggestion – and she convinced L. B. Mayer that it needed to be entirely re-shot (with an additional budget of one hundred and fifty thousand dollars). Although Hepburn offers no further details of what exactly was wrong with the original ending, the synopsis immediately suggests quite a different project to the 'cutting down to size' of Tess/Hepburn. Sam's display of 'weakness' (getting drunk in the face of crisis) not only brings his masculinity into question, but also leads to his public humiliation; Tess, on the other hand, is only trying to support her husband in his hour of need.

The top phoney of them all

The revised ending focuses entirely on Tess's abject failure as a housewife. Her disastrous attempts at making breakfast result in her private humiliation and her exhausted subordination to Sam. Her 'natural' feminine incompetence allows him to take total control and tell her what to do. In many ways, the scene is deeply dishonest: it is beyond the realm of plausibility that someone of Tess's intelligence should believe that coffee-making requires one cup of water to four heaped scoops of coffee. The film's insistence on Tess's failure seems designed to 'punish' Hepburn as well, marking her difference from 'normal' women; as Bosley Crowther put it in his review, 'this is certainly a scene over which the ladies are going to gloat' (1970b: 1845). Tess has gone from one extreme to the other – from independence to incompetence – but neither extreme is acceptable. However, as with *Lady in the Dark*, the final compromise of relative 'equality' is unconvincing. Outweighed by the context of abject subordination, the notion of 'Tess Harding Craig' seems a convenience, not a coherent solution.

There is a significant difference between the resolutions of the two films. While Liza's 'natural' femininity finally emerges, Tess's failure reiterates her exceptional status: she is incapable of performing 'normal' domestic chores. What is particularly interesting about this sequence, then, is the sense in which Tess is attempting to masquerade as a 'normal' woman.[7] Both her performance and her failure undermine essentialist notions of women as 'naturally' domestic creatures. The artificiality of the performance is explicitly recognised by Sam, who tells her to 'drop the curtain' on the act (again, he knows her true identity better than she does). Ultimately, Tess/Hepburn is still different from other women, but she is no longer more powerful than Sam.

Similar tactics are used to resolve *Without Love* and *Pat and Mike*, although in these cases the performance of conventional femininity is self-conscious and knowing, whereas Tess was in earnest. In *Without Love*, Jamie masquerades as a frou-frou French coquette, imitating Pat Jamieson's (Tracy) old flame, Lila. Pat is initially baffled, then irritated – pulling the ringlets from her hair – before they improvise a joint performance at the piano that enables their reunion. (The scene's levels of ambiguity and playfulness foreshadow the resolution of *Adam's Rib*.) In *Pat and Mike*, Pat Pemberton (Hepburn) has previously emasculated her manager, Mike Conovan (Tracy), by saving him from a beating. In compensation, she pretends that she needs rescuing from her fiancé, Collier Weld (William Ching); she shouts for Mike's help and claims to have been frightened. Mike is initially unconvinced by her claims that she needs someone to look after her, but he concludes, 'I don't know if I can lick you, or you can lick me, but [. . .] together we can lick 'em all.' In all three films, the woman's (and Hepburn's) performance of femininity enables the man to take control; in all three films, he is aware that it is only an act.

Textually and extratextually, the lesson learnt seems to be that female power must be kept hidden behind a mask of femininity. 'Natural' gender inequality must be performed if the woman wishes to keep her man – and her career.

Five-oh, five-oh

Woman of the Year is the most extreme of the Hepburn and Tracy comedies, in the sense that she is blamed for everything, while he is proved infallible. 'Tess Harding Craig' is an unconvincing solution because the compromise is one-sided. The later films involve a higher degree of mutual negotiation and a more consistent sense of the couple's equality. For example, the title, *Pat and Mike*, immediately suggests an evenly matched couple, while the androgyny of the name 'Pat' is enhanced by the intertexual reference to Tracy's character in *Without Love*. The film's plot concerns the prodigious sporting talents of Pat Pemberton, again placing Hepburn's character within a conventionally 'masculine' world. However, the film is not about her relinquishing excessive power, but about gaining the self-confidence to win – to increase her power. Part of this process involves discarding an unequal relationship with Collier, for an equal relationship with Mike. The film repeatedly articulates the male–female relationship in economic terms. As Mike puts it, 'This man and woman thing – that's gotta be a fifty–fifty thing. Five-oh, five-oh.' This is an immediate point of contrast with Collier, whom Mike describes as a 75 per cent guy. Indeed, when Mike claims to own 51 per cent of Pat (because of their business contract), Collier responds that he owns all of her (because they are engaged to be married). Their argument reduces Pat to tears, sobbing, 'Nobody owns anything of anybody, except myself.'

Collier and Mike are implicitly linked by their attempts to fix golf matches. Although Collier expects Pat to try her hardest to win, while he aims to lose, the fix is no less dishonest or potentially profitable (Collier is hoping Pat's golfing partner will fund a new college gym). When Pat starts playing golf professionally, Mike asks her if she would be willing to throw the contest for the sake of betting odds; she refuses. In both cases, her best intentions are thwarted by Collier's presence. Desperate to please him, she loses all confidence in her own abilities. The source of her 'neurosis' is made clear during a tennis match against 'Gorgeous Gussie' Moran (one of a number of genuine female sportswomen who have cameos in the film). Moran wears a glamorous white satin tennis outfit and poses for photographers; she is the conventional feminine object of desire. Pat, on the other hand, is wearing a high-necked shirt and shorts (both Collier and Mike have previously complained about Pat wearing trousers to play golf; Collier insists she should wear a skirt, but Mike suggests she could vary her attire to include skirts). Pat wins the first set, and is leading in the second when Collier finally arrives with a group of friends, including two attractive blondes. Seated between these elegant ladies, Collier blows a kiss to Pat; she immediately serves a double fault. Her game collapses and the two blondes laugh when she makes further mistakes. Their laughter reflects on Pat's sexual performance of 'woman' as well as her sporting performance. Flustered and humiliated, Pat begins to hallucinate: the net gets higher and higher, and as Gussie's racquet grows to huge proportions, Pat's shrinks. Such hallucinations symbolise her feelings of inadequacy – her 'littleness' (25 per cent) in Collier's eyes – and when every face becomes Collier's smirking visage we know Pat can never 'win' in a relationship with him. The sequence shifts into nightmarish slow motion, until a spinning ball proliferates into an overwhelming mass of balls, all heading straight for Pat.

Mike is represented as both criminal and god: he is a shady sports promoter with gangster connections, but he also claims to be the 'creator' of Davie Hucko (Aldo Ray).

> MIKE: Who made ya, Hucko?
> HUCKO: You, Mike.
> MIKE: Who owns the biggest piece of ya?
> HUCKO: You, Mike.
> MIKE: What'll happen if I drop ya?
> HUCKO: I go right down the drain, Mike.
> MIKE: And?
> HUCKO: Uh, and . . . stay there! [*he smiles, pleased that he managed to remember*]

This catechism is repeated a number of times in the film. It is intended to keep Hucko motivated, but it is unsuccessful; subjugated by an overbearing father-figure, Hucko keeps losing. It is only when Pat convinces Hucko that the person he should be trying to please – and beat – is himself, that he wins a fight. In contrast to Pat seeing Collier's face everywhere, Hucko's retelling of the fight hinges on the moment when his opponent's face turns into his own. Self-reliance is indicated as the key to winning.

Collier expects Pat to give up her career to marry him and to be the good little wife who will support him in all he does. His patriarchal dominance over Pat mirrors Mike's power over Hucko: neither 'child' can satisfy their 'father', and the anxiety caused by their desire to please only makes things worse. The parallel plots suggest that Pat is not just replacing one man with another; she is replacing an unequal relationship with one that enables her to be more powerful because more autonomous. This may sound at odds with her performance of the damsel in distress that enables the film's resolution, but in fact it is entirely consonant with the film's articulation of complementary equality. Pat's masquerade is in response to Mike's angry claim that he has built her up into a monster: 'You're just a great, big Mrs Frankenstein. [. . .] I just don't like the combination, I thought I would, but I don't. I like everything to be five-oh, five-oh, I like a – he to be a he and a she to be a she.' The source of his anger is that, by emasculating him, she has altered the balance of power in her favour. Paradoxically, her performance of vulnerability restores the 'correct' level of equality. As befits a fifty–fifty partnership, their union is sealed, not with a kiss, but with a firm handshake.

The success of the union is apparent from the coda sequence. Pat finally wins a golf tournament. She appears to be wearing a dress, but in fact it is a neat compromise, a tunic worn over culottes. As she plays, she asks Mike the catechism of four questions, to which he replies in her favour, 'You did.' His final reply, however, suggests their mutual dependence: 'I'd go right down the drain – and take you right down with me, Shorty.'

Who took these pictures?

Mike has never referred to Pat as 'Shorty' before. The nickname echoes the anecdote about Hepburn and Tracy's first meeting (Hepburn has been cut down to size). As Britton notes, both *Pat and Mike* and *Adam's Rib* are 'clearly informed by a tone of insinuating knowingness' (1995: 170) that encourages the interpenetration of the textual and extratextual. 'Most journalistic writing about Hepburn and Tracy has consisted of [. . .] a more or less explicit invitation to read the films as something akin to documentaries about their stars' (Britton 1995: 170).

The 'home movie' sequence in *Adam's Rib* is a key example of these tendencies. Spada claims that 'many filmgoers thought they were seeing actual footage of Kate and Spencer "at home"' (1986: 120). The usual slippage between star persona and 'fact' is complicated here, because Hepburn and Tracy's affair was not public knowledge when the film was made (Berg 2003: 170). Spada's assumption that the public *did* know reinforces the aura of authenticity, mystifying the processes of representation. However, the supposed 'documentary' intimacy of the home movie is disavowed by the on-screen audience: Judge Marcasson (Will Wright) explains that they re-enacted paying off the mortgage for the camera; and, since both Adam and Amanda are usually in frame, Kip expressly asks, 'Who took these pictures? Your cow?' The construction of the home movie is further acknowledged by the inclusion of a shot spliced in upside down and allusions to the clichés of silent melodrama. The sequence is part of the film's systematic exploration of the performance of public and private identities. Its self-reflexivity draws attention to the ways in which the act of filming necessarily transforms reality, including the Hepburn/Tracy partnership. It is equally plausible, then, to read this sequence as foregrounding the fact that it is not a 'documentary' about its stars. The willingness of critics (and the putative 'public') to believe such moments offer some kind of direct access to the 'real' stars says more about the power of stardom, than the 'truth' of the couple's relationship.

These slippages between 'fact' and 'fiction' are mutually reinforcing. Hepburn and Tracy's relationship appears to substantiate the films' representations of sexual equality, but the relationship is always read through the fictions of the films. Thus, the extratextual discourses often make use of similar narrative structures to the career woman comedy. Consider Spada's account:

> For many years Katharine Hepburn had been wrapped up in herself, both as an actress and a woman. Spencer Tracy showed her how to break out of her egotism to give better performances, and by loving him, she learned that caring so much for another person was not only the source of happiness but of optimal personal development as well. Meeting Spencer Tracy turned Katharine Hepburn into a better actress, and a better person. (1986: 89)

Hepburn is characterised as egotistical and self-centred, rather than other-directed; loving Tracy enables her to become 'properly' feminine. However, there is an alternative narrative: Tracy was a married man and an alcoholic, and Hepburn's devotion saved him from himself. Significantly, this version inverts the metaphor of economy and excess, undermining the gender stereotyping of Tracy's 'natural' masculine strength and Hepburn's excessive theatricality. There is space for both narratives within the extratextual discourses, but it is the former which has dominated because it fits more readily with patriarchal structures of gender and power.

It is through such slippages, then, that ideology is reproduced. There is no deliberate, conspiratorial intention to keep men on top and women in their place. Rather, there is a shared ideological field in which assumptions are routinely made about what is 'natural' and 'normal'. The discourses of complementary equality are particularly pernicious, since they naturalise the dominance of men, while appearing to offer gender equality. The 'authenticity' of the Hepburn/Tracy couple is essential to their mythic quality, seeming to guarantee the egalitarian possibilities of heterosexual romance. Their union also resolves the contradictions of class and ethnic inequality by privileging the populist American ideals of individualism and democracy. As Molly Haskell concludes, 'Hepburn and Tracy were nothing if not extraordinary. While preserving their individuality, they united to form a whole greater than the sum of its parts' (1987: 227). Such a structure lends itself perfectly to the notion of complementary equality, but it also exposes the limitations of the ideal. The balance of power is redressed, but the binary *structure* of power is not altered.

Notes

1 The couple made nine films: *Woman of the Year* (1942), *Keeper of the Flame* (1942), *Without Love* (1945), *Sea of Grass* (1947), *State of the Union* (1948), *Adam's Rib*

(1949), *Pat and Mike* (1952), *Desk Set* (1957) and *Guess Who's Coming to Dinner* (1967).

2 The President of the United States gives an annual 'State of the Union' address to the nation. The film's title thus directly links the personal union of the couple to much wider political implications about American democracy.

3 According to Spada (1986: 24), this review refers to *Christopher Strong* (1933), and was written by Regina Crew for the New York *American* (no date given).

4 Block-booking was a system of distribution orchestrated by the major studios: independent exhibitors were forced to rent blocks of films in order to get the film they actually wanted; this provided the major studios with a guaranteed market for their products, but the exhibitors were paying for films their local market did not necessarily want to see.

5 The press book for *Woman of the Year* includes three separate sections on Hepburn's 'exciting' face, long hair (which is described as 'regal and feminine' when up, and 'girlish' when hanging loose) and figure, in addition to her solution to the silk shortage – body make-up on bare legs (MGM 1942: 5).

6 The career woman comedy repeatedly treats marriage as a sacred bond, even when entered into for the wrong reasons (for example, see *The Doctor Takes a Wife*, *Hired Wife* (1940), *Third Finger, Left Hand* and *June Bride*).

7 I am using 'masquerade' here to echo Joan Riviere's psychoanalytical concept, but I am more interested in the cultural significance of her argument than in its theoretical accuracy. It is striking that a professional woman, working in a male-dominated environment in 1929, should choose to analyse a 'particular type of intellectual woman' (1986: 35) who compensates for her professional activities by manifesting excessive 'femininity'. According to Riviere, femininity is always 'put on', to mask the (guilty) possession of phallic power, but she argues this is an unconscious reaction-formation.

Part IV

Desire

Bedroom problems: Doris Day and Rock Hudson in *Pillow Talk* (1959).
Courtesy of Universal.

6

Possess me: consuming desires in the sex comedy

The concerns and interests of the sex comedy are neatly encapsulated in a scene from *The Tender Trap*. Julie Gillis (Debbie Reynolds) is certainly not a career woman; her one desire is to get married, despite a burgeoning stage career. When Julie fails to turn up for rehearsal, her agent, Charlie Reader (Frank Sinatra), eventually finds her at the American Home Show. She has been testing out a living-room suite, but is undecided: 'I love this style of house, and I love this decor, but when a man sits in that chair it just doesn't gel, it sorta goes out of focus.' She has tried five different men in the chair without success, but when Charlie sits down her reaction is extreme. Head tilted, she stares at him as if seeing him for the first time. Magical string-music reinforces the romantic impact, as she says, 'It's amazing, the room seems so *different* now – all at once.' This is the first time Julie has shown any physical interest in Charlie; indeed, she earlier refused his dinner invitation because she felt no 'immediate chemistry' between them. After this consumer epiphany, however, she asks *him* out; the sexual chemistry he lacked is apparently less important than (or perhaps a by-product of) his aesthetic ability to co-ordinate with her dream decor.

This sequence immediately links consumerism with romantic desire. At the same time, Julie's consumption of 'interior' design is matched by the spectator's consumption of 'exterior' design (CinemaScope, Eastman Color, chic decor and costume). The 'plushy look' (*Variety*, 26 October 1955) of *The Tender Trap* is typical of Hollywood's widescreen spectacle of the fifties, especially the sex comedies. Indeed, promotional tours often centred upon the more obviously consumable aspects of a film; for example, during August 1959, the Lincoln Futura automobile featured in *It Started with a Kiss* toured fifteen major US cities (*Motion Picture Herald* 1959: 9). The emphasis on glossy spectacle has led many critics to assume the films are superficial. For instance, Engene [*sic*] Archer considered the films produced by Ross Hunter (which included *Pillow Talk*, the remake of *My Man Godfrey* and a number of Douglas Sirk's melodramas) to be an enigma: 'do American audiences really want to see "bad films" – slick, soap-opera stories peopled with beautiful, artificial characters in stylish wardrobes, moving through rich and colourful furnishings to the strain of "schmaltzy" scores?' (1984: October 1960). The link between Archer's qualitative judgement and the motifs of popular consumerism is clear.

This interaction between textual and extratextual consumption may well be one reason for the sex comedy's relatively low critical standing. While film academics have devoted a good deal of attention to fifties' melodrama, science fiction and horror, relatively little work has been done on the era's romantic comedies. However, once you scratch beneath the Eastman Color, the chic decor and the fashion-plate costumes, the sex comedy reveals anxieties and contradictions comparable to those found in other genre films of the fifties. As John Belton observes, sex comedies are 'sites for a critique of contemporary mass culture' (1994: 159), satirising the relationships between sexual fantasy and the consumption of mass-produced texts and products.

Easy living

In the popular imagination, America in the fifties was a suburban dream of middle-class togetherness: Mom in her ultra-modern kitchen, Dad relaxing with his pipe and newspaper after a hard day's work, and their four freckle-faced kids engaged in a variety of hobbies and pastimes. As Betty Friedan noted in *The Feminine Mystique*, the arguments of Lundberg and Farnham's *Modern Woman* had been 'paraphrased ad nauseam in the magazines and in marriage courses, until most of its statements became a part of the conventional, accepted truth of our time' (1964: 111). Certainly, the moral of *Modern Woman* seemed to have been learned: woman's place was in the home. According to Friedan, 'by the mid-fifties, 60 per cent [of women] dropped out of college to marry, or because they were afraid too much education would be a marriage bar' (1964: 12). By the end of the decade, the average marrying age of men and women had plummeted to just twenty-two and twenty, respectively, and 'nearly one-third of all American women had their first child before they reached their twentieth birthday' (Mintz and Kellogg 1989: 179). The post-war baby boom saw the population of the US grow by almost 30 million in the 1950s (Chafe 1995: 123). Perhaps most telling, though, was the claim that 'fewer than one American in ten believed that an unmarried person could be happy' (Mintz and Kellogg 1989: 180).

The baby boom was matched by economic growth. Gross national product soared 250 per cent between 1945 and 1960 (Chafe 1995: 112) and national income rose by 60 per cent; even more significant was the increase in disposable income, from $160 million to $350 million (Baughman 1997: 42–3).

As Chafe notes, 'consumerism represented one of the primary consequences – as well as one of the essential ingredients – of this prosperity. The initial quest for appliances, automobiles, and new furniture after the war expanded quickly into the mass consumption of services, goods, and recreational materials during the 1950s' (1995: 119). The country had far exceeded its aim of returning to 'normal' as quickly as possible.

This sense of excess overflowed into the era's tastes and style. During the 'Populuxe' decade, as Thomas Hine describes it, 'the objects people could buy took on a special, exaggerated quality. They celebrated confidence in the future, the excitement of the present, the sheer joy of having so much' (1987: 4). This style was epitomised by automobile design: massive cars with chrome bumpers, tail fins and extravagant petrol consumption. The popular icons of the era display a similar, exaggerated quality – described by James Wolcott as 'Hollywood-billboard images in the toothpaste reign of Rock Hudson and Doris Day' (1997: 50). This association of Hudson and Day with toothpaste is revealing. The couple are not only characterised as an idealised, larger-than-life, constantly smiling image, but are also linked directly with consumerism. A similar (though less flattering) effect is given in a contemporary review of *Pillow Talk*: 'when these two magnificent objects [Hudson and Day] go into a clinch [. . .] they look less like creatures of flesh and blood than a couple of 1960 Cadillacs that just happen to be parked in a suggestive position' (*Time*, 19 October 1959). The iconic imagery of the fifties is inextricably bound up with consumerism, size and surface. These icons may seem two-dimensional and ideologically transparent, but closer examination of the stereotypes they embody reveals hidden depths. The figures of the bachelor playboy and the virgin reflect many of the era's deepest anxieties about sexuality and gender.

American masculinity was considered to be in crisis during the post-war period (see Dubbert 1979: 140–69). After the disruptions of the war, it was assumed that 'normal' gender roles would be restored by demobilisation. The feminine mystique returned women to the kitchen and 'domestic bliss', but men found that the nature of the workplace was changing irrevocably. The economic boom, combined with rapid developments in technology, led to the emergence of corporate capitalism. In 1956, the American economy 'crossed the line from an industrial to a "post-industrial" state, with white-collar workers outnumbering blue-collar workers for the first time' (Chafe 1995: 114). Normative masculinity was unequivocally identified with this white-collar, middle-class, suburban breadwinner: the responsible WASP in the Gray Flannel Suit. As Steve Cohan has argued, this identification 'ended up relocating masculinity in what had previously been considered a "feminine" sphere, primarily by valuing a man's domesticity (and consumption) over his work (and production) as the means through which he fulfilled societal expectations of what it took to be "manly"' (1997: xii). Herein lies the source of the tension surrounding masculinity in the fifties: while society defined masculinity in terms of 'maturity' and responsibility, this very definition robbed men of their 'masculine' independence and individuality. The gray flannel breadwinner was left feeling that something was wrong: 'the only word he had to describe the problem was one which, unfortunately, described everything and explained nothing. The word was "conformity," and in the fifties "conformity" became the code word for male discontent' (Ehrenreich 1983: 30).

These discontented men 'Put the blame on Mame'. According to a *Playboy* article by Burt Zollo, 'all woman wants is security. And she's perfectly willing to crush man's adventurous, freedom-loving spirit to get it' (quoted by Ehrenreich 1983: 47). Zollo was not alone in his sentiments: 'a whole possefull of angry male writers took out after the American woman; if it wasn't the corporation that had emasculated American men, it must have been her' (Ehrenreich 1983: 37). For example, in 1958, *Look* magazine published a series of articles by Robert J. Moskin on 'The decline of the American male', including one entitled 'The American male: Why do women dominate him?' An important part of this 'domination' was women's supposed economic power. According to Moskin, *Fortune* magazine had 'credited women with making sixty percent of all consumer purchases and a Gallup poll showed that wives participated in managing seventy-one percent of the funds of American households' (quoted by Dubbert 1979: 255). At the same time, rates of female employment continued to rise, including wives and mothers; although these jobs tended to be part-time, 'the expansion of women's economic roles represented, in many cases, the indispensable prerequisite to families achieving middle-class status' (Chafe 1995: 127).

As *The Tender Trap* sequence indicates, the relationship between women's investment in consumption and men's domestic entrapment is worth further consideration. Friedan critiqued society's 'dream image' of the American housewife who had supposedly 'found true feminine fulfillment. As a housewife and mother, she was respected as a full and equal partner to man in his world. She was free to choose automobiles, clothes, appliances, supermarkets; she had everything that women ever dreamed of' (1964: 13). Friedan's ironic connection between fulfilment and shopping is far from coincidental; the feminine mystique depended upon women believing that domesticity could satisfy their every feminine desire. According to Bailey, 'a husband was necessary, the base of the pyramid on which she [the wife] would pile washer–dryers and refrigerator–freezers and sterling and fine china. [. . .] In this vision the man is not only an interchangeable commodity, he is ultimately less important than the other commodities he makes possible' (1989: 75). As Maggie Putnam (Debbie Reynolds) informs Joe Fitzpatrick (Glenn Ford) in *It Started with a Kiss*, 'Falling in love is no reason to get married [. . .]. If you were a girl, you'd be looking for a beautiful set of things to marry, and you really wouldn't care *what* kind of man went with them.'

Men may have felt that marriage was emasculating, but resisting marriage was considered even worse. As far as Lundberg and Farnham were concerned, 'bachelors of more than thirty, unless physically deficient, should be encouraged to undergo psychotherapy' (1947: 370). Such bachelors were seen as failing to accept their 'natural', mature responsibilities, with severe psychological consequences: 'in the schema of male pathology developed by mid-century psychologists, immaturity shaded into infantilism, which was, in turn, a manifestation of unnatural fixation on the mother, and the entire complex of symptomatology reached its clinical climax in the diagnosis of homosexuality' (Ehrenreich 1983: 20).[1] Kinsey's report on *Sexual Behavior in the Human Male* (1948) shocked many with its claims that over one-third of the men interviewed had had a post-adolescent homosexual experience, and one out of eight were predominantly homosexual for at least a three-year period (D'Emilio and Freedman 1997: 291–2). 'Unhealthy' sexuality and social deviance were certainly major concerns in the fifties, coinciding with the discourses of conformity, popular Freudianism and the Cold War.[2] Neurotic rebels like James Dean and Montgomery Clift personified fifties' angst about immature masculine sexuality (see Cohan 1997: 201–63). And if Jerry Lewis was the excessive expression of the infantilised American male, then the threat of matriarchal dominance – momism gone mad – reached its apotheosis in *Psycho* (1960). Three years before *Psycho* was released, *Movie and TV Spotlight* (27 May 1957) ran the headline 'Is Tony Perkins a Mama's boy?' alongside one declaring 'How Rock Hudson dodges dangerous dames' (reprinted in Klinger 1994: 116). As this begins to suggest, even the status of the bachelor playboy was questionable. Given the low average marriage age, popular wisdom dictated that 'if a man held out much longer [than twenty-three], say even to twenty-seven, "you had to wonder"' (Ehrenreich 1983: 14–15). For example, according to a 1955 *Life* magazine article, 'fans are urging 29-year-old Hudson . . . to get married – or explain why not' (quoted by Cohan 1997: 297). It is worth noting that most of the bachelor playboys in sex comedies are considerably older than this (Charlie Reader admits to being thirty-five).

Remaining single was considered deviant because it was 'irresponsible' and 'immature', but marriage was emasculating. No wonder, then, that the American man was confused. In some ways, the emergence of publications such as *Playboy* served to reassert traditional masculinity: powerful, virile and undomesticated. At the same time, it held a compensatory potential as an over-determined assertion of heterosexuality in a culture that viewed unmarried men with suspicion. However, while *Playboy* proclaimed the bachelor's (hetero)sexual freedom, this often took the form of lifestyle articles showcasing apartments, suitable decor, modern conveniences (including remote controls) and clothing: 'as represented every month in *Playboy* [. . .] the bachelor pad was not a den of iniquity but a site of consumerism' (Cohan 1997: 266). The magazine even included recipes and explanations on how to use a chafing dish. As Hugh Hefner himself put it, in the first *Playboy*, 'We enjoy mixing up cocktails and an *hors d'oeuvre* or two, putting a little mood music on the phonograph and inviting in a female acquaintance for a quiet discussion on Picasso, Nietzsche, jazz, sex' (quoted by Cohan 1997: 271). In other words, the playboy bachelor was highly civilised, preferring indoor pursuits to the more rough and tumble masculine traditions of the great outdoors. There is a fine line, then, between the 'virile' bachelor and the effeminate 'type that likes to collect cooking recipes', as Brad Allen (Rock Hudson) puts it, in *Pillow Talk*. Indeed, 'it has been argued that the playboy lack[ed] personal commitment as an aspect of mature manhood. [. . .] Others saw the playboy of the sixties as only half a man because of his devotion foremost to appearance' (Dubbert 1979: 269). Ultimately, it was the end that justified the somewhat effeminate means; the decisive proof of masculinity was the consummating heterosexual act itself.

The bachelor's need to demonstrate his heterosexuality begins to elucidate the era's 'mammary madness', but there are other factors to consider. Sikov expresses the phenomenon in a nutshell: 'they were big, they were comical, they required euphemisms, and they were simultaneously objects of desire and threat' (1994: 34). As *The Girl Can't Help It* (1956) comically demonstrates, men could be turned into gibbering wrecks by the appearance of a big-bosomed girl like Jayne Mansfield. Men gaze at Jerri Jordan (Mansfield) as she walks down the street, but the power of this gaze is reflected back at them, as if she were Medusa. An iceman stands frozen to the spot as his overheating body melts the block of ice he was about to pick up; the milkman's bottle spurts forth milk; and a third man's glasses shatter when he gazes at her legs ascending the stairs. Given this immediate visual power, it is hardly surprising that such women had to be 'dumbed down' into dimwitted blondes. The Populuxe surface of the dumb blonde works on conflicting levels, then, not only as a slightly ridiculous sexual object, but also as the excessive representation of female sexual potency. There is one other aspect of mammary madness which needs consideration: the economic function of big breasts. Bailey notes that 'big breasts, in the popular conception, signaled that a woman was "expensive." [. . .] By dating women with big bosoms, men showed that they could afford the expense, could command such abundance' (1989: 73–4). Once again, sex and consumption are inextricably linked, this time through the economy of dating.

Bailey has discussed this economy in detail and some of her conclusions bear repeating here. First and foremost, the emergence of dating meant that courtship was largely 'construed and understood in models and metaphors of modern industrial capitalism' (1989: 5). Because dates took place in the public sphere of consumption, money became an issue, shifting the balance of power from whether the girl was willing to receive a caller, to how much the boy was willing to pay for the girl. The acceptability of Dutch dates (splitting the costs) dropped dramatically during the 1950s (Bailey 1989: 111). It was 'unmanly' for the boy to be seen to let the girl pay; at the same time, the girl expected her 'worth' to be reflected in the boy's expenditure. The corsage encapsulates the dating system's emphasis on competing through conspicuous consumption: 'almost every description of a "big date," from the 1920s through the 1950s, features the kind of corsage the girl or woman wears, and sample budgets for major dates allot anywhere from $2 to $10 for corsages. These flowers were not private gifts [. . .] but public symbols. They said, for the man, "See what I can afford," and for the woman, "See how much I'm worth" (1989: 65). In this way, the dating system becomes intimately tied to public display. As Mead observed, 'the boy who longs for a date is not longing for a girl. He is longing to be in a situation mainly public, where he will be seen by others to have a girl, and the right kind of girl, who dresses well and pays attention' (1971: 263). This kind of date is in itself a commodity, a status symbol to flaunt. More importantly, the woman also becomes a commodity: 'like his car and hi-fi, the playboy's women are status possessions, generally, depersonalized objects of pleasure to show off to other males' (Dubbert 1979: 269). As Bailey notes, this 'equation of women and cars was common in mid-century American culture. Both were property, both expensive; cars and women came in different styles or models, and both could be judged on performance' (1989: 70). This equation is directly acknowledged in *It Started with a Kiss*. When Joe asks, 'Speaking of possessions, how would you like to possess mine?', Antonio Soriano (Gustavo Rojo) mistakenly thinks Joe is offering him his wife, rather than his red Lincoln Futura.

Given the economic basis of heterosexual romance, it is hardly surprising that dating also led to male expectations of 'getting their money's worth' in sexual favours from their date. Against this expectation, the moral impetus against premarital sex was placed firmly in the hands of the woman: it was only 'natural' that a man would seduce women, but women had to protect their values – in both senses of the word. 'If a woman maintained her virtue (making sex a scarce commodity) her value to men would rise, and she would realize a long-term gain greatly exceeding her "cheap" sisters' one-time bonanza' (Bailey 1989: 94). The economic value of virginity was expressly acknowledged by contemporary advice columnists, and one 1948 advice book 'put it bluntly: sex was "something a man should pay for." The author's suggested selling price was, of course, a high one: marriage' (Bailey 1989: 95). This explicit connection between the laws of supply and demand and female worth in the sexual exchange meant that (the appearance of) virginity was the best way for a young woman to maintain her social and economic value.

As this contextual overview demonstrates, even those cultural icons which seem most stereotypical reveal profound contradictions and tensions on closer examination. While society demanded that women fulfilled their traditional domestic role, they were simultaneously criticised for 'enslaving' the male in marriage. The mature man had to be supportive and responsible, but the suburban breadwinner had become emasculated and trapped. The dumb blonde wielded a paralysing power over men, which they seemed to enjoy in a masochistic desire for domination. The bachelor had to demonstrate his 'masculinity' by co-ordinating his environment to assert his heterosexual prowess. Women were expected to remain virgins until marriage, but the virgin was also a rarity to be prized above all other women. As Chafe argues, 'the effort to reinforce traditional norms seemed almost frantic, as though in reality something very different was taking place' (1995: 125). In a similar vein, Sikov suggests a reason for America's obsession with popular Freudianism: 'psychoanalysis clearly distinguishes between two perceptual levels: the calm facade of everyday life is not only accompanied by *but actively opposed by* its darker underpinnings, the revelation of which was evidently gratifying in the postwar era' (1994: 22, emphasis in original). The Populuxe surfaces of the culture of consumption mask a severe identity crisis.

Professional virgins

It is important to emphasise the extraordinary status of the heroine in the sex comedy. Most critics have recognised female virginity as the cycle's thematic core, but very few have engaged with the economic and cultural dimensions. These films repeatedly acknowledge the sexual commodification of women. *The Moon Is Blue* sets the tone: Patty O'Neill (Maggie McNamara) asks Don Gresham (William Holden) what Cynthia Slater (Dawn Addams) meant by calling her a 'professional virgin'.

> DON: 'It's not necessary to advertise it' – that's really all the phrase means.
> PATTY: What's wrong with advertising?
> DON: [*enunciating clearly, because exasperated*] People who advertise are anxious to sell something.
> PATTY: Oh. Oh, I see, I see what you mean. Maybe I do yap about it too much.

While few sex comedies are this explicit in drawing attention to the heroine's virginity, most do single her out as 'different' from other women. For example, in *That Touch of Mink*, Philip Shayne (Cary Grant) tells Cathy Timberlake (Doris Day), 'You have rare qualities. You're direct, sincere, uncomplicated.' This kind of frankness and honesty typically connotes the heroine's 'virginity' (which may or not be literal) and her exceptional status is often accentuated by her unusual perspective on life (*The Moon Is Blue*, *The Tender Trap*, *Ask Any Girl*, *Sunday in New York*). It is her rareness which sets her apart not only as someone to love, but also to marry.

Female sexuality is explicitly linked to consumerism in *Ask Any Girl*. References are made to 'you-know-whats' (prostitutes) and Meg Wheeler (Shirley MacLaine) herself is accidentally arrested for such 'moral turpitude'. The film goes further, recognising marriage as an economic transaction. When one of Meg's best friends, Jeannie Boyden (Elizabeth Fraser), announces she is going to marry an old beau – Alvin the Square – Meg and her other friend, Terri Richards (Dody Heath), are shocked and ask why. Jeannie explains, 'I know he's no bargain, but who am I to complain? [. . .]. I used to think it was us girls who did all the shopping around. We're just pieces of merchandise on a shelf. The men come in, take a look – if we have something they want, they take us home. All I know is, I was getting pretty scared of staying on that shelf.' Throughout the sequence, the shelf metaphor is visually reinforced by the spatial blocking: facing the camera, the three women are lined up at a diner counter with Jeannie flanked by Meg and Terri. In the very next scene, Meg asks her boss, Miles Doughton (David Niven), for help: 'I would like to sell myself [. . .] – as a wife.' Meg's potential customer is Miles's brother, Evan (Gig Young). The brothers own a market research agency and Miles has already boasted that he can sell anything through 'motivation research' using 'scientific methods aimed at the subconscious'. In other words, by researching what Evan finds attractive in other women, Miles will market Meg as the ideal product to satisfy Evan's desires.

This concept of motivation research was extremely popular in the advertising industry during the fifties. As Vance Packard observed in *The Hidden Persuaders*, 'the use of mass psychoanalysis to guide campaigns of persuasion has become the basis of a multi-million dollar industry' (1957: 3). According to Packard, the 'high apostle' of such image-building was Pierre Martineau, who 'analyzed the problem with startling candor in talking to Philadelphia advertising men in early 1956. [. . .] "Basically, what you are trying to do," he advised, "is create an illogical situation. You want the customer to *fall in love* with your product and have a profound brand loyalty when actually content may be very similar to hundreds of competing brands"' (Packard 1957: 47, my emphasis). In effect, this brand loyalty was attached to the product's image, not its content. Certainly, this is the process involved in making Evan fall in love with 'any-girl' Meg; Miles decides to 'start not with the product, but with the outer wrapping'. The first stage of attack involves changing Meg's perfume, clothes, jewellery and make-up, but Miles's 'field research' (dating all Evan's girlfriends himself) eventually leads to more intimate marketing, including dancing style and seduction techniques. It is only when Miles attempts to teach Meg how Evan likes to be kissed that he advises her, 'Try not to improve [. . .] on a good thing.'

Although not necessarily as explicit as *Ask Any Girl*, marketing an empty image is integral to a number of sex comedies. For example, in *The Girl Can't Help It*, Tom Miller (Tom Ewell) is hired to market Jerri (whose real name is Georgie) as a singing star, even though she cannot sing; Jerri's magnificent surface is all that is required to make her a star. Her sexual image is belied by her own desire: 'I just want to be a wife, have kids – but everyone figures me for a sexpot. No one thinks I'm *equipped* for motherhood!' The irony embedded in this line is simultaneously blatant and complex. In one sense, Jerri/Mansfield's mammary glands mean she is very well equipped for motherhood; in another, the 'natural' function of her breasts has been superseded by their excessive size, causing a disjunction between the female body and the Populuxe image of female sexuality. From any other star, the desire to be a wife and mother might seem reactionary, but from the extremely artificial Mansfield it exposes the constraints of image and ideology.

The gap between artifice and identity is more directly exposed in *Lover Come Back*. The film's plot hinges on Jerry Webster's (Rock Hudson) invention of a non-existent product called Vip, in order to placate one of his girlfriends, Rebel Davis (Edie Adams). He even goes so far as to have five commercials made starring Rebel as the 'Vip girl'. In the first advert (a beach set), Rebel disrobes to reveal the gold lamé swimsuit beneath her wrap and announces, 'Everything I've got, I owe to Vip' – the 'everything' pointedly referring to her voluptuous figure. In each of the successive commercials (shown without interruption), she continues to wear the swimsuit, but in combination with a variety of sets and props designed to add another facet to the benefits Vip will bring the consumer. Chained to a golden bedstead, she declares, 'I'm just a slave to any man who uses Vip!' Lying on a *chaise-longue*, with a fur coat behind her shoulders and dangling jewellery from her hand, she murmurs, 'Mmm, good things have been happening to me since I started using Vip.' Still in the swimsuit, but wearing a bridal veil and clutching a bouquet, she announces, 'I got my man, when I got Vip'. Finally, she is shown holding a baby and standing next to a cradle: 'Oh yes, folks. *Everything* I got [*looking down at the baby and then back to camera*] I owe to Vip!' Using sex to sell a product is, of course, a standard marketing ploy, but here the standard is taken to extremes, with each successive advert promising ever more ludicrous consequences. (The irony is that Vip finally does give Carol everything the commercials promised: sex, marriage and pregnancy – as well as 25 per cent of the American liquor industry's advertising.) In the adverts, Rebel's sex appeal stands in for the product, but 'Vip' also functions as a euphemism for her sex appeal. The product is sold to men and women, promising to satisfy a number of 'normal' desires – sex, wealth, marriage and children – but without any indication of what the product actually is. Content is nothing, image is all.

This same interest in seductive surfaces informs the romance strand of the narrative. It is only after forty minutes of screen time that Jerry and Carol Templeton (Doris Day) actually meet, but they have already established an antagonistic relationship through their business rivalry. Both work for advertising agencies, but while Carol depends on hard work and business research, Jerry plies clients with alcohol and girls. Having lost out on a major account, Carol is determined to win the Vip account and tracks down the scientist she believes invented it; in fact, Dr Linus Tyler (Jack Kruschen) has been hired by Jerry to invent a product to fit the commercials. Jerry masquerades as Dr Tyler, pretending to be naïve, innocent, and easily led. He uses this persona to manoeuvre Carol into doing things she would not normally do, initially to get the Vip account (going to a strip club) and then because she loves him (teaching him how to kiss). He sells her an image, but instead of the Populuxe surface of the Vip adverts, he utilises an outmoded sense of naturalness and 'authenticity' (from a beard and second-hand suit, to innocence and awkwardness). The paradox of this artificial authenticity is epitomised by the seduction scene. Jerry/Linus tells Carol that he can never marry, knowing that this will pique her curiosity. His reason is sexual insecurity: 'I'm afraid, afraid I'll be a failure.' He even uses 'Jerry Webster' as a point of comparison, because 'He's a *real* man. [. . .] Do you know what Jerry Webster would do? In two minutes he'd manoeuvre you into that bedroom!' (the bright-red door to the bedroom is framed between them as he speaks). Exactly two minutes later (emphasised by cutaways to a clock), Jerry/Linus has succeeded in this manoeuvre: he is lying face down on the bed, in the dark, with Carol perched next to him. By feigning such unmanly traits as insecurity and virginity, Jerry convinces Carol to sleep with him. As Carol wavers on the point of 'Surrender' (the song she sings to herself as she battles with her conscience), the telephone rings. It is her boss (Howard St John), ringing to inform her that she is fired because the man in her apartment is *not* Dr Linus Tyler.

Miscommunication

Considering the cycle's satirical interest in consumer image, it is unsurprising that there should be a repeated discrepancy between appearance and truth.

This has consequences for the representation of the couple, since the cycle's thematic interest in miscommunication means they rarely manage to have a conversation that does not operate at cross-purposes. The 'virgin' will often inadvertently make suggestive comments and misunderstand the bachelor's intentions (not least because he will often be deliberately misleading her). For example, in *That Touch of Mink*, when Philip tells Cathy he will have a sunken bath tub in his new apartment, Cathy replies, 'Oh, I love taking sunken baths – you'll always find me in it.' Only moments later, she mistakes his invitation to go around the world and live in the apartment upon their return as a proposal of marriage. The disjunction between their expectations is the cause of confusion: while good girl Cathy assumes living in his apartment involves marriage, playboy Philip assumes a jet-set lifestyle is emblematic of freedom. Cathy's mistake is perfectly understandable since it is governed by social convention, but within the context of the film this convention is made to seem foolish; it is implausible that the aloof Philip would ask her to marry him, since they only met that morning.

Similar miscommunications occur in *All in a Night's Work* (1961). Through a series of coincidences, Tony Ryder (Dean Martin) has come to believe that Katie Robbins (Shirley MacLaine) was with his uncle the night he died in a hotel bed, and that she is trying to extort money in return for keeping quiet. Katie, on the other hand, thinks Tony has been meeting with her purely to discuss trade-union business. The disjunctions between their expectations and understanding is repeatedly made clear to the audience as a series of events are 'misread' by a variety of different people. When Katie bursts into uncontrollable tears at Colonel Ryder's funeral, Tony and the company board read this as 'proof' that she was the woman in the hotel room; however, the previous scene established to the audience that Katie always cries at events like this (she even cried at a hockey match). When she comes to apologise for her outburst, Tony thinks she has come to extract a pay-off. Consequently, their conversation operates at cross-purposes. He suggests she was 'dazzled' by his uncle, but she queries the word:

> TONY: Or shall we say 'impressed'?
> KATIE: Well, that is a better word, I guess. But, you see, the real trouble, Mr Ryder – Sir – is that I'm . . . I'm too sentimental.
> TONY: 'Sentimental'? Oh, I'm sure *you* could think of a better word.
> KATIE: Oh. Well how about 'emotional'? That's what I am, that's it – I'm overemotional.

They may both be speaking English, but they are certainly not 'learning to speak the same language'. The ambiguities of the replacement words allow the conversation to continue without either party realising that they are talking about different things. The words become loaded with innuendo, as if 'sentimental' and 'emotional' are euphemisms for something unrespectable such as gold-digging. More importantly, Katie's words are not accepted by Tony at face value: we recognise her sincerity (her 'innocence' and 'virginity') but he does not; he cannot tell a 'good girl' from a 'bad girl'.

The couple's miscommunication occurs not only at the level of verbal misunderstandings, therefore, but also at the level of visual signifiers. For example, Katie is sent a mink coat by a lecherous old man whom she saved from drowning. She tries to return it to the store, but finds it difficult to explain why she cannot keep it: 'I haven't done anything to earn it. Oh! er, oh . . . I mean, all I did was take him up to his room and put him to – oh!' The manager assumes she wants the money instead (assuming the type of girl who is sent a mink coat will inevitably be a gold-digger). Eventually, she insists on paying for it herself in ten-dollar instalments, even if it will take forty-five years. Her honourable intentions are not only misconstrued by the shop assistants and customers, but also by Tony's chauffeur, O'Hara (Ian Wolfe); watching through the shop window, he completely misreads the visual signifiers. All he sees is Katie buying a mink coat: 'She paid cash for it! Must have been thousand dollar bills.' When Tony queries how she could afford it on her salary, O'Hara replies, 'Overtime.' The insinuation (reinforced by the film's title) is that she has earned it through 'night work'.

In this respect, sex comedies embody anxiety around female sexual experience: 'Does she or doesn't she?', as the question is posed in *Sex and the Single Girl*. *All in a Night's Work*, *Ask Any Girl* and *That Touch of Mink* all touch on issues around sexual harassment and the fragility of respectability for women. For example, in *That Touch of Mink*, when Cathy breaks out in a rash in Bermuda, her anxiety is not just about her 'fear' of sex; it is also about becoming a different kind of person altogether – a kept woman. To become involved with Philip is to commit herself to an 'unrespectable' illicit relationship (hence her hallucinations in which she imagines everyone 'knows', causing a lilo, a carriage and the elevator to transform into the four-poster bed from their room). The seductive powers of this kind of life are again encapsulated in a mink coat, the ultimate object of feminine consumer desire in fifties' America. The scene in which Cathy succumbs to this desire is fascinating, since it incorporates the spectacle of *haute couture* fashion, as various models parade for her benefit. First, we see her watching from the shadows at the edge of the frame (aligning the female spectator with her position as consumer) and then the scene intercuts medium close-up reaction shots. As the parade continues, her reactions become ever more ecstatic: her eyes widen, her mouth is parted, gasping in delight, she sits up straighter as if the experience is lifting her physically 'higher' – reaching an orgasmic climax when the mink coat is displayed. There are even tears of happiness in her eyes.

These mink coats operate as complex signs, therefore, loaded not only with connotations of luxury, wealth and extravagance, but also symbolic associations with female sexuality: fur as tactile, sensual, something to be 'stroked' (not to mention indirect associations with female genitalia, as suggested by such slang terms as 'pussy' and 'beaver'). It is striking too that the 'queering' of Roger (Gig Young) in *That Touch of Mink* and Jerry in *Lover Come Back* includes the idea of them wearing mink coats. Part of the spectacle of Cathy's mink coat is achieved by having interchangeable overcoats of black, emerald, scarlet and cream, with the fur lining the coat. Cathy is seen wearing the cream version, hugging the coat to herself: the colour paradoxically suggests both her innocence and her potential fall, since it is off-white; keeping the fur on the 'inside' suggests a kind of discreet sexual modesty (not frigidity). The coat also maintains a level of ambiguity – 'Is she or isn't she?' – especially in contrast to the more obvious flaunting of fur by the other woman (Laurie Mitchell) in the elevator in Bermuda. Significantly, when Cathy breaks out in a rash, she is shown using her now uncovered mink as a blanket. In a sense, she has been paid for, too, but the rash is a somatic expression of her resistance to being commodified and her inability to become that other kind of woman.

Consuming passion

Colin Campbell argues that most theories of consumerism fail to address the integral phenomenon of modern consumption: 'the mystery [. . .] concerns the very essence of modern consumption itself – its character as an activity which involves an *apparently endless pursuit of wants*; the most characteristic feature of modern consumption being this insatiability [. . .] which arises out of a basic inexhaustibility of wants themselves' (1990: 37, my emphasis). This proves immediately suggestive in relation to the Vip adverts (with each one promising a different form of satisfaction), but also to the representation of the insatiable desires of the bachelor. The playboy has an endless stream of girlfriends on tap, each with her own appeal: for example, *The Tender Trap* opens with Charlie kissing a honey blonde; minutes later a Southern brunette arrives, eager to clean his apartment; then a serious red-head comes to walk his dog; but he goes out for the evening with a sophisticated platinum blonde.

As Bruce Babington and Peter William Evans point out, the fifties were 'overridingly the age of almost instant everything, of innumerable domestic gadgets and devices to save time and labour and allow more human energy to be channelled into expanding leisure time' (1989: 202). The playboy's bachelor pad is often fitted with such gadgets, notably Tony's clocks/dimmer switches in *All in a Night's Work* and Brad's remote-controlled sofa-bed in *Pillow Talk*. The connection between 'instant' consumerism and desire is made explicit in *Teacher's Pet*, when Peggy (Mamie Van Doren) bumps and grinds her way through the song 'The girl who invented rock'n'roll':

> Now, you've heard of instant coffee,
> You've heard of instant tea –
> See hear, you guys,
> Just feast your eyes
> On little ol' instant me!

While these sentiments construct the woman as the object to be consumed, the sex comedy does not exclusively gender this relationship as male consumer, female object. For example, in *Pillow Talk*, when Brad asks the telephone inspector, Miss Dickenson (Karen Norris), what she would like to inspect, she replies (virtually salivating), '*You!*'. Brad masquerades as 'Rex Stetson' in order to seduce Jan Morrow (Doris Day). Rex is very definitely presented as an object of desire, but he is also explicitly one to be consumed, as Jan's cleaner, Alma (Thelma Ritter) acknowledges:

> ALMA: Takes only one sip of wine to tell if it's a good bottle.
> JAN: [*smiling knowingly*] This is a good bottle.
> ALMA: Well, what're you waitin' for? Drink up!

Indeed, in the age of 'beefcake' (images of muscular men, like Hudson, stripped to the waist), the question of female desire is explicitly redirected in fifties' culture to include *active* physical (and implicitly sexual) attraction.

The visible effect of male physical beauty on women even became part of Cary Grant's star persona; throughout the fifties, he 'continued to attract the gaze of the female spectator, on screen as well as in the audience, often making her and not him the sexual aggressor' (Cohan 1997: 30). For example, when Roger Thornhill (Grant) tries to sneak through a hospital room in *North by Northwest* (1958), the female patient demands that he stops twice, the second time (after she has put on her glasses) with a lustful sigh in her voice. Grant has a similar effect on Day in *That Touch of Mink*: Cathy's anger and self-possession dissipate completely upon first sight of Philip (her reaction emphasised by a medium close-up of her misty-eyed, glowing face). In both *Pillow Talk* and *Lover Come Back*, the playboy's creation of an *alter ego* is expressly designed to gratify the heroine's idealised desires. Thus, the male masquerade is not only about disrupting masculine identity, but also about becoming an object of female desire (as amply demonstrated by Tony Curtis's Cary Grant impression in *Some Like It Hot*).

Beefcake and breadwinners

The objectification of the male body has serious repercussions for the status of masculinity, since the erotic gaze has traditionally been privileged as male (see Dyer 1982; Neale 1992b; Cohan 1993). The anxiety is two-fold: that the woman's gaze will subordinate (and feminise) the male object; and that the male gaze will remain erotic. The sex comedy repeatedly emphasises the physical spectacle of the male body – even Frank Sinatra gets his chest out in *The Tender Trap* – but the male body is also the site of anxiety about visible difference. Chapter 7 will consider some of these issues in relation to Rock Hudson, but first there is a more general tendency which needs to be explored. A number of sex comedies contrast a puny male body with a hypermasculine body. In some cases, it is the hero/playboy who has the hypermasculine body, while the sidekick or other man is presented as physically weaker, as well as neurotic. In films such as *The Seven Year Itch*, *Will Success Spoil Rock Hunter?* and *I Married a Woman*, however, it is the puny body of the hero which is contrasted with a 'he-man' figure. This splitting of different types of masculinity – the corporate breadwinner and the playboy or male object of desire – might seem to suggest a dichotomy between 'acceptable' and 'unacceptable' masculinity, but in fact neither version proves adequate. Instead, this splitting registers as recognition of conflicting social expectations about what makes a 'real' man.

The Seven Year Itch plays out this conflict in detail, not only through the external contrasts between Richard Sherman (Tommy Ewell) and Tom MacKenzie (Sonny Tufts), but also through the internal conflict of Richard's fantasy life. Richard is torn between fulfilling two sets of social expectations: the 'feminine' expectations (voiced through his wife) that he will be a good breadwinner by working hard, eating well and avoiding alcohol and cigarettes; and the 'masculine' expectations of freedom (represented through the desire to chase girls, drink and smoke). At first glance, it may seem that the film is offering a Freudian explanation for this split, between the social instincts of the superego and the 'natural' instincts of the id, because Richard is reading a manuscript entitled *Of Man and the Unconscious*, and specifically a chapter on 'The repressed urge in the middle-aged male: Its roots and its consequences'. However, Richard's overactive imagination is quickly established, and, in this sense, reading the manuscript is simply a stimulus for his fantasies, not an explanation. For example, Richard soliloquises about how he has never cheated on his wife, but certainly could have; as he says this, he hears a woman's laugh, and imagines his wife, Helen (Evelyn Keyes) is sitting nearby, laughing at the idea that women find him attractive. He tries to convince her (and himself) by imagining a series of encounters with women who threw themselves at him; in each case, he resisted their advances. The paradox here is clear: if these fantasies are the return of Richard's 'repressed urges' then his urge is 'unmanly' chastity. The third of these encounters is particularly relevant, since it parodies the famous beach scene in *From Here to Eternity* (1953). The original scene stars Burt Lancaster – the epitome of fifties' beefcake – in figure-hugging swimming trunks, embracing Deborah Kerr as the surf pounds over them; the embrace is adulterous because Kerr's character is married. In *The Seven Year Itch* version, Helen's best friend, Elaine (Roxanne), embraces Richard as he lies on the beach; he is wearing an old-fashioned swimming costume that covers his chest, and he breaks away from her to stumble weakly down the beach. Where Lancaster was strong and dominating, Richard is weak and dominated.

Richard's fantasies become focused on The Girl (Marilyn Monroe). The fact that The Girl has no name indicates her symbolic function, but it also suggests the ways in which women are routinely objectified by men. What is particularly interesting is the discrepancy between Richard's fantasy and what actually takes place when The Girl comes for a drink. In the fantasy, the grandeur of Rachmaninoff's Second Piano Concerto is matched by Richard's suave dressing gown and cravat, distinguished greying hair and phoney English accent – but The Girl is transformed, too, from dumb blonde to *femme fatale*. She is wearing a tiger-print sheath dress with black gloves and her hair is in sleek kiss-curls; she is smoking a cheroot and her voice is lower and more alluring. Richard's fantasy of seduction is overblown, but it is completely undercut by reality. While the fantasy girl recognised Rachmaninoff and was immediately affected by it ('It shakes me! It quakes me! It makes me feel goose-pimply all over!'), The Girl realises, 'This is what they call classical music, isn't it?' In the fantasy, Richard plays the concerto himself; in reality he plays chopsticks – but *this* gives The Girl goosebumps. Repeating his fantasy, Richard stops playing to kiss her, but her shocked reaction knocks them both off the piano-stool instead. The gap between the seductive fantasy of male potency and the awkward reality of chopsticks satirises populist Freudian explanations of 'natural' masculine instincts. The discourses of 'natural' urges can be just as repressive as the breadwinner ethic. At the same time, the film's plot involves the rejection of the Populuxe image of The Girl as idealised consumer object (she advertises Dazzledent toothpaste) and the recognition of her as an autonomous human being with her own opinions, including the ability to see through the vanity of the 'great big lunk in a striped vest' (as she describes the hypermasculine, Tom MacKenzie type of man).

The collapse of masculinity in the sex comedy also enables queer possibilities, particularly when the playboy takes centre stage and the figure of emasculation becomes the neurotic sidekick. The Dean Martin/Jerry Lewis star couple provide an influential model for this kind of relationship, particularly in the films directed by Frank Tashlin. For example, in *Artists and Models*

(1953), Rick Todd (Martin) wants to move out of the apartment (and bedroom) he shares with Eugene Fullstack (Lewis). While Eugene (wearing an apron) stands silently in the doorway, Rick packs a suitcase and declares that 'divorce is the only way out'; Rick cannot go through with it, though, and as he throws the clothes back on to the bed, the reverse shot of Eugene is finally shown, smiling through his tears. The sex comedy rarely treads as close to the edge as this, but the sidekick's relationship with the playboy is sometimes misconstrued by others, as in *That Touch of Mink*, when Dr Gruber (Alan Hewitt) mistakes Roger's hypothetical speech about Cathy's relationship with Philip, thinking instead that Roger has been invited to Bermuda by a 'forceful, dynamic' and very wealthy man.

That Touch of Mink raises another aspect of male anxiety: the playboy's resistance to marriage can prove just as 'uptight' as the virgin's resistance to premarital sex. The figure of the uptight virgin has more commonly informed criticism of the cycle but, by the standards of the era, the bachelor playboy is no less problematic. Krutnik asserts that when Cathy breaks out in a nervous rash in Bermuda it 'successfully "saves" the evening for her and "ruins" it for him [Philip]. The implication is that sexual pleasure is the exclusive province of the male and that women "put up" with being fucked solely in order to "trap" men into marriage' (1990: 60). Quite apart from the facts that Philip has expressly told Cathy he has no intention of marrying her and that Cathy is distraught at having 'failed' to be a real woman, Krutnik overlooks the recurrence of the rash after the couple are married. The scene is set up to imply that Cathy *is* still afraid of sex. Doctor Richardson (Jack Livesey) again emerges from the bedroom saying, 'Nothing serious, just another rash. Quite common on honeymoons.' However, the reverse shot reveals that he is speaking to Cathy. From behind the closed door, Philip apologises to her – 'It never happened before!' – but as Cathy points out, he has never been married before. The implications of impotence coincide with the bachelor's fear of marriage as emasculation. Philip's 'horrible thought' is significant in this respect: 'You break out when we're not married, and I break out when we are. We may never get together!' The inherent contradiction between their desires (and their neuroses) appears to render satisfaction of both (or either) impossible. Cathy's reaction is revealing, insisting, 'If *that's* what you think, you don't know the girls in Upper Sandusky!' To prove her point, the film immediately cuts to the consequences: their baby in its pram.

Satisfaction guaranteed?

The contradiction between male and female desires in the sex comedy exaggerates sexual difference to such an extent that it may seem the couple are wholly incompatible. However, these desires are shaped by cultural ideology. For example, in *The Tender Trap*, Julie is the feminine mystique personified: 'I mean, a career is just fine, but it's no substitute for marriage [. . .]. A woman isn't really a woman at all until she's been married and had children. And why? Because she's fulfilled.' However, as Charlie's best friend, Joe McCall (David Wayne), sarcastically points out, 'In order to be fulfilled you have to have a man, and it might be just possible that what fulfils you might not fulfil him.'

Before considering how these contradictory desires can be surmounted, the complex interaction between consumerism and desire needs to be formulated in more depth. Campbell points out that modern consumerism is associated with the consumption of luxury items (rather than necessities) and connotes both superfluity and sensuous, pleasurable experience. He argues that this emphasis on pleasurable experience – on the emotion, rather than the object – binds modern consumerism to modern hedonism. While traditional (medieval) hedonism was based upon (often excessive) sensation, modern hedonism (in a world where sensation can be gratified easily) relies upon sustaining the emotion of pleasure. In order for emotions 'to be employed to secure pleasure, it is necessary for individuals to attain that level of self-consciousness which permits the "willing suspension of disbelief"; disbelief robs symbols of their automatic power' (1990: 76). In other words, modern hedonism is dependent upon the 'skilful use of the faculty of imagination' (1990: 76) – upon the anticipation of gratification through an idealised object of desire. Most importantly, it is the *process* of hedonism (the imagining, the anticipation, and so on) that is pleasurable; 'the gap between wanting and getting never actually closes' (1990: 38) because even when the want is gratified, the reality is unlikely to match the perfect fantasy.[3] Campbell concludes that 'individuals do not so much seek satisfaction from products, as pleasure from the self-illusory experiences which they construct from their associated meanings' (1990: 89).

According to this model, consumer desire is based on self-gratification and self-illusion; the fantasy of the idealised object is, in part, about the power to control the meanings associated with the object through the 'willing suspension of disbelief'. By mapping consumer desire on to heterosexual romance and seduction, the sex comedy repeatedly signals the dehumanising tendencies of such self-centred structures of commodified desire. The bachelor treats women as novelty items for instant gratification, while the 'virgin' searches for the ideal home man. In both cases, consumerism is bonded with sexualised, hedonistic pleasure. However, by recognising the limitations of consumerism – its reliance on image and artifice – the sex comedy also suggests that the object of desire can never fulfil the subject's idealised expectations. Thus, the hero and heroine must reject their consumerist fantasies if they are to form a couple.

In most cases, this process is accomplished by distinguishing between seduction and love. While seduction is associated with consumerism, commodification and artifice, love is represented as a 'natural' reaction that overcomes the stated intentions of the playboy and the 'virgin', almost against their will. The power of love is symbolised through the kiss, which is often presented as having an excessive and 'magical' effect on both parties. The framing usually conforms with romantic conventions in terms of the man embracing and enfolding the woman (see Chapter 2), but the reaction shots include the man's face, giving a stronger sense of mutual pleasure.[4] For example, in *It Started with a Kiss*, Maggie may have claimed that she is looking for a beautiful set of things to marry and Joe has just described himself as a 'devout' bachelor, but the moment he kisses her, 'magical' glockenspiel music starts. The power of this kiss/music is so strong that it breaks the rules of diegetic realism: the music is clearly non-diegetic, and yet three men standing at the bar turn around as if they have heard it. They sense the erotic potency of the kiss and gaze in the direction of Maggie and Joe. As the couple break from kissing, Joe seems as overwhelmed as Maggie – but it is Maggie who initiates further kissing. Again the music starts, but this time a brief snatch of 'The Wedding March' is worked in. The scene dissolves (with magical mist) to a new location: the camera tracks past discarded stockings, clothes and shoes to the edge of a bed; a man's hand lies over a woman's. An alarm clock rings and the man moves his hand away, revealing a wedding ring on the woman's hand. The kiss is expressly sexual, therefore, but it is also potent enough to override Joe and Maggie's previous desires and assertions about marriage.

'Love' conquers all

The problem with heterosexual romance in the sex comedy is three-fold: there is an extreme disjunction between the culturally determined desires of the male and female ('instant' sex versus long-term commitment); this disjunction renders satisfaction of both impossible; and even when these original desires are fulfilled, there is no guarantee of satisfaction because new desires may have taken their place. For example, in *Lover Come Back*, Jerry and Carol's ostensible desires are satisfied simultaneously. They wake up in bed together after consuming too much Vip (the alcoholic candy invented by the real Dr Tyler). Although neither of them remember what happened, Jerry finds a marriage certificate. While Jerry is relieved by, and even happy about, this discovery (partly because he assumes it will placate Carol), Carol is horrified. Being 'had' by Jerry Webster is nothing compared to being married to him.

Carol refuses to have anything more to do with Jerry and he leaves for California. There seems to be no way to resolve this narrative happily, but then – without any explanation of time passing – the film abruptly cuts to Carol's secretary, Millie (Ann B. Davis) telephoning Jerry to inform him that he is about to become a father. Dashing to Carol's side, Jerry only manages to convince her to remarry him at the very last minute, the ceremony taking place as she is being wheeled into the delivery room (luckily he brought a judge with him). The film ends with an orderly commenting, 'Man! That's what I call cutting it close.' Paradoxically, the insinuations of premarital sex happen to be false, but as usual in the sex comedy it is appearances which are at stake. What is most striking is the bluntness of this resolution, which is motivated purely by Carol's pregnancy; their remarriage is determined by the need to legitimate the child, rather than the desire to form a couple. However, the style of this ending undercuts the conservative meaning of the narrative. By breaking the classical codes of temporal and spatial continuity (omitting any dissolve or intertitle to explain that nine months have passed) the film refuses to make this union credible. Indeed, although we have seen Carol kiss 'Linus', we never see her kiss Jerry. Their relationship remains passionless; it is only about reproduction. In this sense, the bluntness of the resolution exposes the extent to which heterosexuality and marriage are 'compulsory' (Rich 1986: 67), not only in romantic comedy, but also in fifties' society.

The conditions of the couple's formation have altered quite dramatically since screwball comedy, from mutual companionship to apparently irreconcilable difference. Needless to say, this makes the resolution of the sex comedy extremely difficult. What is entirely missing from most of these films is any sense of private conversation and 'learning to speak the same language'. The cycle's interest in miscommunication means that the couple's dialogue remains at cross-purposes and their misconceptions are frequently maintained until the last moment. In these cases, the only diegetic explanation for the couple's union is the magic of 'true' love – despite the fact their relationship has been based on deceit and false impressions. The couple's union is made plausible through generic verisimilitude; the couple must be united simply because this is romantic comedy. While this places great strain on the happy ending, within the logic of the sex comedy it can be seen as part of the cycle's interrogation of heterosexual romance, as closer analysis of *Pillow Talk* will reveal.

Notes

1 Such diagnosis has very little to do with sexual preferences. Hereafter, such references will be placed in inverted commas, to signify that I am referring to the

cultural construction of *any* deviance from the norm (including effeminacy or emasculation) as 'homosexual'.

2 The connections between McCarthyism and homophobia have been well documented. See Corber (1997), Klinger (1994: 112) and D'Emilio and Freedman (1997: 292–3).

3 Campbell's arguments bear obvious comparison to Freudian and Lacanian models of desire (in which the quest for lost unity results in the endless postponement of satisfaction and the death drive) particularly in terms of the psychoanalytical models' emphasis on narcissism and sexual overvaluation (see Freud 1991, Grosz 1990, Lacan 1982). However, Freud's and Lacan's assumptions of a 'normative' (white, male, heterosexual) individual are notoriously ahistorical and universalising (see Grosz 1995: 145 and Jackson 1995: 57); my approach is more concerned with the specific cultural formations of desire.

4 For other examples of these 'magical' kisses, see *Ask Any Girl* (*c.* 84 mins), *Pillow Talk* (*c.* 63 mins) and *All in a Night's Work* (*c.* 77 mins).

7

There *must* be a boy! Doris Day and Rock Hudson

> Tony, Rock, and I were made for each other. (Doris Day, quoted by A. E. Hotchner 1975: 195)

In some respects, the centrality of the Doris Day/Rock Hudson pairing to critical understanding of the sex comedy is misleading. Day and Hudson only made three films together – *Pillow Talk*, *Lover Come Back* and *Send Me No Flowers* – and in the latter they play a married couple. Although they form a heterosexual union in each film, the dynamics of this coupling are complicated by the presence of Tony Randall, who co-stars in all three. The films are very conscious of the cultural discourses around masculinity and sexuality and repeatedly place Hudson and Randall in queer positions; in *Send Me No Flowers*, they even share a bed. Hudson's homosexuality was an open secret in Hollywood at the time, but it did not become public knowledge until 1985, when it was announced he had AIDS. Similarly, rumours have persisted about Day's sexuality, and she has gained a lesbian following through her roles in such films as *Calamity Jane* (1953). The extratextual resonances of Day's and Hudson's star personae add another dimension to the sex comedy's themes of masquerade and identity. While this chapter remains centrally concerned with the formation of the heterosexual couple in *Pillow Talk*, the Day/Hudson/Randall threesome also enables queer readings that recognise and resist the social construction of 'normative' gender and sexuality.

What virgin?

In *Pillow Talk*, Jan Morrow (Day) and Brad Allen (Hudson) share a party-line telephone. She is an interior designer; he is a composer. She thinks he is a sex maniac; he thinks she is an uptight spinster. She desires love, entailing commitment; he desires unrestricted, short-term sex. Unknown to either, they are both friends with Jonathan Forbes (Randall), who is also paying for their professional services. Brad and Jan's conflicting desires are complicated when Brad discovers Jan is very attractive and he decides to masquerade as her ideal man, 'Rex Stetson'. Jan is on the verge of going 'all the way' with Rex when she discovers the deception, but by this point true love has struck and sex is no longer the issue. Desperate to make amends, Brad abandons his playboy lifestyle and arranges for Jan to redecorate his bachelor pad. Having wreaked her revenge, the couple are united.

For the first twelve minutes of the film, the spectator is positioned with Jan. Although Day has become identified as the archetypal sex comedy virgin, there is little in these opening scenes to suggest Jan's literal virginity. The title song is sung by Day and the lyrics expressly deal with a woman's sexual and personal desires: she wants a man in her bed, but someone she can also talk to, and specifically within the framework of marriage ('Talk about the boy I'm gonna marry'). Until that time, she has to make do with 'talking' to her pillow, fantasising about who the boy might be. The repetitive structures of the song reinforce the increasingly desperate tone of the lyrics, as Day finally declares, 'There must be a boy – there *must*!' With the end of the credit sequence and the cut to the first story shot, the song continues, but fades; the melody is picked up diegetically, however, as Jan gently hums it to herself, thereby linking the lyrics specifically to Jan (not just Day).

Given this overt concern with getting a man into her bed, it is only fitting that the film should open with the sexually charged image of a woman's leg, extended across the frame to show its shape, as the unseen woman, perched on the edge of an unmade bed, smoothes her stocking sensually into place. While Babington and Evans are quite right to note that this is a 'highly conventional image of female sexuality' (1989: 203), it is less conventional that it should be Doris Day's leg that is so revealed – a star whose persona was built on tomboy naturalness and healthy, girl-next-door values. This opening image, then, is a deliberate assertion of Day's sexual attractiveness. As Ross Hunter (the film's producer) bluntly pointed out, 'for Doris, it was an enormous departure from the kind of films she'd been doing for a dozen years. A sophisticated sex comedy. Doris hadn't a clue as to her potential as a sex image and no one realized that under all those dirndls lurked one of the wildest asses in Hollywood' (quoted in Hotchner 1975: 200). The spectator is given a very privileged introduction to Jan. The camera pulls back to reveal her, dressed only in a baby-blue slip and stockings, in an intimate location (her bedroom) and at a private moment (connoted not only by her state of undress, but also by the little touches of unselfconscious vanity, such as when she briefly preens in front of the mirror). While Jan's confident briskness and the sunny-yellow and pale-blue decor counteract any overly sensual response to the shot, we are definitely presented with a highly attractive, stylish, vivacious woman, who does not seem in the least repressed or spinsterly.

These images clash with the later calcification of Day's image into the 'constant virgin' desperately clinging to her maidenhood.[1] There is nothing to signify that Jan Morrow is chaste out of choice; it is rather the lack of choice that proves to be the problem. 'There *must* be a boy' suggests her personal sexual frustration, but also reflects on the unsuitability of the men surrounding her: Jonathan has been married three times as a revolt against his mother; Tony Walters (Nick Adams) is oversexed and underage; and her employer, Pierot (Marcel Dalio) is both too old and too 'French', the codification of queerness reinforced by his career as an 'interior designer'. As for Brad, he is only interested in one thing and expects that 'five, six dates ought to do it'. Diana Simmonds expresses the dilemma well: 'Day's refusal to give in and lie down was not that of the "constant virgin" [. . .] but of a woman refusing to be had – in every sense of the word' (1980: 870). Given the potential consequences of actually having sex (underlined in *Pillow Talk* by the coda pregnancy), the heroine's hesitancy is understandable.[2] Krutnik asserts that the sex comedy locates men 'as the active agents of the Fuck, whereas women are established in relations of resistance to it or negotiated compliance with it. They cannot initiate or control it [. . .]. The question of female desire is thus defused or deflected' (1990: 61). This assertion fails to recognise anything positive or active in 'resistance', perhaps because the situation is reduced to its most banal common denominator ('the Fuck') while the wider concerns of the female (not to be 'had') are neglected. More importantly, his statement implies that the question of female desire is not an issue in the sex comedy – but, as the song 'Pillow Talk' demonstrates, female desire is integral. Moreover, this desire is not limited to marriage and security; Brad's physical size is repeatedly commented on and the display of Hudson's admirable torso provides a visual counterpoint to the fetishised images of Day's legs and 'wild ass'.

The predominant critical approach to the sex comedy is to reduce the sexual conflict to a fantasy of male phallic power, whereby the woman to be conquered is only interested in avoiding sex. Krutnik goes so far as to assert that films like *Pillow Talk*, *Lover Come Back* and *That Touch of Mink* 'insinuate that women do not actually enjoy sexual intercourse' (1990: 60). Not only does this ignore the behaviour of secondary characters, such as Brad's girlfriends, it again misses the underlying issues of trust, risk and respectability involved in the heroine's acknowledgement of desire. Certainly, within *Pillow Talk*'s narrative Jan proves willing, giving Jonathan the chance to help her 'hit the moon'. More importantly, it is her questioning that invites the 'magical' kiss with Rex/Brad at The Hidden Door nightclub – and no one could call *that* kiss repressed (even the musicians are struck dumb). Furthermore, Jan makes her own decision to go to Connecticut and 'convinces' Rex by saying that 'we're both over twenty-one'. The sirenic song 'Possess me' should allay any remaining doubts about her intentions.

Jan is a successful, independent career woman, but she is never other than 'feminine'. Her confidence, practicality and efficiency in the hands of a Katharine Hepburn may well have appeared austere, extreme and 'unwomanly', but as embodied by Day they are full of bounce and energy and eminently attractive. Where the career woman comedy marked the heroine as different from other women, Day connotes the everyday and all-American – the girl-next-door grown up and moved to New York. Her characters' careers are rarely treated as problematic and, in *Pillow Talk*, Jan's career is so thoroughly integrated into the narrative and stylistic form that the resolution depends upon it. Babington and Evans (1989: 198) assume that the conventional ending of marriage and pregnancy signals the end of Jan's career, but this is not implied by the narrative. It is equally plausible to assume that Jan will (at the very least) have to redecorate Brad's apartment. (Day's publicity frequently emphasised her own family values as a working mother, and she also played working mothers in, for example, *It Happened to Jane* (1959) and *The Thrill of It All* (1963); the question of her character's abandoned career following marriage is central to *The Man Who Knew Too Much* (1956).)

The characterisation of Jan as practical and sincere is accentuated by the film's system of costume. Her clothes are well tailored, with clean lines and plain fabrics, with few if any lacy frills, flounces or unnecessary adornments; they are bright, pastel shades of 'innocent' colours such as white and pale blue, occasionally complemented with dashes of bold red or leopard skin accessories. In the first sequence, Jan's appearance is directly contrasted to that of Brad's girlfriends, Eileen (Valerie Allen) and Yvette (Jacqueline Beer): both are dark-haired, wearing more conventionally sexy négligés of lacy salmon pink and black, respectively; while Jan usually stands, the girls recline on boudoir chaises, surrounded by pink satin or purple cushions. However, these girls are made to seem foolish by the blind ardency of their adoration and the ease with which the insincere Brad manipulates them. Eileen and Yvette, along with the elderly Mrs Walters (Lee Patrick), are also the only women in the film who do not seem to work; we tend to agree with Jan's implication that there should be more important things for these women to be doing at nine o'clock in the morning than listening to a very bad love song.

You are my inspiration . . . Eileen/Yvette/Marie

The fact that Brad tries this song on each girl in his life is the first signal that *Pillow Talk* intends to treat romance as a construction, and seduction as manipulation. Consequently, while Brad is certainly the image of masculine virility, the substance of this image is constantly called into question by his lack of sincerity and integrity. When Eileen asks him to sing it to her, Brad seductively sighs 'Oh, now?', while looking at his watch, as if he has better things to do; when Marie (Julia Meade) asks him to sing it, he struggles to remember her name. It is not only the song's repetition, but the exaggerated style of Brad's performance which alerts us to his insincerity. He sings with the affected charm of a Las Vegas cabaret entertainer, flourishing his hands into shot at the end of almost every phrase. The predictability and blandness of the song are subtly underlined when Jan first interrupts. She politely waits until the end of the song line, but as soon as Brad finally sings 'Eileen', she cuts in, pitching the 'I' of 'I do hate to interrupt' perfectly in tune with the 'Ei' of Eileen. In another kind of film, the idea of writing a song inspired by love would be the ultimate vindication of romance, emotional truth and artistic creativity. In *Pillow Talk*, the romantic convention is used purely as a prop for seduction, the supposed 'inspiration' belied by the banal lyrics ('Your eyes, your hair, are beyond compare') and the interchangeable muse. It is only fitting that the song should prove to be the petard by which Brad is hoisted.

Romance is made ridiculous elsewhere in the film as well. Conventionally romantic situations, such as the hansom cab ride, are undercut by the deception involved and particularly by the conflicting opinions expressed by the thought-overs.

> JAN: Hmm, there's something so . . . wholesome about a man who loves animals.
> BRAD: I hope this stupid horse knows where he's supposed to go.
> DRIVER: [*seated behind them*] Hangs on to the reins like a subway strap. I don't know what he's up to, but I'm sure glad she ain't my daughter!

Throughout the film, there is a tension between authentic emotion and manipulative appearances, and this tension is often focused upon the issue of seduction. For example, Brad's seduction scene with Marie is juxtaposed with the scene of Tony Walters mauling Jan in his sports car. While Brad's seduction is smooth and conventionally romantic (dimmed lights, soft music), Tony is all over Jan, as she squeals in displeasure and repeatedly fends him off. Two shots of each couple are joined by a cut, but the transition carries a surprising sense of continuity because, as one shot ends and the next begins, the camera tracks in (increasingly fast) on the kissing couples. The comparison is clear: Brad's and Tony's aims are the same; their technique makes the difference. Tony's seduction routine is limited to the juvenile method of getting Jan drunk, a technique which Jan sees through at once (presumably having been in this situation before). Brad, on the other hand, is so experienced as to have reduced romance to an automated modern convenience. Next to his sofa, Brad has two switches: one dims the lights, turns on the phonograph and locks the front door, the other turns the sofa into a fold-out bed with baby-blue sheets. Whether the method is alcohol or electricity, seduction and romance become linked with consumption.

Objects of desire

This link raises the question of the playboy and his bachelor pad. The consumer objects that define Brad's living space are the piano, the tasteful selection of post-impressionist art (nothing too avant-garde, unlike the painting delivered to Jonathan's office) and, most importantly, that sofa-bed and the remote-control switches. To paraphrase Hugh Hefner, Brad enjoys putting a little mood music on the phonograph and inviting in a female acquaintance for a quiet discussion on Picasso, bad love songs and sex. Consumerism functions thematically to privilege seduction and appearance, not only at the level of social environment, but also in relation to the cultivation of identity. Brad's apartment may be a fully functional 'spider's web' (one of Jan's descriptions) but it also aims to reinforce his image of heterosexual virility. As the finale riot of bad-taste exotica–erotica shouts at the top of its purple voice, the apartment's interior decoration is all about controlling meaning through appearance. Jan's redecorated version reveals the blatant objective beneath the smooth 'bachelor playboy' facade, by evoking the imagery of the harem, the honky-tonk brothel and the cheap saloon.

The question of taste proves vital to this thematic concern with consumerism and decorative appearances. When Brad asks Jan to redecorate his apartment, he explicitly tells her to get rid of those things she considers 'bad taste'. She does quite the reverse. While her own apartment is fashionably practical and carefully co-ordinated, anger and revenge allow Jan to let loose with a riot of tasteless colour when redecorating Brad's apartment. The use of clashing colours is excessive (dominant red, sickly green, orange, blue and puce), expressing Jan's loss of self-control. This return of the repressed suggests that taste is a question of 'respectability' and social constraints. It is no coincidence that Jan chooses the wooden fertility goddess as the finishing touch to Brad's apartment. Earlier, Mrs Walter's animal instincts led her to select the statue (Pierot thinks she has the 'taste of a water buffalo'). When Jan enlightened her to the fact that 'a fertility goddess is the last thing you need in Scarsdale', she immediately changed her mind and denounced the object as a 'savage little thing'. The connotations of class, gender and repression are especially interesting. Sexual fertility is apparently particularly inappropriate in the refined Scarsdale suburbs, and Mrs Walters must repress her instinctual interest in the statue. However, while sex may be savage and primitive, it is not alien to either Mrs Walters or Jan (who shows no embarrassment in admitting the statue's symbolic function). Indeed, it is a fertility *goddess*, fundamentally linking sex with women and pregnancy; it implies that sex is not just a masculine prerogative, but that the modern woman feels unable to display such sexual instincts in public. This kind of 'keeping up appearances' is typical of the sex comedy and the prevalence of the interior design, fashion and advertising industries signals that image has become all-important. If 'you are what you consume', then identity becomes a fashion accessory – the performance of a socially determined image through the consumption of *haute couture*, decor and modern art to signify personal, sexual, social and economic status.

It is this aspect of signified identity which relates the film's consumerism to the wider theme of communication by emphasising the processes of meaning. Indeed, the relationship between consumerism and communication is symbolised by the film's key motif, the telephone. Telephones are everywhere in this film (with the exception of Jonathan's cabin); they are always framed prominently and often shown in close-up. A private telephone line is Jan's most sought-after consumer object because it would allow her to control communication with the outside world and particularly with men (both Pierot and Jonathan fail to reach her by telephone). The narrative conceit of sharing a party line foregrounds the title's concern with 'talk', at the same time as obfuscating communication between the sexes by creating three-way conversations, interruptions, eavesdroppers and busy signals.[3] Thus, when Jan interrupts Brad's conversations with Eileen and Yvette, the sense of her intrusion is reiterated visually. Although the triangular split-screens slide in from left and right while Jan's shot continues, because she is contained within the central, downward-pointing triangle, the overall effect is of her coming between Brad and the girl. The effect is reinforced by the *mise-en-scène*: the vertical hang of the curtains behind Jan reinforces the drive downwards of the triangle point, while the bright yellow and blues of her environment stand out against the more muted pinks, purples and browns of the adjacent screens.

The plot and themes are both concerned with (mis)representation and (mis)communication, underlining the processes of constructing – and controlling – meaning. Even the structures of language and dialogue foreground the gap between the word and meaning; *double entendre*, innuendo and Freudian slips abound. For example, when Jan goes to complain to the telephone company, Mr Conrad (Hayden Rorke) asks her if Brad has made 'immoral overtures' (an unwitting pun):

JAN: Well . . . [*implying yes*] – Oh! Not to me!
MR CONRAD: And you're bothered by this?
JAN: Yes [*firmly*] – I mean, no. What do you mean 'bothered'?

This kind of confusion not only suggests that Jan's unconscious desires have found a voice, but also implies the inherent impossibility of saying what you mean (and meaning what you say). This impossibility becomes central to the representation of Brad and Jan's relationship. There is a gap, too, between the individual's projected appearance and their instinctual reactions, as in the moment when Jan tells herself to make 'casual conversation', comments on the lovely evening and then blurts out, 'You married?' The crossed wires of communication are most often figured by Brad and Jan's thought-overs. Not only do their private thoughts reveal the disjunction between their perceptions, their behaviour and reality, but also the conflict between their desires.

While Jan's desire for a 'boy I'm going to marry' has been established by the theme song, it is quite clear that Brad, although instantly attracted to Jan, has no intention of a committed relationship. On the contrary he sees her as a challenge:

> BRAD: [*off-screen thought-over*] So *that's* the other end of your party line. [*Cut to reverse angle . . . pause in thought*] How're you going to get on friendly terms with that?

Brad's sexual objectification of Jan into 'that' is emphasised by the framing. Before Brad's thoughts are heard, we see a medium shot, roughly from his point of view, of Jan's back as she dances; the camera tilts down to fill the frame with Jan's 'end' as she sways rhythmically to the music, at which point Brad's thoughts are voiced. Thus, when Brad wonders how to get on friendly terms with 'that', he is implicitly referring to a sexual act with Jan's rear end, rather than any emotional relationship with her as an autonomous individual. Indeed, Brad's estimate of 'five, six dates ought to do it' proves spot on: if the montage sequence of dates is broken down into separate occasions then the trip to Connecticut would be date number six. Brad's desire is a self-gratifying fantasy of sexual conquest, made all the more challenging by the necessary deceit. He reduces Jan to a sexual object to be 'had', partly in order to regain confidence in his own seductive prowess, since Jan has rejected him repeatedly; even when he turns on the charm, she forthrightly rebuffs his telephone invitation for a drink. Brad's pursuit of Jan involves a displacement of his masculine anxiety on to the phallic fantasy of the 'virgin' territory to be conquered.

Brad's creation of an *alter ego* is expressly designed to gratify Jan's idealised desires. Rex Stetson combines the gallant charm of the Southern gentleman with the physical attributes of the cowboy and the economic benefits of the oil tycoon. He is considerate, sensitive and polite, and interested in more than sex. Admittedly, Rex is a conventional ideal – the feminised, non-aggressive type – and this stereotyping is accentuated by Brad's assumption of what Jan will find attractive. However, the film itself acknowledges this level of stereotype through Rex's caricature name and obviously phoney

Southern accent. The accent is not a matter of poor acting, since in *Giant* (1956) Hudson's Texan drawl seems authentic. Moreover, secondary characters, such as the hansom cab driver and the singer at The Hidden Door, see through Brad's masquerade to his underlying purpose of seduction. This begs the question, 'How dumb is Jan?' Since all other evidence in the film points to her common sense and intelligence, it seems reasonable to assert that Jan's desire that 'there *must* be a boy' finds its potential gratification in the concept of Rex, but it is a hedonistic fantasy process which demands the willing suspension of disbelief (see Chapter 6). Once Brad plants doubt in her mind, the power of the ideal is rapidly undercut by his manipulation of the signifiers: politeness becomes impotence; sexual control becomes a mother-fixation; and sensitivity becomes 'homosexuality'. Rex may well be Jan's ideal man; the only problem is he does not really exist.

It is not just a question of Jan's and Brad's asserted goals (commitment versus freedom) being incompatible; ultimately, both objects of desire are unattainable, because they are rooted in fantasy, not in the reality of the autonomous individual. If the couple are to form a relationship by the end of the film, both consumer fantasies must be overcome. Ironically, it is Brad's masquerade which allows this learning process to take place, not least because of the liberation from patriarchal logic that it entails.

Acting like a man

Brad seems to enjoy pretending to be someone else. Certainly, part of his enjoyment stems from his deception of Jan – the wicked glee he derives from 'interrupting' her telephone conversation with 'Rex', for example. There is more to his enjoyment than simple revenge or mockery, though, and it is the sheer intricacy of the masquerade that reveals his pleasure. Cohan argues that 'the effort, not to say expense, that Brad undertakes in wooing her indicates that he has more of an investment in his masquerade than he ever realizes' (1997: 289), citing as prime evidence the rental of a hotel room for Rex. Brad tells Jan that Rex is not to be trusted, that he will find an excuse to take her up to his room – 'And that, Miss Morrow, is when the pay-off comes' – implying that Rex is a wolf just like him. When Rex only shows Jan the view of Central Park, picks up his coat and makes for the door, Jan is taken aback, declaring, 'I should've known that you're not like the others.' There are multiple levels of irony in this moment. Rex is *not* different; he is Brad. His apparent courtesy is in fact a double bluff designed to seduce Jan. Simultaneously, Rex *is* different, because that is how Brad constructs him, but he is not different for the reasons Jan thinks he is. Moreover, while Jan may appreciate Rex's courtesy, her line already carries the innuendo of deviance from heterosexual masculine 'norms' (a 'difference' that will become more explicit later on). Brad's manipulation of the situation plays not only with Jan's expectations, but also with the era's ideological assumptions surrounding masculinity: Rex's behaviour may be 'unmanly', but Brad's performance as Rex is the ultimate display of playboy seduction.

The Brad/Rex pairing is amplified by Brad's relationship with Jonathan, particularly with regard to the question of sexuality. The disruptive potential of Brad's masquerade as the increasingly effeminate and 'homosexual' Rex might finally be contained as a seduction tactic, if it were not for the presence of Jonathan. For if Rex is *not* like the others, how exactly is he different from Jonathan? As Cohan notes, Jonathan 'mirrors Rex's persona in many respects (both are millionaires, both are gentle with Jan, both talk about their mothers)' (1997: 290). Indeed, despite his failed marriages – or perhaps because of them – Jonathan is implicitly coded as 'homosexual' by the same cultural standards that Brad later manipulates to tease Jan. When Brad tells her that there are some men who are 'devoted to their mothers', the spectator understands the cliché, partly because the same conclusion has already been jumped to in relation to Jonathan (moreover, Jonathan's employment of both Jan and Brad demonstrates his interest in interior design, modern art and musical theatre). Clearly, the primary difference between Rex and Jonathan is physical. Jan describes Rex as 'six foot six, handsome, intelligent, owns a mountain' – phallic proportions to say the least; Jonathan is short and plain (but does own a cabin in Connecticut). While the *visible* difference of the male body may be enough to initiate Jan's desire, it is not enough to prove heterosexuality, and the possibility that Brad/Rex's perfect body cannot authenticate his normative masculinity is pushed even further by the possibility of Brad's pregnancy. Jonathan partly functions as a safety valve for the implications of Brad's masquerade and misrecognition by others. Anxieties about male performance (in both senses of the word), effeminacy and homosexuality are finally incongruent with the formation of the heterosexual couple, and are displaced on to the slightly ridiculous, expressly neurotic figure of Jonathan. Jonathan is the typical sex comedy sidekick, 'the site of all that [is] suppressed in the figure of the hero' (Neale 1992a: 292), but he is also Brad's *alter ego* (Brad is looking in the mirror when Jonathan first arrives at his apartment). At the same time as providing an outlet for cultural anxiety about 'deviant' masculinity, Jonathan's presence reiterates these issues.

This complex interaction of the Brad/Rex/Jonathan characters raises the question of masculine identity. While women have traditionally been associated with duplicity and deceit (from Eve to *The Lady Eve*), Western philosophical thought has privileged identity (connoting self-unity) and integrity as 'masculine'. As Moi observes, the 'integrated self is in fact a phallic self, constructed on the model of the self-contained, powerful phallus. Gloriously autonomous, it banishes from itself all conflict, contradiction and ambiguity' (1988: 8). Thus, the opposition between masculine identity/feminine duplicity is rooted in phallocentric logic, particularly as revealed in the Freudian theory of sexual difference: with a man, what you see is what you get; with a woman, you see 'nothing' and are left in the realm of mystery. The privileging of visible difference within this formulation plays an important part in the sex comedy's anxiety about masculinity, as signalled by the disjunction between Brad/Rex's body and the possibilities of pregnancy and homosexuality. If the eye cannot be trusted to recognise the 'truth' of identity, then the phallic potency of masculinity becomes undermined. For example, in *Lover Come Back*, two middle-aged businessmen, Fred (Jack Albertson) and Charlie (Charles Watts), provide a chorus of admiration for Jerry's masculine virility; when Jerry finally strides past dressed only in a woman's fur coat, they are dumbfounded, Fred remarking, 'He's the last guy in the world I would've figured' (see Dyer 1993). Their astonishment stems primarily from the visual undermining of Jerry's masculine identity in relation to both femininity and 'homosexuality'.

Harry Brod explores this conception of masculine identity as pure, honest and obvious, specifically in relation to masquerade: 'the masculine self has traditionally been held to be inherently opposed to the kind of deceit and dissembling characteristic of the masquerade. Philosophers such as Plato and Rousseau have, for example, considered any sort of playacting or pretension to be corrupting of the masculine virtues' (1995: 13). Consequently, as Michael Malone argues, acting itself carries 'a stigma of effeminacy in the sense that it is thought to be frivolous, unuseful, unserious, and therefore unmanly. [. . .] If acting itself is seen as tinged with unmanliness, then allowing oneself to be made into a sex object is [considered] far, far worse' (1979: 4, 6; see also Creekmur 1995). To counteract the taint of effeminacy, 'masculine' discourses of acting tend either to emphasise the physical rigours of acting (doing your own stunts and so on) or to downplay the effort involved. Spencer Tracy epitomises the latter tendency: the 'naturalness' of his acting is now almost mythic, implying that his gruff, masculine appearance is authentic; Spada describes him as 'an actor whose talent lay in his never seeming to act at all' (1986: 89).

Rock Hudson's career, on the other hand, was initially built upon his beefcake image. When Raoul Walsh 'discovered' Hudson, he reportedly told Hudson's agent, 'He's green, but he's juicy. Even if he can't do anything he'll be pretty scenery' (quoted by Hicks 1975: 270). Hudson's publicity figured him as 'natural' and 'authentic' – and, therefore, overtly 'masculine' – at the same time as this masculine integrity was being undermined by the exposure of his spectacular torso on screen and in publicity stills.[4] The cultural tension is implicit in this comment from *Life* magazine: 'students of fan appeal are undecided whether Hudson's lies primarily in his "basic honesty" or his bare chest' (quoted by Cohan 1997: 164–5). Barbara Klinger links this 'basic honesty' to the 'nature boy' image with which he became associated in the fifties: 'magazine stories explicitly presented discourse on [Hudson's] home as discourse on the "natural" man. We see Hudson the bachelor living on top of a mountain in a redwood house with a dog, eating steaks. [. . .] [He emerges as] a quasi-Paul Bunyan figure who has maintained innate masculine characteristics unpolluted by fame or civilization' (1994: 104). Two meanings of 'natural' ('pertaining to nature' and 'inborn') often seem to be collapsed in this discourse; an association with the natural world seems somehow to validate the authenticity of male identity. As posterity has accentuated, this assertion of 'natural' living and archetypal American masculinity, especially heterosexual 'normalcy', is a double bluff, no less constructed and manipulative than Rex's gentlemanly conduct in the hotel room.[5]

What becomes particularly interesting is the interaction of the extratextual star persona with the textual masquerade, destabilising masculine identity by self-consciously playing with cultural perceptions of 'Rock Hudson' and 'masculinity'. If Hudson's star persona during the fifties negotiated an inherent tension between the overtly sexualised symbol of male beauty and the authentic, honest, 'natural' man, then, to an extent, *Pillow Talk* deconstructs the contradiction into the separate terms of 'Brad' and 'Rex', respectively (see Cohan 1997: 299). Thus, at the most apparent level of narrative, Brad's ability to perform Rex as the authentic American nature boy inherently contradicts the concept of masculine identity. The performative status of 'Rex' is further underlined by the film's parodic intertextual reference to Hudson's earlier role in *Giant*, as the exemplary Texan oilman, Jordan Benedict. This kind of self-conscious reflexivity is quite typical of Hollywood romantic comedy, but here it specifically reminds the spectator that while Rex is being performed by Brad, Brad is being performed by Rock Hudson.

The status of *Brad's* 'male identity' is brought into question as well – diegetically, by his willingness and ability to pretend to be someone he is not, and extra-diegetically, by the film's foregrounding of Rock Hudson's performance. In this respect, it is important to recognise another aspect of intertextuality: while the references to *Giant* function in relation to Rex, the oft-noted allusions to *All that Heaven Allows* (1955, also produced by Ross Hunter) function specifically in relation to Brad. In Sirk's film, Hudson plays Ron Kirby, a gardener who is repeatedly associated with tree imagery; the film's interest in Ron's 'natural' masculinity revolves around his Thoreauvian self-reliance and integrity, but ends with his symbolic castration, enabling his reunion with Cary Scott (Jane Wyman). In *Pillow Talk*, Brad, too, is associated with tree imagery, beginning with his speech to Jonathan:

> Before a man gets married, he's uh . . . he's like a tree in the forest. He – he stands there, independent, uh – an entity unto himself. And then he's chopped down. His branches are cut off, he's stripped of his bark, and he's thrown into the river with the rest of the logs. Then this tree's taken to the mill. And when it comes out, it's no longer a tree. It's the vanity table, the breakfast nook, the baby crib, and the newspaper that lines the family garbage can.

No one could call Brad Allen a 'nature boy', but he is still able to adopt the ideology surrounding the concept. The imagery invokes the idea of the 'natural man' (the sturdy, upright tree) but the music and *mise-en-scène* clearly signal that this is a speech which Brad performs: as he begins to speak, a dignified orchestral soundtrack begins; he stands, walks over to the piano and then turns to deliver the rest of the speech to his one-man audience, Jonathan; finally, the extended metaphor and even the vocabulary ('entity unto himself') indicates the speech's rhetorical status. Thus, the most 'authentic' ideals of 'natural' American masculinity (bound up here with connotations of transcendentalism, the mythology of the western and even political mythology – George Washington's inability to lie about chopping down that cherry tree) are treated ambivalently. The myth of monolithic masculinity is dismembered.

The ambivalence of the sequence extends to include the prevailing cultural issues surrounding the role of the 'mature' male in society, namely, the conflict between the 'responsible breadwinner' ethos and the emasculated husband. Certainly, the explicit concern of Brad's speech is that marriage is equivalent to castration and his concern is specifically framed in terms of domestic consumerism. But as Jonathan explains, 'That's what it means to be adult. A wife, a family, a house. A mature man wants those responsibilities.' It is, of course, significant that it is the thrice-divorced, supposedly mother-fixated Jonathan who spouts the conventional wisdom. The responsible/irresponsible dichotomy is played out in the scene by Jonathan's attempts to 'educate' Brad, who can only respond with childish contrariness, or irrefutable logic, 'Why?' The humour of this dialogue overtly challenges the breadwinner ethos, but (as suggested above) Brad's rhetorical response is no more seriously presented or authoritative. The sequence raises the prevalent cultural questions surrounding masculinity and domesticity, only to highlight the inherent ideological contradiction, not to solve the dilemma. Thus, the film never asserts that a relationship with Jan would not involve being chopped down to size – quite the reverse. Jonathan argues that because Jan is 'extra special [. . .] you *look forward* to having your branches cut off' and (although both men look slightly dumbfounded by the possibility) the film tends to endorse that position. It is hardly coincidental, for example, that just at the moment when Jan realises who Rex really is, Brad walks in carrying logs for the fire. But what exactly does this symbolic 'castration' signify? Certainly not a loss of *sexual* potency, as the coda pregnancy makes clear. Instead, it is linked to being 'found out' and involves the loss of phallic power as Jan finally sees through the masquerade of authentic masculinity.

Possess me

So far, all things seem to point to the discord between the couple. Their asserted goals are incompatible, their objects of desire are rooted in unattainable fantasy, and their methods of communication involve deceit, misconstruction and misunderstanding. Indeed, their romantic relationship is intrinsically based on artifice and fantasy, since Jan has fallen in love with the man she thinks is Rex, not Brad. Moreover, both Jan and Brad seem to be afraid of something: Jan fears being 'had' and cast aside; Brad fears being 'hooked' and castrated. Essentially, the conflict between the male and female is one of power. Jan and Brad want to maintain control of the situation, without becoming subject to someone else's will: the consumers fear being consumed. Considering the variety of conflicts and misunderstandings involved, the possibility of their negotiation and resolution becomes doubtful. However, while the plot continually undercuts the possibility of an equal relationship between Jan and Brad, the *mise-en-scène* functions to bring them together, implying physical attraction and underlying compatibility.

The film's use of split screen is perhaps the most important and obvious device in this process (see p. 135). While the telephone conversations Jan and Brad/Rex have during these sequences frequently involve conflict and miscommunication, the split screen visually unites them (with the exception of the third-party girlfriends, the split is not used for conversations with other characters). The primary benefit of the split screen is to have two characters, divided by diegetic space, present on screen at the same time. Consequently, the split screen functions as part of the romantic comedy's dual-focus narrative, allowing equal attention to the hero and heroine and suggesting that their desires are equally important. Additionally, the style of the split can reflect the status of the relationship between Brad and Jan. Thus, when Jan first talks to Rex on the telephone, he is shown in a box, apparently lying on top of her; later, they appear to take a bath together. In Jan's conversations with Brad, the verbal conflict is often counteracted by a co-ordinated use of costume and colour. For example, when Jan is shown visually coming 'between' Brad and his other girlfriends, the yellow shades of Jan's apartment complement the deep browns of Brad's 'manly' living-room (wood panelling and the piano); more importantly, both Jan and Brad are wearing pale blue – as they are in the credit sequence, again in a later split-screen sequence and, most significantly, during their reunion. Finally, the two telephone wires often meet at the edge of the split, emphasising the 'connection' between Jan and Brad. During the bath sequence, the spatial divide represented by the split screen is even transgressed. Jan and Rex/Brad are shown in long shot, each stretched out in the bath with one foot placed on the wall (corresponding to the split in the screen). As Rex comments on what a friendly town New York has turned out to be, the sequence cuts to a close-up of their feet, and on the word 'friendly' he appears to tickle Jan's foot with his own. Jan quickly withdraws her foot (as if in surprise) and the film cuts back to the long shot; Jan then responds, 'You'll find that most people are willing to meet you [*returning her foot to the wall*] half way – if you let them!'[6]

Similar spatial effects are used throughout Jan and Rex's courtship, and the camera framing develops a system of progressive intimacy. This is most clearly seen if their first taxi journey is compared to the final drive to Connecticut. In the back of the taxi, Jan and Rex are first shown in a straight-on medium shot; in effect, the widescreen is still split, as Jan retains her position on the left of the screen, and Brad/Rex stays on the right. Throughout the journey, the camera articulates the conversation by intercutting this shot with a series of obliquely angled close-ups of either Jan or Brad. The spatial disjunction between the couple is matched by their wandering eyelines (their eyes rarely meet and they frequently look up, down and out of the window) and especially by the contradiction of their external and internal dialogue:

> REX: [*looking out of window*] All those buildings filled with people. [*She looks out of his window too*] Kind of scares a country boy like me, you know it? [*He casts a look back at her before closing his eyes, cringing at his words*].
> JAN: [*thought-over*] Ah, isn't that sweet? So unpretentious . . . [*looking to the front and smiling dreamily; at the same time, Brad looks to the front with an incredibly innocent, blank look on his face*] and honest. [*Looks back at him – down and up*] What a relief after a couple of monsters like that Tony Walters [*freezes and clenches jaw at her next thought*] and that . . . Brad Allen!

Brad seems to react to the 'mental' mention of his name, breaking his blank look by casting his eyes down, before catching Jan's eye; the sequence ends with them looking at each other and smiling. These techniques are repeated throughout the film, with straight-on two-shots placing Jan on the left, and Rex/Brad on the right of the frame (for example, when they are seated at the piano in The Hidden Door). At first, the journey to Connecticut follows the same pattern, with a 'split' designation of space in a straight-on medium shot; however, the cut to an oblique-angle close-up now includes *both* Jan and Brad and these shot/reverse shots become increasingly tight. Jan's thought-over is now used to signal something quite different – 'If only he knew what I was thinking!' – and this thought initiates the song 'Possess me'. Throughout this song, the spatial split between Jan and Brad is gradually transgressed, primarily by Jan. She moves in closer, finally taking Rex's arm and snuggling up to him, and he then puts his arm around her. As the song ends and the visual space has become intimately occupied, even the privacy of the thought-over seems to be overcome:

BRAD: [*speaking in his normal voice*] What did you say?
JAN: [*still in reverie*] Hmm?
BRAD: Didn't you say something?
JAN: Who, me?

When we next see Jan and Rex/Brad, at the cabin, she is sitting across his lap, completely mingling the previous left–right split, to form a centrally framed, sexually integrated couple, brought together by Jan's active surrender to desire and her willingness to be 'possessed'.

What bride?

But this is not the end of the story; having visually united the couple, the plot again intervenes. From thinking she has 'hit the jackpot', Jan now realises she has been 'had' after all. However, the complete destruction of her willing suspension of disbelief in the symbolic power of Rex's masculine identity is matched by Brad's symbolic 'castration' (the armful of logs). Thus, it is vital that Brad and Jan have not yet fully consummated the relationship. Both their initial goals – to have sex and to find love – are simultaneously denied to them.

Having rejected the impossible fantasies, the film is still left with the question of how to reunite the couple. It is never in doubt that the couple will be reunited, of course. The real question is *why* the couple should be reunited, and the answer (as always) is love. 'Love' is taken for granted in a way that romance and seduction have not been. Beneath the masquerade and deception, beneath the fantasy and manipulation, there is the necessity that Jan and Brad must have fallen in love, in order to validate their final union. The almost accidental nature of this fall is signalled by the fact that neither party recognises their true feelings themselves; Jonathan tells them and they confirm his opinion. The symmetry is heightened by the visual image. As Jan and Brad come to admit their feelings, they are seated on the exact-same spot on Jonathan's office window sill. Furthermore, the question of Brad's commitment is neatly elided with love: Jonathan declares, 'You're in love. The mighty tree has been toppled', expressly connecting love to the earlier marriage-as-castration imagery.

Once Brad's love has been established, the film is still left with the problem of reconciling Jan to having a relationship with him. The fact remains that Jan apparently fell in love with another man (Rex) and – if the film's resolution is to be convincing – this problem must be negotiated. However, the final section does not address the question of exactly who, or what, Jan loves, instead focusing on the processes of revenge and rehabilitation whereby Brad can become an acceptable compromise. Suddenly, the last thing Jan wants is to get married and the only thing Brad wants is to be chopped down. The method Brad selects to win back Jan is also connected to the tree imagery: redesigning his domestic environment to suit her taste (presumably including a vanity table, breakfast nook and baby crib). He is willing to be domesticated and his rehabilitation is further signalled by the ritual of breaking off relations with the other girls. However, this sequence is intercut with the vengeful Jan's shopping for the most 'nauseating' items of decor with which to bless Brad's home. The discord between the couple is signalled visually by canted frames: shots featuring Jan slant to the right, while shots featuring Brad slant to the left. Consequently, when Brad beholds 'the work of a woman in love', there is yet another potential source of conflict, not a solution to their problems.

Ultimately, the plot has set up so many obstacles between the sexes, who are placed in such opposing positions, that the compatibility of the couple still seems in doubt. Krutnik argues that the sex comedy relies 'upon broad physical comedy as a means of "pulling off" a resolution in lieu of an adequately motivated and convincing conclusion. [. . .] In such instances, the concluding sexual union seems more blatantly forced than it does in the screwball films' (1990: 61). Apart from the implication that such 'adequately motivated and convincing' endings do occur in screwball comedy, Krutnik's point seems valid. In *Pillow Talk*, Brad reverts to caveman mode, kicking down Jan's door and carrying her off. His primitive instincts even inspire the elevator man, Harry (Allen Jenkins), to 'sweep' Alma off her feet, as the speed of his elevator knocks her to the floor. When he helps to pick her up again, Alma is impressed: "Why, Harry, you're so strong!". As Babington and Evans note, her words 'seem more a projection of her culture-bound fantasies than a reflection of reality' (1989: 213). Harry's aggressive action is immediately subverted by his claim that Alma needs a 'man to take care of' (not one to take care of her), and the couple's distinctly anti-romantic appearance reinforces the discrepancy between Alma's clichéd compliment and the facts. Rather than reaffirming primitive masculine power, therefore, this moment makes it faintly ridiculous, implying that this is just one more cultural performance of identity. Furthermore, the incident interrupts and comments upon Brad's macho display, emphasising the far-fetched lengths to which the plot has now resorted in order to reunite the couple; indeed, the conspiracy between Brad, Jonathan, Alma and Pierot is now extended to include the entire narrative population; even a smiling policeman condones Brad's actions. Once inside his apartment, Brad's overtly 'masculine' performance is again countermanded. Having dumped Jan on the bed, he fails to follow the caveman act with a suitable show of sexual attack, instead turning to leave, in a moment reminiscent of Rex's 'unmanly' behaviour in the hotel room. Jan must take control of the relationship, flipping one of his modified switches to lock him in. While Brad has been taking the 'female' part by talking about marriage, the role reversal is completed by Jan's activation of the remote controls of seduction. Suddenly, Jan and Brad want the same thing and they have had to occupy each other's position to realise this. The process of compromise is complete.

Exactly how convincing this process has been is another question entirely. All the conflicts of the plot seem to have been magically solved by the flick of a switch. This instability is implicitly signalled by the film, as a closer look at the final consummation of the relationship demonstrates. As Brad and Jan embrace, the shot starts to dissolve and the title '3 months later' begins to appear on screen, before Jan and Brad have even kissed. Thus, the consummation is rapidly elided with the consequence: pregnancy. Moreover, given that the fertility goddess was visible on a pedestal right next to the bed, the implication is that marriage came after the fact.

Jan's repeated question, 'What bride?', continues to resonate after the accelerated dissolve into the coda sequence. Not only is the wedding completely omitted, the intended bride disappears altogether. The film apparently does not want to end with the happy heterosexual couple. Instead, it ends with the possibility of a pregnant man and this pregnancy is specifically framed within a 'homosexual' couple: if Brad is the male mother, then Jonathan is the feminised father.

Premature climax

Close analysis of the relationships between artifice, image and identity in *Pillow Talk* reveals a high degree of instability. The discourses around masculinity remain confused and the question of Brad's 'identity' is never really resolved. Jan's anger and her dislike of Brad magically disappear at the mention of marriage, but then she disappears, too, and her sexual desire is displaced on to reproduction. The ideological contradictions raised by the film are not fully negotiated and the happy ending is hardly reassuring: instead of Bordwell's well-defined classical resolution and stable epilogue, *Pillow Talk* ends with a pregnant man – except this is not 'The End'. The credit sequence superimposes the words 'The' and 'End' on to two pillows, but then displays an ever-growing pillar of pink and blue cushions, each saying 'Not Quite'. This erection is paradoxically phallic (soft, not hard) and polysemic: the alternating blue and pink cushions could signify further children and/or further gender confusion; 'Not Quite' could refer to sexual climax (or rather its postponement). Ultimately, *Pillow Talk*'s meaning, like the pillar of cushions, is far from stable.

This is not to say that the film is incoherent. Unlike the unresolved contradictions of *Woman of the Year*, the ideological confusion of *Pillow Talk* is entirely deliberate. At a formal level, the film's narrative and stylistic systems are carefully interwoven to draw attention not only to the construction of meaning, but also to its collapse. The gap between image and identity cannot be bridged because ultimately the film *wants* to expose the fallacy of 'authentic' identity.

Three's company

The endings of both *Pillow Talk* and *Lover Come Back* (see Chapter 6) refuse to affirm the stability and 'naturalness' of the heterosexual couple, instead parodying the generic and cultural requirements of heterosexual union. The forced quality of these unions may be one reason why the Day/Hudson couple have been caricatured as two-dimensional, but it is precisely these traits which expose the social constraints of heterosexuality and enable queer readings. In this respect, the presence of Tony Randall proves crucial.

The love triangle is a conventional trope of Hollywood romantic comedy, but in most cases it is constructed to privilege the heterosexist Oedipal structures of a woman passing from the Wrong Man to Mr Right. The Wrong Man is usually coded as less virile than the hero: he may be effeminate, or older, or just a buffoon, thereby allowing and reinforcing a binary power structure in which the woman ultimately chooses her 'opposite'. *Pillow Talk* and *Lover Come Back* operate very differently, because Hudson plays both men: Brad/Rex and Jerry/Linus. Moreover, these pairings blur the distinctions between 'right' and 'wrong'. Brad and Jerry are more conventionally 'manly' than Rex and Linus, but Jan and Carol fall in love with the 'nice' guys, rather than the 'real' men. In the process, the structures of binary logic are destabilised.

This effect is heightened by Randall's presence. It is only in *Pillow Talk* that there is any possibility of romance between Day's and Randall's characters; instead, Randall is more closely associated with Hudson's characters, creating the potential for a queer love triangle. In *Lover Come Back*, for example, we never even see Day and Randall on screen together. Randall plays Jerry's titular boss, Peter Ramsey. Peter is very like Jonathan in *Pillow Talk*: they have both inherited vast wealth which has prevented them from becoming self-made men; they are both in analysis; and they are both relatively emasculated. Initially, Pete seems quite commanding, but he needs his chauffeur to fulfil his threat of giving a taxi driver a 'fat lip' and, when he prods a sleeping Jerry with his silver-topped cane, Jerry snatches it away and breaks it in two. The symbolism of the cane is explained by Pete: 'Do you realise what you just broke? My psychiatrist gave me that to build up my confidence.' 'Normative' masculinity is again linked to phallic potency. Later,

Pete takes Jerry away for a holiday at his (dead father's) shooting lodge. Here, urban masculinity is contrasted with a more 'natural' rugged masculinity: both men have grown beards and are wearing hunting jackets, but Pete's chauffeur-driven car is following them at a distance; Pete blows a horn to simulate a moose mating call, but his intention is to shoot the moose with a camera, not a gun. The son's 'weakness' compared to the dead father's conventional masculine 'strength' is emphasised by the fact that the bull moose chases after him. As Jerry points out, 'He's not running twenty miles to get photographed.'

The homosocial bonds between Randall's and Hudson's characters encourage a degree of queerness, especially in *Send Me No Flowers*. Arnold Nash (Randall) is married, but his wife is away; he lives next door to Judy and George Kimball (Day and Hudson) and throughout the film functions as George's confidante. George is a hypochondriac and believes he is dying (which we know is not true). Hudson's body is again the site of irony and contradiction, his physique contrasting with the supposed failure of his health. This emphasis on the healthy/sick male body raises questions about sexuality and potency, resonating with the cultural discourses around homosexuality as a neurotic 'sickness'. His 'illness' leads him to search for a new husband for Judy and he is aided in this search by Arnold. They watch (gaze at) a succession of men, sizing them up before discounting them; in George's opinion, one man is 'reasonably good looking', but according to Arnold, 'Not as reasonable as you, George.' Their search is interrupted when Judy's college sweetheart appears out of nowhere on horseback to save her from a runaway golf cart. As his name suggests, Bert Power (Clint Walker) is the epitome of hypermasculine potency. Power is even taller and broader than George (no mean feat) and the scene in which they meet reinforces the comparisons. While Judy and Bert are placed together on the right-hand side of the frame, they are visually balanced by the other couple, Arnold and George. As Bert takes Judy's hands in his, Arnold takes hold of George's elbow; and when Judy puts her arm around Bert as they walk towards the club house, Arnold trots after George and follows suit. At lunch, Arnold suggests he and George need to powder their noses, in order that they can talk privately about Bert: 'Our worries are over! We've found a man for Judy!' Again, Arnold physically clings to George.

It should be emphasised that these queer possibilities are not made explicit by the plot. On the contrary, the plot maintains a heterosexual discourse: Judy thinks George is having an affair with Linda Bullard (Patricia Barry); and George implies that Arnold had an affair with a waitress the year before. Instead, the queer meanings are produced through the camp style of the film and through the repetition of the Day/Hudson/Randall formula. As Alexander Doty argues, 'camp's central interests are taste/style/aesthetics, sexuality, and gender – or rather, sexuality as related to gender role-playing (via style codes). Camp's mode is excess and exaggeration' (Doty, 2000: 82). Thus, the Day/Hudson/Randall films' emphasis on performance and masquerade, image and identity, intertextuality, and *mise-en-scène* invites the viewer to read against the grain. If the trio had only made one film together, then these meanings would seem more incidental, but across three films they gain resonance.

The camp meanings of *Pillow Talk*, *Lover Come Back* and *Send Me No Flowers* are part of the films' interrogation of compulsory heterosexuality. As Doty notes, 'camp's ironic humor always foregrounds straight cultural assumptions and its (per)version of reality – and therefore seeks to denaturalize the work of dominant (patriarchal, heterocentrist) ideologies' (2000: 82–3). However, because the camp humour in these films is predominantly focused on masculinity and the male body, there is a sense in which this queer meaning is at the expense of the usual generic emphasis on gender equality. There is a definite imbalance in the dual focus of the Day/Hudson films, caused not only by Randall's presence, but also by the levels of deception involved in the plot. Day's characters spend most of each film under some kind of misapprehension about the status of Hudson's characters, while we know the truth. The imbalance is most problematic in *Lover Come Back*: the narrative focus is firmly placed with Jerry, and yet his motivations seem obscure; it is not clear whether he is primarily interested in keeping Carol busy while Dr Tyler invents Vip, or in seducing her – and, if the latter, whether this is to prove that he can, or to make a fool of her. At the same time, Carol is less sympathetically presented than Jan, seeming quite prudish and easily shocked (as when she hides her eyes while Sigrid Freud, the 'Id Girl' strips); moreover, her hatred of Jerry Webster has far more substance, and stronger grounds, than Jan's dislike of Brad Allen.

The progressive potential of the Day/Hudson/Randall films lies in the films' interrogation of the ideology of 'normative' gender and sexuality. Ultimately, this potential is limited, however, because the queer possibilities are focused only on the male body, at the expense of the heterosexual couple's equality. Moreover, if the queer triangle enables space for male homosexuality, it closes down the options for the heroine.[7] Heterosexuality remains the only choice for Jan, Carol and Judy, but at least the films expose the extent to which this 'choice' is compulsory. As far as these women are concerned, 'There *must* be a boy.'

Notes

1 By 1968, Day's virginal status was the subject of parody: in *Where Were You When the Lights Went Out?*, Day plays Margaret Garrison, an actress starring in a Broadway show called *The Constant Virgin*.

2 This sexual risk reflects the fact that female contraception was quite limited in the 1950s; the Pill was not introduced until 1961.
3 In the fifties, the demand for telephones was so great in New York, that people sometimes had to share a telephone line: these 'party lines' were not necessarily connected spatially, hence Jan and Brad do not live in the same building.
4 Similar discourses about 'naturalness' surrounded William Holden's persona in the fifties; Cohan (1993 and 1997: 164–200) has analysed these in detail, specifically in relation to the spectacle of Holden's waxed chest in *Picnic* (1955).
5 This 'normalcy' is not only in relation to Hudson's own hidden sexuality, but more specifically in relation to the cultural construction of Hudson as a prime example of 'healthy' heterosexuality, in comparison to the disturbed and disturbing sexuality of other rising stars such as Marlon Brando, James Dean and Elvis Presley. For more on this, see Klinger (1994: 104–9). See also Meyer (1991).
6 The convention of using split screen for telephone conversations had been put to similar use the year before in *Indiscreet* (1958): Philip Adams (Cary Grant) and Anna Kalman (Ingrid Bergman) share an intimate conversation in bed, but the visual innuendo is more blatant and contrived. The split-screen method of sharing a bed had been utilised even earlier by Rouben Mamoulian in *Love Me Tonight* (1932): Princess Jeanette (Jeanette MacDonald) and Maurice Courtelin (Maurice Chevalier) lie in separate beds singing a love song, but a blurred diagonal split places their pillowed heads side by side.
7 There are a number of romantic comedies in which the centrality of the triangle presents queer possibilities. In most cases, these triangles consist of two men and one woman, as in *Sylvia Scarlett* (1935), *Lucky Lady* (1975) and *Victor/Victoria* (1982). On the other hand, *Old Acquaintance* (1943) provides a fascinating (and rare) opportunity for a queer/lesbian reading, but the presence of Bette Davis and Miriam Hopkins inevitably steers the film away from career woman comedy into the realm of melodrama.

Conclusion: the extraordinary couple

According to André Bazin, 'comedy was in reality the most serious genre in Hollywood – in the sense that it reflected, through the comic mode, the deepest moral and social beliefs of American life' (1982: 35). Hollywood romantic comedy's articulation of the ideology of heterosexual love, marriage and desire is far from consistent, and certainly reflects many of the deep-seated anxieties of the culture(s) which produced it. However, where the realist Bazin implies that Hollywood comedy's seriousness lies in its accurate reflection of ordinary American beliefs, the instabilities and excesses of the films with which I have dealt imply something more complex. Hollywood romantic comedy not only 'reflects' American ideology, but also interrogates and negotiates its contradictions. These couples are extraordinary because they somehow manage to find happiness *despite* the 'deepest moral and social beliefs of American life'.

Bearing this in mind, I want to draw some final conclusions about the ideological implications of this extraordinary status from three different perspectives: the ideology of romantic love; the structures of romance; and the limitations of the ideal.

The ideal couple

The ideology of love has proved remarkably adaptable to changing circumstances. It is only in the last two hundred and fifty years that the ideal of romantic love culminating in marriage has become a conventional expectation in Western society, and this conventionalisation was achieved (in part) through the processes of mass production and the rise of consumer capitalism. Germaine Greer credits Samuel Richardson's novel *Pamela* (1740–41), and the love-novels that followed it, with being the source of the romantic 'marrying-and-living-happily-ever-after myth' (1971: 213). The fairytale connotations of the phrase 'happily ever after' suggest fantasy, but the distinction made by Greer can be explained as the attachment of this myth to a realist genre (the bourgeois novel) creating a 'genuine' expectation.

Considering the increased emphasis placed on love as the basis of marriage, it was perhaps inevitable that companionate marriage should itself become romanticised. Elizabeth Owens' fan magazine article, 'Why the perfect wife's marriage failed', is particularly revealing. Writing in the early 1940s, Owens describes how, upon finally marrying Arthur Hornblow Jr, Myrna Loy was determined to be 'a perfect wife. She would create a perfect marriage. She and Arthur, she swore, would be no average man and wife. They would be sweethearts forever, playmates and partners in love forever. Theirs would be a romance that would never be allowed to die' (1970: 145). Apart from the overblown romanticism, the description could equally apply to Nick and Nora Charles. The fact that Loy could not prevent the 'death' of romance and the failure of her marriage leads Owens to wonder 'if romance is the right basis for marriage after all' (1970: 145). Despite this note of pessimism, Owens clearly assumes that something called romance – not companionate love – is the basis of marriage. Loy's supposed desire for a playmate and partner is now an inherently romantic (and impossible) ideal. Herein lies a major shift in the structure of idealised desire. With the romanticisation of companionate marriage, the object of desire is no longer an objectified, external 'other': it is the couple itself.

The impossible couple

Screwball comedy represents this companionate couple as escaping the logic of patriarchal society. The unstable endings of films such as *Libeled Lady*, *The Awful Truth*, *Bringing Up Baby* and *The Lady Eve* leave the couple in 'limbo', in a liminal space that is neither here (patriarchal society) nor there (an alternative society). The 'other' spaces of romantic comedy (in any of their manifestations) are decidedly utopian in nature, not only in the sense of articulating a 'better' way of life, but also in the sense that this space has no material existence. This kind of strategy is not unique to screwball comedy (although the specific connotations of privacy and the green playground most certainly are): as Jackie Stacey and Lynne Pearce have argued, literary lovers are similarly 'depicted as occupying an "empty time" cut off from the diachronic processes of the material world' (1995: 34). Here, too, the other space/place can be 'highly politicized, representing both an exotic "otherness" [. . .] and a territory in which alternative sexualities/gender relations can be explored' (1995: 34). While the progressive potential of such explorations are limited because of their inability to change material reality, the importance of imagining alternative realities should not be underestimated. The spatial structure of romance narratives can enable the extraordinary couple to get away with non-patriarchal heterosexuality.

The 'natural glory' of the couple

The limits of this romantic space are the potential for idealisation. The mythic dimensions of the extraordinary couple have been noted by Britton: 'Hepburn and Tracy have come to embody [. . .] "the natural glory of the couple"' (1995: 174). The phrase is taken from Roland Barthes' 'Conjugations', where Barthes uses it to describe the mythic meanings of the marriage between Miss Europe and her childhood sweetheart. Their 'natural' glory is contrasted with the 'ephemeral' glory of her (renounced) career. 'Here love-stronger-than-glory sustains the morale of the social status quo: it is not sensible to leave one's condition, it is glorious to return to it. [. . .] Happiness, in this universe, is to play at a kind of domestic enclosure [. . .] glorifying the closing of the hearth, its slippered introversion [. . .] excusing it from a broader social responsibility' (Barthes 1979: 24–5). This talk of enclosure and introversion is immediately suggestive in relation to Shumway's description of screwball comedy as 'thoroughly bourgeois [. . .]. Marriage is a private matter' (1991: 16). However, Barthes' emphasis on the domestic hearth of the petite bourgeoisie contrasts with the recreational (anti-domestic) pleasures of the more upper-class screwball couple. The extraordinary couple in screwball comedy is an exception. They manage to leave their previous conditions of existence behind, to start afresh elsewhere. Instead of a reassuring return, the extraordinary couple's privacy is a transforming removal. The same cannot be said for all romantic comedies. The Cinderella cycle of the thirties, for example, fits very well with Barthes' arguments.

The star couple provides a potent site of ideological negotiation in this respect. Because stars exist in the real world (they are flesh and blood, not just fiction), the values embodied in the star couple's persona are lent a 'factual' dimension. Publicity and biographical materials seem to give access to the 'real person', but this material is no less mediated than the fictional characters portrayed on screen; appropriate information is selected and presented to best maintain the star's power. Dyer notes the prevalence of love as a theme in Hollywood fan magazines: 'the magazines carry the implication that these are the only kinds of relationship of any interest to anyone – not relationships of, for instance, work, friendship, political comradeship, or, surprisingly enough, parents and children' (1979: 51). In this way, the textual and extratextual discourses around the star couple naturalise certain patterns of behaviour as important and appropriate, while negotiating, masking or excluding values that may contradict or threaten current social norms. The material realities of institutionalised social inequality are displaced on to the personal realm, where the ephemeral power of 'love' magically enables individual equality without the need for systemic change.

Most importantly, as Robin Wood notes, the couple's 'natural glory' mythologises the ideology of 'legalized heterosexual monogamy' (1976: 23) and therefore performs an ideological function in itself: 'its ideological power can be suggested by the fact that for most people in our society that is automatically what the term "marriage" conveys' (1976: 23). If this is the sense in which the extraordinary couple has been mythologised, then the ideal is a limited one indeed.

Coda

None of these three conclusions are entirely adequate explanations of the extraordinary couple, but each sheds light on the representation of heterosexual romance in Hollywood romantic comedy. To quote Adrienne Rich:

> The question inevitably will arise: Are we then to condemn all heterosexual relationships, including those which are least oppressive? [. . .] We have been stalled in a maze of false dichotomies which prevents our apprehending the institution as a whole: 'good' versus 'bad' marriages; 'marriage for love' versus arranged marriage; 'liberated' sex versus prostitution [. . .]. Within the institution exist, of course, qualitative differences of experience; but the absence of choice remains the great unacknowledged reality. (1987: 67)

The 'natural glory' of the couple is essential to the phallocentric, binary logic of compulsory heterosexuality. In some cases, romantic comedy's extraordinary couples can draw attention to this ideology, exposing its contradictions and repressions, as well as its economic imperatives. As the example of Doris Day, Rock Hudson and Tony Randall suggests, even those comedies that have been treated as most superficial and sexist by critics may contain a realm of possibility in the gaps between signifier and signified. Indeed, the more central the love triangle becomes to a romantic comedy's plot, the more overtly queer the possibilities, confounding the phallocentric logic of compulsory heterosexuality.

Appendix: the cycles

This appendix lists the films used as primary sources for analysing the three main cycles. It is not intended as a complete filmography. Films are arranged by year and then in alphabetical order (to give some sense of each cycle's development). The director is listed, followed by the distributor and production company (where there is more than one production company, the names are separated by an oblique; where the distributor was not involved in production, the production company is placed in parentheses). For reference purposes, I have also included details of the career woman's occupation and details of the colour and widescreen systems used for each sex comedy.

Screwball comedy

Forsaking All Others (1934) W. S. Van Dyke. MGM
It Happened One Night (1934) Frank Capra. Columbia
The Thin Man (1934) W. S. Van Dyke. MGM/Cosmopolitan
Twentieth Century (1934) Howard Hawks. Columbia
If You Could Only Cook (1935) William A. Seiter. Columbia
Red Salute (1935) (a.k.a. *Arms and the Girl*, UK: *Arms and the Girl*) Sidney Lanfield. United Artists (Reliance)
Ruggles of Red Gap (1935) Leo McCarey. Paramount
She Married Her Boss (1935) Gregory La Cava. Columbia
Libeled Lady (1936) Jack Conway. MGM
My Man Godfrey (1936) Gregory La Cava. Universal
Theodora Goes Wild (1936) Richard Boleslawski. Columbia
The Awful Truth (1937) Leo McCarey. Columbia
Breakfast for Two (1937) Alfred Santell. RKO
Double Wedding (1937) Richard Thorpe. MGM
Easy Living (1937) Mitchell Leisen. Paramount
Nothing Sacred (1937) William A. Wellman. United Artists (Selznick International)
Topper (1937) Norman Z. McLeod. MGM (Hal Roach Studios)
Woman Chases Man (1937) John Blystone. Samuel Goldwyn/Howard Productions

Bluebeard's Eighth Wife (1938) Ernst Lubitsch. Paramount
Bringing Up Baby (1938) Howard Hawks. RKO
Four's a Crowd (1938) Michael Curtiz. Warner Bros
Holiday (1938) (a.k.a. *Unconventional Linda.* UK: *Free to Live*) George Cukor. Columbia
Joy of Living (1938) Tay Garnett. RKO
The Mad Miss Manton (1938) Leigh Jason. RKO
You Can't Take It with You (1938) Frank Capra. Columbia
Fifth Avenue Girl (1939) Gregory La Cava. RKO
Midnight (1939) Mitchell Leisen. Paramount
His Girl Friday (1940) Howard Hawks. Columbia
I Love You Again (1940) W. S. Van Dyke. MGM
My Favorite Wife (1940) Garson Kanin. RKO
Ball of Fire (1941) Howard Hawks. Samuel Goldwyn
The Bride Came C.O.D. (1941) William Keighley. Warner Bros/First National
The Lady Eve (1941) Preston Sturges. Paramount
Love Crazy (1941) Jack Conway. MGM
Mr and Mrs Smith (1941) Alfred Hitchcock. RKO
Two-Faced Woman (1941) George Cukor. MGM
I Married a Witch (1942) René Clair. United Artists/Masterpiece
The Palm Beach Story (1942) Preston Sturges. Paramount

Career woman comedy

Honeymoon in Bali (1939) (a.k.a. *My Love for Yours.* UK: *Husbands or Lovers*) Edward H. Griffith. Paramount. (Vice-President of department store)
Ninotchka (1939) Ernst Lubitsch. MGM. (Russian envoy)
The Doctor Takes a Wife (1940) Alexander Hall. Columbia. (Best-selling author)
Hired Wife (1940) William A. Seiter. Universal. (Executive's assistant)
Third Finger, Left Hand (1940) Robert Z. Leonard. MGM. (Magazine editor)
Design for Scandal (1941) Norman Taurog. MGM. (Judge)
She Couldn't Say No (1941) William Clemens. Warner Bros (First National). (Lawyer)
This Thing Called Love (1941) (UK: *Married but Single*) Alexander Hall. Columbia (Grand National Pictures). (Insurance agent)
Take a Letter, Darling (1942) (UK: *Green-Eyed Woman*) Mitchell Leisen. Paramount. (Advertising executive)
They All Kissed the Bride (1942) Alexander Hall. Columbia. (Managing executive)
Woman of the Year (1942) George Stevens. MGM. (Political correspondent)
No Time for Love (1943) Mitchell Leisen. Paramount. (Magazine photographer)
Lady in the Dark (1944) Mitchell Leisen. Paramount. (Magazine editor)
She Wouldn't Say Yes (1945) Alexander Hall. Columbia. (Psychiatrist)
Lover Come Back (1946) (a.k.a. *When Lovers Meet*) William A. Seiter. Universal. (Fashion designer)
Without Reservations (1946) Mervyn LeRoy. RKO/Jesse L. Lasky Productions. (Best-selling author)

The Bachelor and the Bobby Soxer (1947) (UK: *Bachelor Knight*) Irving Reis. RKO/Vanguard. (Judge)
A Foreign Affair (1948) Billy Wilder. Paramount. (Congresswoman)
June Bride (1948) Bretaigne Windust. Warner Bros/First National. (Magazine editor)
Let's Live a Little (1948) Richard Wallace. Eagle-Lion/United California. (Psychiatrist)
Adam's Rib (1949) George Cukor. MGM. (Lawyer)
The Lady Says No (1952) Frank Ross. United Artists (Stillman). (Best-selling author)
Pat and Mike (1952) George Cukor. MGM. (College coach and professional sportswoman)

Sex comedy

The Moon Is Blue (1953) Otto Preminger. United Artists/Holmby Productions. (Black and white)
The Seven Year Itch (1955) Billy Wilder. 20th Century Fox. (De Luxe Color, CinemaScope)
The Tender Trap (1955) Charles Walters. MGM. (Eastman Color, CinemaScope)
The Girl Can't Help It (1956) Frank Tashlin. 20th Century Fox. (De Luxe Color, CinemaScope)
Designing Woman (1957) Vincente Minnelli. MGM. (Metrocolor, CinemaScope)
Will Success Spoil Rock Hunter? (1957) (UK: *Oh! For a Man!*) Frank Tashlin. 20th Century Fox. (De Luxe Color, CinemaScope)
I Married a Woman (1958) Hal Kanter. RKO/Gomalco. (Black and white with Technicolor sequences, RKOscope)
Teacher's Pet (1958) George Seaton. Paramount/Perlberg-Seaton Production. (Black and white, Vistavision)
Ask Any Girl (1959) Charles Walters. MGM/Euterpe. (Metrocolor, CinemaScope)
It Started with a Kiss (1959) George Marshall. MGM/Arcola. (Metrocolor, CinemaScope)
Pillow Talk (1959) Michael Gordon. Universal-International/Arwin. (Eastman Color, CinemaScope)
All in a Night's Work (1961) Joseph Anthony. Paramount. (Technicolor)
Come September (1961) Robert Mulligan. Universal-International/7 Pictures/Raoul Walsh Enterprises. (Technicolor, CinemaScope)
Lover Come Back (1961) Delbert Mann. Universal-International (7 Pictures/Nob Hill/Arwin). (Eastman Color)
That Touch of Mink (1962) Delbert Mann. Universal-International (Granley/Arwin/Nob Hill). (Eastman Color, Panavision)
Come Blow Your Horn (1963) Bud Yorkin. Paramount/Essex/Tandem. (Technicolor, Panavision)
Sunday in New York (1963) Peter Tewksbury. MGM/Seven Arts. (Metrocolor)
Kiss Me, Stupid (1964) Billy Wilder. United Artists (Mirisch/Phalanx/Claude Productions). (Black and white, Panavision)
Man's Favorite Sport? (1964) Howard Hawks. Universal/Gibraltar/Laurel. (Technicolor)
Sex and the Single Girl (1965) Richard Quine. Warner Bros/Reynard. (Technicolor)

References

Adams, Samuel Hopkins. (1979) 'Night bus', reprinted in William Kittredge and Steven M. Krauzer (eds) *Stories into Film*. New York: Harper Colophon, 32–91. Originally published in *Cosmopolitan*, August 1933

Albert, Katherine. (1970) 'What's wrong with Hollywood love?', reprinted in Martin Levin (ed.) *Hollywood and the Great Fan Magazines*. London: Ian Allan, 60–2, 183–4. Originally published in *Modern Screen* [*c.* 1933]

Altman, Rick. (1987) *The American Film Musical*. Bloomington: Indiana University Press

—— (1999) *Film/Genre*. London: BFI Publishing

Anderson, Karen. (1981) *Wartime Women: Sex Roles, Family Relations, and the Status of Women during World War II*. Westport: Greenwood Press

Archer, Engene [*sic*]. (1984) 'Hunter of love, ladies, success', reprinted in Gene Brown (ed.) *The New York Times Encyclopaedia of Film 1958–1963*. New York: Times Books. Originally published in *New York Times*, 9 October 1960

Aristotle. (1983) *Poetics* (trans. Gerald F. Else). Ann Arbor MI: Ann Arbor Paperbacks/University of Michigan Press

Babington, Bruce and Peter William Evans. (1989) *Affairs to Remember: The Hollywood Comedy of the Sexes*. Manchester: Manchester University Press

Bailey, Beth L. (1989) *From Front Porch to Back Seat: Courtship in Twentieth Century America*. Baltimore: The John Hopkins University Press

Bakhtin, Mikhail. (1984) *Rabelais and His World* (trans. Hélène Iswolsky). Bloomington: Indiana University Press

Barnett, James Harwood. (1968) *Divorce and the American Divorce Novel 1858–1937: A Study in Literary Reflections of Social Influences*. New York: Russell & Russell.

Barthes, Roland. (1979) *The Eiffel Tower: And Other Mythologies* (trans. Richard Howard). New York: Hill and Wang; Toronto: McGraw-Hill Ryerson

Basinger, Jeanine. (1994) *A Woman's View: How Hollywood Spoke to Women, 1930–1960*. London: Chatto & Windus

Baughman, James L. (1997) 'The frustrated persuader: Fairfax M. Cone and the Edsel advertising campaign, 1957–59', in Joel Foreman (ed.) *The Other Fifties: Interrogating Midcentury American Icons*. Urbana: University of Illinois Press, 27–52

Bazin, André. (1982) *The Cinema of Cruelty: From Buñuel to Hitchcock.* New York: Seaver

Belton, John. (1994) *American Cinema/American Culture.* New York: McGraw Hill

Berg, A. Scott. (2003) *Kate Remembered.* London: Simon & Schuster

Bordwell, David. (1982) 'Happily ever after, part two'. *The Velvet Light Trap*, 19, 2–7

Bordwell, David, Janet Staiger and Kristin Thompson. (1988) *The Classical Hollywood Cinema: Film Style and Mode of Production to 1960.* London: Routledge

Britton, Andrew. (1986) 'Cary Grant: Comedy and male desire'. *CineAction!*, 7, December 1986, 36–51

—— (1995) *Katharine Hepburn: Star as Feminist.* London: Studio Vista

Brod, Harry. (1995) 'Masculinity as masquerade', in Andrew Perchuk and Helaine Posner (eds) *The Masculine Masquerade: Masculinity and Representation.* Cambridge, MA: MIT Press, 13–19

Campbell, Colin. (1990) *The Romantic Ethic and the Spirit of Modern Consumerism.* Oxford: Blackwell

Cavell, Stanley. (1981) *Pursuits of Happiness: The Hollywood Comedy of Remarriage.* Cambridge, MA: Harvard University Press

Chafe, William H. (1977) *Women and Equality: Changing Patterns in American Culture.* New York: Oxford University Press

—— (1991) *The Paradox of Change: American Women in the 20th Century.* Oxford: Oxford University Press

—— (1995) *The Unfinished Journey: America Since World War II.* Third edition. Oxford: Oxford University Press

Cixous, Hélène. (1997) 'Sorties: Out and out: Attacks/ways out/forays' (trans. Betsy Wing), reprinted in Catherine Belsey and Jane Moore (eds) *The Feminist Reader: Essays in Gender and the Politics of Literary Criticism.* Second edition. Basingstoke: Macmillan, 91–103. Originally published in Hélène Cixous and Catherine Clément (1986) *The Newly Born Woman.* Minneapolis: University of Minnesota Press, 63–4, 83–8, 91–7

Cohan, Steven. (1993) 'Masquerading as the American male in the fifties: *Picnic*, William Holden and the spectacle of masculinity in Hollywood film', in Constance Penley and Sharon Willis (eds) *Male Trouble.* Minneapolis: University of Minnesota Press, 203–29

—— (1997) *Masked Men: Masculinity and the Movies in the Fifties.* Bloomington: Indiana University Press

Corber, Robert J. (1997) *Homosexuality in Cold War America: Resistance and the Crisis of Masculinity.* London: Duke University Press

Creekmur, Corey K. (1995) 'Acting like a man: Masculine performance in *My Darling Clementine*', in Corey K. Creekmur and Alexander Doty (eds) *Out in Culture: Gay, Lesbian, and Queer Essays on Popular Culture.* London: Cassell, 167–82

Crowther, Bosley. (1970a) 'Review of *Three Loves Has Nancy*', reprinted in *The New York Times Film Reviews, 1913–1968: Volume 2, 1932–1938.* New York: New York Times and Arno Press, 1527. Originally published in *New York Times*, 2 September 1938, 23

—— (1970b) 'Review of *Woman of the Year*', reprinted in *The New York Times Film Reviews, 1913–1968: Volume 3, 1939–1948*. New York: New York Times and Arno Press, 1845. Originally published in *New York Times*, 6 February 1942, 23

Dabakis, Melissa. (1993) 'Gendered labor: Norman Rockwell's *Rosie the Riveter* and the discourses of wartime womanhood', in Barbara Melosh (ed.) *Gender and American History since 1890*. London: Routledge, 182–204

Deleyto, Celestino. (1998) 'Love and other triangles: *Alice* and the conventions of romantic comedy', in Peter William Evans and Celestino Deleyto (eds) *Terms of Endearment: Hollywood Romantic Comedy of the 1980s and 1990s*. Edinburgh: Edinburgh University Press, 129–47

Dell, Floyd. (1973) 'Love in the machine age', reprinted in Warren Susman (ed.) *Culture and Commitment, 1929–1945*. New York: Braziller, 209–19. Originally published in Floyd Dell (1930) *Love in the Machine Age: A Psychological Study of the Transition from Patriarchal Society*. New York: [n. pub.], 6–12, 42–7, 67–9, 403–5

D'Emilio, John and Estelle B. Freedman. (1997) *Intimate Matters: A History of Sexuality in America*. Second edition. London: The University of Chicago Press

de Rougemont, Denis. (1983) *Love in the Western World* (trans. Montgomery Belgion). Revised and augmented edition. Princeton: Princeton University Press

Dignam, Dorothy. (1948) 'Woman's place in advertising', in Mary Margaret McBride (ed.) *How To Be A Successful Advertising Woman: A Career Guide for Women in Advertising, Public Relations, and Related Fields*. New York: Whittlesey House, 203–23

Doane, Mary Ann. (1988) *The Desire to Desire: The Woman's Film of the 1940s*. London: Macmillan

Doty, Alexander. (2000) *Flaming Classics: Queering the Film Canon*. London: Routledge

Dubbert, Joe L. (1979) *A Man's Place: Masculinity in Transition*. Englewood Cliffs: Prentice-Hall

Dulles, Foster Rhea. (1952) *America Learns to Play: A History of Popular Recreation, 1607–1940*. New York: Peter Smith.

Dyer, Richard. (1979) *Stars*. London: BFI Publishing

—— (1982) 'Don't look now'. *Screen*, 23: 3–4, 61–73

—— (1993) 'Rock – The last guy you'd have figured?', in Pat Kirkham and Janet Thumim (eds) *You Tarzan: Masculinity, Movies and Men*. London: Lawrence & Wishart, 27–34

Ehrenreich, Barbara. (1983) *The Hearts of Men: American Dreams and the Flight from Commitment*. London: Pluto Press

Eitzen, Dirk. (1999) 'Comedy and classicism', in Richard Allen and Murray Smith (eds) *Film Theory and Philosophy*. Oxford: Oxford University Press, 394–411

Elliot, George. (1988) *Middlemarch*. Oxford: Oxford University Press

Epstein, Cynthia Fuchs. (1970) *Woman's Place: Options and Limits in Professional Careers*. Berkeley: University of California Press

Ferguson, Otis. (1971) 'While we were laughing', reprinted in Robert Wilson (ed.) *The Film Criticism of Otis Ferguson*. Philadelphia: Temple University Press, 18–24. Originally published in *Accent*, Autumn 1940

Filene, Peter G. (1998) *Him/Her/Self: Gender Identities in Modern America*. Third edition. Baltimore: The John Hopkins University Press

Fowler, Alastair. (1982) *Kinds of Literature: An Introduction to the Theory of Genres and Modes*. Oxford: Clarendon Press

Freud, Sigmund. (1991) 'On narcissism: An introduction' (trans. James Strachey), reprinted in Angela Richards (ed.) *On Metapsychology*. Penguin Freud Library 11. Harmondsworth: Penguin, 59–97

Friedan, Betty. (1964) *The Feminine Mystique*. New York: Dell

Frye, Northrop. (1965) *A Natural Perspective: The Development of Shakespearean Comedy and Romance*. New York: Columbia University Press

—— (1984) 'The argument of comedy', reprinted in D. J. Palmer (ed.) *Comedy: Developments in Criticism*. London: Macmillan, 74–84. Originally published in *English Institute Essays, 1948*. New York: [n. pub.], 1949, 58–73

—— (1990) *Anatomy of Criticism: Four Essays*. Harmondsworth: Penguin

Gabler, Neal. (1996) *Walter Winchell: Gossip, Power and the Culture of Celebrity*. London: Papermac

Gaines, Jane Marie and Charlotte Cornelia Herzog. (1982) 'Hildy Johnson and the 'man-tailored suit': The comedy of inequality', in Jae Alexander *et al.* (eds) *Film Reader 5: Film and Cultural Studies; Feminist Film Criticism*. Evanston: Northwestern University, 232–46

Galerstein, Carolyn. (1989) *Working Women on the Hollywood Screen: A Filmography*. New York: Garland Publishing

Gehring, Wes D. (1986) *Screwball Comedy: A Genre of Madcap Romance*. Westport: Greenwood Press

Greer, Germaine. (1971) *The Female Eunuch*. London: Paladin

Grosz, Elizabeth. (1990) *Jacques Lacan: A Feminist Introduction*. London: Routledge

Groves, Ernest R. (1928) *The Marriage Crisis*. New York: Longmans, Green

Hall, Mordaunt. (1970) 'Review of *It Happened One Night*', reprinted in *The New York Times Film Reviews, 1913–1968: Volume 2, 1932–1938*. New York: New York Times and Arno Press, 1035. Originally published in *New York Times*, 23 February 1934, 23

Hammett, Dashiell. (1935) *The Thin Man*. Harmondsworth: Penguin

Harvey, James. (1998) *Romantic Comedy: In Hollywood, From Lubitsch to Sturges*. Paperback edition. New York: Da Capo Press

Haskell, Molly. (1987) *From Reverence to Rape: The Treatment of Women in the Movies*. Second edition. Chicago: The University of Chicago Press

Henderson, Brian. (2001) 'Romantic comedy today: Semi-tough or impossible?', reprinted in Gregg Rickman (ed.) *The Film Comedy Reader*. New York: Limelight Editions. Originally published in *Film Quarterly*, 31: 4, Summer 1978, 11–23

Hepburn, Katharine. (1992) *Me: Stories of My Life*. Harmondsworth: Penguin

Hicks, Jimmie. (1975) 'Rock Hudson: The film actor as romantic hero'. *Films in Review*, 26: 5, May 1975, 267–89

Hine, Thomas. (1987) *Populuxe*. New York: Knopf

Honey, Maureen. (1984) *Creating Rosie the Riveter: Class, Gender, and Propaganda During World War II*. Amherst: The University of Massachusetts Press

Horton, Andrew. (1991) 'Introduction', in Andrew Horton (ed.) *Comedy/Cinema/Theory*. Berkeley: University of California Press, 1–21

Hotchner, A. E. (1975) *Doris Day: Her Own Story*. New York: William Morrow
Huizinga, Johan. (1970) *Homo Ludens: A Study of the Play Element in Culture* (trans. George Steiner). London: Maurice Temple Smith.
Hurley, Joseph. (1982) 'Nora on Nick: Myrna Loy talks about her co-star'. *Films in Review*, 33: 8, October 1982, 464–9
Jackson, Stevi. (1995) 'Women and heterosexual love: Complicity, resistance and change', in Lynne Pearce and Jackie Stacey (eds) *Romance Revisited*. London: Lawrence & Wishart, 49–62
Jacobs, Lewis. (1969) *The Rise of the American Film: A Critical History*. New York: Teachers College Press
Jagendorf, Zvi. (1984) *The Happy End of Comedy: Jonson, Molière and Shakespeare*. Newark: University of Delaware Press; London: Associated University Presses
Jakobson, Roman. (1978) 'The dominant' (trans. Herbert Engle), reprinted in Ladislav Matejka and Krystyna Pomorska (eds) *Readings in Russian Poetics: Formalist and Structuralist Views*. Ann Arbor: Michigan Slavic Publications, 82–7
Kanin, Garson. (1972) *Tracy and Hepburn: An Intimate Memoir*. Toronto: Bantam
Karnick, Kristine Brunovska and Henry Jenkins (eds). (1995) *Classical Hollywood Comedy*. New York: Routledge
Kettunen, Marietta. (1941) *Fundamentals of Dress*. New York: McGraw-Hill
Kirchwey, Freda (ed.). (1925) *Our Changing Morality: A Symposium*. London: Kegan, Paul, Tranch, Trubner
Klinger, Barbara. (1994) *Melodrama and Meaning: History, Culture, and the Films of Douglas Sirk*. Bloomington: Indiana University Press
Kotsilibas-Davis, James and Myrna Loy. (1988) *Myrna Loy: Being and Becoming*. New York: Knopf
Krutnik, Frank. (1990) 'The faint aroma of performing seals: The 'nervous' romance and the comedy of the sexes'. *Velvet Light Trap*, 26, Fall 1990, 57–72
Lacan, Jacques. (1982) *Feminine Sexuality: Jacques Lacan and the École Freudienne* (Juliet Mitchell and Jacqueline Rose (eds); trans. Jacqueline Rose). London: Macmillan
Landay, Lori. (1998) *Madcaps, Screwballs, and Con Women: The Female Trickster in American Culture*. Philadelphia: University of Pennsylvania Press
Lapsley, Robert and Michael Westlake. (1992) 'From *Casablanca* to *Pretty Woman*: The politics of romance'. *Screen*, 33: 1, Spring 1992, 27–49
Leach, Jim. (1977) 'The screwball comedy', in Barry K. Grant (ed.) *Film Genre: Theory and Criticism*. Metuchen, NJ: Scarecrow Press, 75–89
Lewisjohn, Ludwig. (1925) 'Love and marriage', in Freda Kirchwey (ed.) *Our Changing Morality: A Symposium*. London: Kegan, Paul, Tranch, Trubner, 197–203
Lichtenberger, J. P. (1931) *Divorce: A Social Interpretation*. New York: Whittlesey House
Lindsey, Judge Ben B. and Wainwright Evans. (1928) *The Companionate Marriage*. New York: Brentano's
Lundberg, Ferdinand and Marynia F. Farnham. (1947) *Modern Woman: The Lost Sex*. New York: Harper
Malone, Michael. (1979) *Heroes of Eros: Male Sexuality in the Movies*. New York: Dutton
Maltby, Richard. (2003) *Hollywood Cinema*. Second edition. Oxford: Blackwell

Mast, Gerald. (1979) *The Comic Mind: Comedy and the Movies*. Second edition. Chicago: The University of Chicago Press

Matthaei, Julie A. (1982) *An Economic History of Women in America: Women's Work, the Sexual Division of Labour, and the Development of Capitalism*. New York: Schocken; Brighton, UK: Harvester Press

May, Elaine Tyler. (1980) *Great Expectations: Marriage and Divorce in Post-Victorian America*. Chicago: University of Chicago Press

Mead, Margaret. (1971) *Male and Female: A Study of the Sexes in a Changing World*. Harmondsworth: Penguin

Meyer, Richard. (1991) 'Rock Hudson's body', in Diane Fuss (ed.) *Inside/out: Lesbian Theories, Gay Theories*. London: Routledge, 258–88

MGM (1942) *Press Book: Woman of the Year*. Microfiche. BFI Library

Mintz, Steven and Susan Kellogg. (1989) *Domestic Revolutions: A Social History of American Family Life*. New York: The Free Press; London: Collier Macmillan

Mirza, Candace. (1990) 'The collective spirit of revolt: An historical reading of *Holiday*'. *Wide Angle*, 12: 3, July 1990, 98–116

Moi, Toril. (1988) *Sexual/Textual Politics: Feminist Literary Theory*. London: Routledge

—— (1997) 'Feminist, female, feminine' in Catherine Belsey and Jane Moore (eds) *The Feminist Reader: Essays in Gender and the Politics of Literary Criticism*. Second edition. Basingstoke: Macmillan, 104–16

Motion Picture Herald. (1959) 'Promotion'. 8 August 1959, 9

Mulvey, Laura. (1989) *Visual and Other Pleasures*. Basingstoke: Macmillan

Munby, Jonathan. (1999) *Public Enemies, Public Heroes: Screening the Gangster From Little Caesar to Touch of Evil*. Chicago: The University of Chicago Press

Murphy, James E. (1984) 'Tabloids as an urban response', in Catherine L. Covert and John D. Stevens (eds) *Mass Media Between the Wars: Perceptions of Cultural Tension, 1918–1941*. Syracuse: Syracuse University Press, 55–69

Neale, Steve. (1992a) 'The big romance or something wild?: Romantic comedy today'. *Screen*, 33: 3, Autumn 1992, 284–99

—— (1992b) 'Masculinity as spectacle: Reflections on men and mainstream cinema', in Steven Cohan and Ina Rae Hark (eds) *Screening the Male: Exploring Masculinities in Hollywood Cinema*. London: Routledge, 9–20

—— (1995) 'Questions of genre', reprinted in Barry Keith Grant (ed.) *Film Genre Reader II*. Austin: University of Texas Press, 159–83. Originally published in *Screen*, 31: 1, Spring 1990, 45–66

Neale, Steve and Frank Krutnik. (1990) *Popular Film And Television Comedy*. London: Routledge

Neupert, Richard. (1995) *The End: Narration and Closure in the Cinema*. Detroit: Wayne State University Press

Owens, Elizabeth. (1971) 'Why the perfect wife's marriage failed', reprinted in Martin Levin (ed.) *Hollywood and the Great Fan Magazines*. London: Ian Allan, 144–5, 215. Originally published in *Photoplay* [*c*. 1940]

Packard, Vance. (1957) *The Hidden Persuaders*. New York: David McKay

'The Production Code'. (1996) in John Belton (ed.) *Movies and Mass Culture*. London: Athlone Press, 138–49

Pye, Douglas. (1975) 'Genre and movies'. *Movie*, 20, Spring 1975, 29–43
Reid, James. (1970) 'He wants to be alone', reprinted in Martin Levin (ed.) *Hollywood and the Great Fan Magazines.* London: Ian Allan, 156–8, 218. Originally published in *Modern Screen* [*c.* 1937]
Renov, Michael. (1988) *Hollywood's Wartime Women: Representation and Ideology.* Ann Arbor: UMI Research Press
Rich, Adrienne. (1987) 'Compulsory heterosexuality and lesbian existence', reprinted in *Blood, Bread, and Poetry: Selected Prose, 1979–1985.* London: Virago, 23–75
Riviere, Joan. (1986) 'Womanliness as a masquerade', reprinted in Victor Burgin, James Donald and Cora Kaplan (eds) *Formations of Fantasy.* London: Methuen, 35–44. Originally published in *The International Journal of Psychoanalysis*, 10, 1929
Rowe, Kathleen. (1995) *The Unruly Woman: Gender and the Genres of Laughter.* Austin: University of Texas Press
Sanger, Margaret. (1927) *Happiness in Marriage.* London: Jonathan Cape
Sarris, Andrew. (1962) 'The world of Howard Hawks: Part 1'. *Films and Filming*, 8: 10, July 1962, 20–3, 48–9
—— (1998) *'You Ain't Heard Nothin' Yet': The American Talking Film: History and Memory, 1927–1949.* Oxford: Oxford University Press
Schatz, Thomas. (1981) *Hollywood Genres: Formulas, Filmmaking and the Studio System.* Philadelphia: Temple University Press
Schickel, Richard. (1985) *Common Fame: The Culture of Celebrity.* London: Pavilion
Seidman, Steven. (1991) *Romantic Longings: Love in America, 1830–1980.* New York: Routledge
Sennett, Ted. (1973) *Lunatics and Lovers: A Tribute to the Giddy and Glittering Era of the Screen's 'Screwball' and Romantic Comedies.* New Rochelle, NY: Arlington House
Shumway, David R. (1991) 'Screwball comedies: Constructing romance, mystifying marriage'. *Cinema Journal*, 30: 4, Summer 1991, 7–23
Sikov, Ed. (1989) *Screwball: Hollywood's Madcap Romantic Comedies.* New York: Crown Publishers
—— (1994) *Laughing Hysterically: American Screen Comedy of the 1950s.* New York: Columbia University Press
Simmonds, Diane. (1980) 'Perfect pairing: The stormy romances of Doris Day and Rock Hudson'. *The Movie: The Illustrated History of Cinema*, 44, 870–1
Sklar, Robert. (1978) *Movie-Made America: A Cultural History of American Movies.* London: Chappell
Spada, James. (1986) *Hepburn: Her Life in Pictures.* London: Columbus
Stacey, Jackie and Lynne Pearce. (1995) 'The heart of the matter: Feminists revisit romance', in Lynne Pearce and Jackie Stacey (eds) *Romance Revisited.* London: Lawrence & Wishart, 11–45
Susman, Warren. (1984) *Culture as History: The Transformation of American Society in the Twentieth Century.* New York: Pantheon
Thomas, Deborah. (2000) *Beyond Genre: Melodrama, Comedy and Romance in Hollywood Films.* Moffat: Cameron & Hollis
Thumim, Janet. (1986) '"Miss Hepburn is humanized": The star persona of Katharine Hepburn'. *Feminist Review*, 24, Autumn 1986, 71–102

Thurber, James and E. B. White. (1960) *Is Sex Necessary? Or Why You Feel the Way You Do*. Harmondsworth: Penguin

Time. (1959) 'Review of *Pillow Talk*'. *Pillow Talk* press cuttings microfiche. BFI library. Originally published 19 October 1959

US Department of Commerce. (1975) *Historical Statistics of the United States: Colonial Times to 1970: Part 1*. Bicentennial edition, Washington: Bureau of the Census

'Variety's' Film Reviews. (1983) 20 Vols. New York: Bowker

Vasey, Ruth. (1997) *The World According to Hollywood, 1918–1939*. Exeter: University of Exeter Press

Viederman, Milton. (1988) 'The nature of passionate love', in Willard Gaylin and Ethel Person (eds) *Passionate Attachments: Thinking About Love*. New York: The Free Press, 1–14

Walsh, Andrea S. (1984) *Women's Film and Female Experience, 1940–1950*. New York: Praeger

Wexman, Virginia Wright. (1993) *Creating the Couple: Love, Marriage, and Hollywood Performance*. Princeton: Princeton University Press

Winokur, Mark. (1995) *American Laughter: Immigrants, Ethnicity, and 1930s Hollywood Film Comedy*. Basingstoke: Macmillan

Wolcott, James. (1997) 'Waiting for Godard'. *Vanity Fair*, April 1997, 46–53

Wolfenstein, Martha. (1955) 'Fun morality: An analysis of recent American child-training literature', in Margaret Mead and Martha Wolfenstein (eds) *Childhood in Contemporary Cultures*. Chicago: The University of Chicago Press, 168–76

Wood, Robin. (1976) 'Old wine, new bottles: Structuralism or humanism?'. *Film Comment*, 12: 6, November–December 1976, 22–5

—— (1989) *Hitchcock's Films Revisited*. London: Faber and Faber

Wylie, Philip. (1955) *Generation of Vipers*. Twentieth edition, newly annotated. London: Muller

Young, Kay. (1994) 'Hollywood, 1934: "Inventing" romantic comedy', in Gail Finney (ed.) *Look Who's Laughing: Gender and Comedy*. Langhorne, PA: Gordon and Breach, 257–74

Index

Note: 'n.' after a page reference indicates the number of a note on that page.